Between Threads and Tortillas

Memories and Recipes of a Mexican Immigrant

Monica Ocejo

DISCLAIMER

Some names have been changed, not to erase them, but to protect those who have passed through these pages.

What follows is a tapestry woven from memory, threaded with truth as I lived it and colored by my experiences. We each carry our own version of the world; this one is mine.

Table of Contents

Prologue

In the process of writing this book, I revisited many events in my life. Most of them brought me joy and even a chuckle, but there were times when it became painful to go back and relive the challenging moments. I had to stop and remind myself for whom I was writing this book.

Whether you feel you are not good enough, not smart enough, not pretty enough, not skinny enough, or just "not enough," this book is for you.

If you feel you're not going to make it, you're full of self-doubt, you've fallen a million times, and you've had to get up a million and one, this book is for you.

If you have no hope left, no faith left, and you feel afraid, alone, powerless, in pain, this book is for you.

Know that you ARE enough, that you ARE beautiful just the way you are. That there is hope out there, that there is love out there, that there are angels in all colors, shapes, and forms; you just need to look hard enough not to miss them.

YOU, ME, WE, ARE NOT ALONE

Know that you ARE powerful, you ARE strong, you ARE the architect of your own life, and with a lot of sacrifice and hard work, you can make your dreams a reality.

Power resides within yourself. The power to be happy, the power to be strong, the power to be your true self. Don't let anybody or anything tell you otherwise. And if they do, don't believe them, believe you.

Believe you! Believe in all the good that lives inside you, believe in your power, believe in all the abilities and characteristics that make you different, that make you special.

That is where your true power resides, in yourself. Don't look for power outside yourself because even if you do find it, you can lose it, as it was never yours to begin with.

I give you all my struggles, all my loss, all my blessings, all my challenges. I share with you all my joy, all my dreams, all my doubts, all my failures, and yes, all my triumphs. My goal is that you can find a little bit of hope or inspiration, and why not? We can share a good laugh.

I love all you crazy, amazing, inspiring, awesome fighters out there.

CHAPTER 1

What Lives Within Me

In the midst of hate, I found there was,
Within me, an invincible love.
In the midst of tears, I found there was,
Within me, an invincible smile.
In the midst of chaos, I found there was,
Within me, an invincible calm.
I realized, through it all, that
In the midst of winter, I found there was,
Within me, an invincible summer.
And that makes me happy. For it says that no matter
How hard the world pushes against me, within me, there's
something stronger—something better, pushing right back.
                                        —Albert Camus

One week ago, on a sun-filled, ordinary morning, my life split open in an instant. While in the shower, my hand brushed over my soapy skin, and I felt something that shouldn't be there—a hard, clearly outlined lump in my right breast. The size of an olive. Solid. Unmistakable. A sinking feeling overtook me. Blood rushed down my body. Something wasn't right.

I called my husband right away. "Don't worry; it's probably nothing," he said. "Just schedule a mammogram to rule anything out." In his twenties, he had Hodgkin's lymphoma, so cancer was part of our vocabulary, but never in a million years did I think it could happen to me. There was no major cancer history in my family.

We had moved from Mexico City to Miami just two years before. I didn't even have a proper doctor in the States. I scrambled and booked the next available appointment for a mammogram two days later.

The clinic was inside a Spanish colonial-style building. While I filled out endless forms, my husband sat in the waiting room scrolling through his phone. A nurse called my name. I followed her into a locker room, stripped from the waist up and put on a paper-thin robe.

I was a little bit nervous, but I had convinced myself that my lump was probably nothing.

The nurse then took me into a small room with a robotic cold mammogram machine sitting comfortably like a torture instrument. She grabbed my boob and placed it between two plastic trays as if she was molding Play-Doh. She pressed a button, and the plastic trays started to close in—my face and chin plastered on the cold steel of the statuesque machine.

"Don't move, honey," she said. "Hold your breath. Hold . . . hold . . . got it! You felt the lump in your right breast, right? I see it perfectly."

Crap! Not a great sign if she sees the lump perfectly.

I was hoping for something more discreet, more incognito, perhaps. She continued to do the hold-hold-squish-release procedure, not a fun affair.

"Ok, honey, we are done; please get dressed and wait in the seating area," she said sweetly.

I sat down and immediately started to imagine the worst-case scenarios.

After a while, a nurse interrupted my dark speculations.

"Sweetie, did somebody come with you today?" she asked.

"Yes, my husband is outside in the waiting room."

"Please go get him; the doctor wants to have a word with you."

What doctor? I came for a mammogram, not to see a doctor.

My husband and I sat down in a dark office with multiple full-size screens hanging from the wall, with only the brilliance of those images lighting the room. There were several images of X-rays that we couldn't read. We turned to each other with a what-the-hell-is-happening? look.

An older woman with short dark hair and big square glasses abruptly came in.

"Hi, I am Doctor Shitty, nice to meet you both. This image you see here is of your right breast. Do you see what appears to be a spider web over here? Well, that is a tumor. You have cancer."

She kept talking like her discovery stimulated her, but I stopped hearing and watched her thin lips moving, my mind blank.

Who is this woman? What am I doing here?

"What do you mean, I have cancer? How do you know if this is only an X-ray? Don't you need more tests to determine that?"

"Of course. We must do a biopsy to confirm the diagnosis. But in my experience, from what I can see from that X-ray, it looks like cancer. I can tell you that because the margins are. . ."

"But I had a mammogram seven months ago in Mexico, and they found nothing."

"Well, that was Mexico. Who knows how they did the mammogram?"

"They do it the same as you do," I said, feeling defensive.

"I am not sure about that, but your tumor is not small; if I were you, I would act quickly. You don't want it to spread everywhere."

The room started to spin. I could feel myself shrinking, disappearing, like a bad dream as the earth beneath me opened and swallowed me whole. I turned to my husband. He was asking questions, his voice steady, but I couldn't hear a word. A loud ringing filled my ears.

I stood up, heart hammering.

"Please — no more," I said. "When's the biopsy?"

"Well, today is Friday. Maybe we can fit you in on Monday," she said coldly.

"Ok," I walked straight to the reception desk, clutching onto any shred of air.

"Excuse me, is there another doctor who can do the biopsy? Is Dr. Shitty the only one available?"

The receptionist smiled like she understood, catching my drift.

"Dr. John is available."

"Please book my procedure with him. "

There is no good way to hear that you have cancer, but when you receive the news with not an ounce of empathy or compassion, it makes it much harder to digest. You feel meaningless as they give you devastating news that will alter your life and those around you forever.

I came out bad-mouthing Dr. Shitty, taking all my anger out on her.

"*Flaquita*, let's take it one day at a time," my husband said. "It sucks that the weekend is coming, and we will have to wait for the biopsy."

I called my friend Cris, my partner-in-crime since we moved to Miami.

Her son and my youngest son, Juan, were best friends; they went to kindergarten together. In a couple of hours, I was hosting a baby shower for her at my house, complete with tacos and tamarind margaritas.

"Moni, calm down. Breast cancer is very treatable nowadays. But, forget about hosting my baby shower tonight. I'm canceling it," she said.

"Cris, I've already made the taquitos and guacamole you love. You can't cancel it. Let me find someone else to host. I even bought a margarita machine. But I am in no mood to see anyone."

"Ok, but please take it easy," Cris replied as we hung up.

We found another mom willing to host the baby shower. I dropped everything off — food, drinks, even the brand-new margarita machine. Later, they told me that they couldn't figure out the machine.

What a pity.

Monday came, and my biopsy was done by Dr. John, an infinitely nicer doctor than Dr. Shitty. After it was done, the receptionist asked me for my phone number so they could call me with the biopsy results.

"Can you call my husband instead?" I joked weakly. "I'm afraid I'll crash the car if I get bad news while driving."

"Of course," she said, laughing, "we will call him as soon as we know."

As I was coming down the stairwell early in the morning, I could feel the stairs' warm wood under my bare feet. I hadn't been sleeping well for the last couple of days, foreseeing the final verdict. As I reached the bottom of the stairs, I heard my husband's phone ringing.

Could this be the dreaded call we had been waiting for? It couldn't be; it's too early for the lab to make this type of call.

"Hello," I heard him say. "Oh, so that means she does have it?" he said before he hung up.

He was sitting at the table, framed by soft sunlight, his breakfast untouched. As I reached him, he turned to me with a sad, resigned look.

"It was them, flaquita; you do have it," he gently said.

It was official. I had breast cancer. I hugged him and started crying. I called Cris and told her the news. She probably drove like a maniac because she arrived at my house within a couple of minutes. After a good cry, I calmed down.

"Moni, remember you have a meeting at your office at ten," My husband reminded me. "You need to cancel."

Suddenly, I was dragged back to planet Earth.

"No, there is no way I am going to cancel that meeting; it is too important. I'll take a quick shower, and we can figure out this mess later."

"Are you sure?" Cris asked me, stunned.

"Absolutely. There is no way I am canceling," I said.

I wasn't going to let this freaking cancer get in the way of making my dreams come true.

Recipe for any type of scare

Tamarind margaritas (serves six)

For Rim

- 6 teaspoons of lime chili seasoning (Tajin)
- 3 slices of lime
- 2 teaspoons of sea salt

Margarita

- 8 fl oz tequila
- 8 oz tamarind paste
- 10 fl oz of Sprite or lemon soda
- 2 teaspoons of Tajin
- 3 teaspoons Chamoy or Miguelito sauce (optional if you can't find it)

Instructions

1. Mix the Tajin with sea salt on a small plate in a circle. Rub the rim of the glasses with a slice of lime and dip in the chili mixture.
2. Place the tequila, tamarind paste, soda, Tajin, and Chamoy in a blender. Mix until smooth. Incorporate the ice into the mix little by little until smooth.
3. Pour the Margarita into the rimmed glasses. Enjoy!

CHAPTER 2

México Lindo y Querido
Mexico Beautiful and Beloved

I was born in Mexico, a land of contrasts, one of the most beautiful places on earth. Rich in tradition with a legendary history. A country bursting with vibrant colors, where my grandparents and great-grandparents emigrated from Spain in search of a better life for themselves and their children.

Though poverty is an everyday reality, family, happiness, laughter, and fiestas are the norm. The delicious cuisine is a form of art, and art is a way of living. Its culture, customs, music, humor, and everything that embodies the Mexican spirit feels like magical realism. To understand it, you must experience it—to live it.

Mexico distinguishes itself with its juxtapositions—from the Aztecs to Our Lady of Guadalupe. From the pyramids of Teotihuacan to its modern architecture. From a boundless zest for life to its reverence towards death. Mexican people possess a great sense of pride. I've never met a Mexican who has left their country without carrying that pride with them. On the downside, the astronomical differences between social classes collide. It is not a surprise that the most absurd opulence lives side by side with the most painful poverty. You have the privileged class and, long after that, the rest of the country. A microcosm exists with granted privileges and a lifestyle that is rare to find anywhere else in the world. I was born inside that small bubble, in a privileged family that seemed picture-perfect to the common bystander.

My mom is the second child of two sisters, born beautiful with classical facial features that never took away from her warm demeanor. She reminds me of a first-generation Disney princess: sweet, well-mannered, and regularly contained. Her grandparents, Roberto and his wife Hilaria, fueled by necessity, left Spain and entered through America's gate, Ellis Island. They settled in Connecticut, where Roberto found a steady factory job. But the bitter cold and language barrier proved too much for Hilaria, so she pleaded with her husband to immigrate somewhere warm, where Spanish was spoken. So, to Mexico they went. They settled in Mexico City, a place pulsing with possibility. There, they built an aluminum factory that produced pots and pans that eventually grew into one of the largest manufacturers of its kind in Latin America. My abuelo Eduardo eventually took over the business alongside his brothers.

My mom and her sister Paty had an unconventional childhood. While my *abuelos* traveled the world, the girls stayed behind in Mexico, cared for by their nannies. At a time when very few people could travel, my abuelos would go on extraordinary adventures, climbing the Great Wall of China or riding camels past the Egyptian pyramids. Their trips sometimes lasted months. Once in a while, the girls would accompany them on their travels dressed in their bonbon hats and tailored coats, to Barcelona. There, they would be left for long periods with Tía Tica while my abuelos would enjoy the good life. They had a nomadic lifestyle and would travel the world without any regard for their girls' stability.

Years later, I remember my grandmother narrating stories about their trips at our weekly family lunch.

"You know, girls, once we went on a cruise that crossed the

Atlantic Ocean. Elizabeth Taylor and Richard Burton were on board and assigned to our table for the daily formal dinners. Elizabeth would wear her famous jewelry to these dinners. She was quite a beauty, her eyes a distinct shade of blue. But I became annoyed by her because she blatantly flirted with your Abuelo Eduardo right in front of everyone. He didn't pay much attention to her, but she kept going at it, the whole trip."

I was impressed by her story and name-dropping. I turned to see my abuelo's reaction, and he just smiled and kept calmly eating his soup. I am convinced that this story about my Abuelo Eduardo was true. There was something unique about him. He was like a Mexican Paul Newman, with big green eyes. He was a distinguished gentleman, well-liked by almost anyone, a fair and hardworking family man.

My mom and Aunt Paty grew up attending the Sacred Heart boarding school in Paris, followed by boarding school in New York. School was intended to be a pastime until they found a respectable suitor from the Spaniard community in Mexico, so they could formally take their place in society.

When my dad saw my mom, he was dazzled by her beauty and instantly knew that he would marry her. It was at a family wedding, and it was love at first sight, as he would later recall.

"You and I are going to get married and have four children together," he said when they were introduced.

What a conceited, pompous guy! my mom thought. *I wouldn't marry him even if I were crazy.*

But it seems that she secretly liked his confidence, because they lived a passionate and rocky love story for over 52 years.

After a while, my sister Isabel and I were born. As a chubby, wide-eyed girl, my priorities were to play with my friends, watch cartoons, and eat Mexican goodies like *chamoy, pulparindos* and *churros with cajeta*. I remember a joyous childhood with my parents, sister, grandparents, and many cousins and uncles with whom we traveled during the holidays, celebrated Christmas, and had lunch every Sunday.

We lived in a light-filled house in an upscale suburb on the outskirts of Mexico City. We grew up surrounded by lovely nannies who sweetly took care of us. They would cook, clean, and even dress us for school. I remember how Deme, a petite and pleasant *señorita*, would enter quietly and wake us up early in the morning as soon as a little ray of light came through the small opening of our pink and green drapes.

"*Niñas*, it's time to go to school," Deme whispered, trying with no success to wake us up and get us ready.

"Deme, please, five more minutes, just five," I would beg her with my eyes closed.

"Okay, but take your foot out of the covers so that I can put on your socks so you won't be late."

Still inside my bed, asleep, I stuck a foot out, and she would put a sock on. I then offered the other foot, and she put the other sock on, giving me a generous head start to my day.

Our nannies were like family; my mom exemplified for us how to treat everyone with respect and consideration by how she warmly treated the staff. Pedro, the driver, would chat and joke with us on the way to school, where we would see the day go by.

An indivisible bond unites Mexico and the USA. We are united by land; we have merged our cultures and our people in many ways. We are neighbors, siblings, and sometimes rivals. As we grew up, we had a very close and natural relationship with the United States. For my parents, that we spoke fluent English remained a priority. They sent us to summer camp in Boston for a couple of summers with my cousins. Later, when I attended seventh grade, they sent Isabel and me to a boarding school in a little town on the outskirts of Cleveland, Ohio.

"Hey, Monica, do you ride cars or donkeys in Mexico?" my American friends would ask me.

They had this image of a little *pueblo* with *sombreros* and people taking a *siesta* on their *hamacas*. It made me laugh, but it bothered me that they thought that way. If they knew how incredible and modern Mexico was, they would surely be impressed and inevitably fall in love with it. They also asked me if *mariachis* were playing on the street.

"Only when someone falls in love with you," I would say. "

The United States was our second home. We loved the culture, the movies, and mastered the language. It was exhilarating to bring back American sweets like Milky Ways, Snickers, or my personal favorite, SweeTARTS, to fill your piñata for your birthday party. We could quote Hollywood movies by memory, sing along to Madonna or the Backstreet Boys, play with the ultimate gadgets like Atari or Nintendo, or do our homework on the new Mac. We grew up between two worlds and experienced the best of the two cultures. American culture and values were ingrained in us since practically birth.

Back then, I thought that Mexicans were the luckiest people in the world. Every Wednesday and Sunday, we enjoyed heavenly, delicious homemade food in our abuelos' house, where we would gather with extended family. My childhood and adolescence were surrounded by friends with whom we shared this alternate reality in a close-knit and manicured environment. What I didn't realize was that the reality I lived in was only for a select few. Many Mexicans were struggling and suffering, and there was an abysmal gap between my reality and the reality of the majority of Mexicans.

CHAPTER 3

Holy Drunken Retreat

S ince kindergarten, I attended a small Catholic school for girls with my sister, nestled among trees and ravines in the heart of my neighborhood. The daughters of many important businessmen in Mexico attended the school. The general ambiance was demure and discreet, and being braggadocious was not something that was encouraged.

Between sleepovers, *fiestas*, and trips to Acapulco, we couldn't ask for more. On weekends, we attended parties or drove to Valle de Bravo, a magical colonial town situated on the shores of a lake near Mexico City, where we would water ski and go out dancing.

By this time, a conservative Catholic order had bought my school. The role that women played in the order was confusing. They were not nuns because they were not habituated, but they couldn't go alone to eat sushi and see a movie with friends. They dressed in long skirts, their shirts were closed to the top button, and they had bowl-cut mullets, short with bangs. The consecrated women were a version of the Flying Nun but without the flying part. In short, we referred to them as UROs: Unidentified Religious Objects.

During my junior year, on the week of my 17th birthday, a three-day spiritual retreat was planned. We would go away to sleep in a retreat house, and the UROs prepared talks and activities. A week before the retreat, a URO caught me off guard on the way out of class.

"Hi, Monica, there is a retreat that falls on your birthday, and all your friends say that if you go, they'll go, but if you stay, they'll stay. Think about how you can bring them closer to Jesus. He is counting on you; don't disappoint him."

Ughh! I thought. *It would be totally uncool to disappoint Jesus.*

I went up to my friends and told them, "Hey, the URO came up to me and told me about the retreat. What do you think? It could be cool. We hang together, and we celebrate my birthday." I proposed.

"Perfect, let's go!" all of them agreed. They didn't need much convincing.

In Mexico, alcohol is viewed very differently from the US. Some parents allow their teenagers to drink, supposedly, so they can learn to handle alcohol. Our parents forbade us to drink, and we obeyed them... until this retreat.

None of us drank, so we were clueless. Nothing, nada, zilch. We heard stories that in some of our school retreats and in schools like ours, kids took alcohol to make the retreat tolerable or more fun. At the time, in our pubescent minds, it did not seem like a bad idea. On the contrary, it seemed like an excellent idea!

Hey! I can bring my friends closer to Jesus and celebrate my birthday at the same time. It's a win-win for all, I thought.

We gathered at recess to plan the celebratory retreat. I remember sitting with our legs crisscrossed on the paved floor in a circle, wearing our plaid skirt uniform with a white polo shirt, loafers, and white socks pulled up to our knees. With eight of my closest friends, we began to conspire.

"So, Monica, you decided to go to the retreat, right?" Julie asked. "Why don't we take something to toast with?" Gigi suggested.

Did I mention that we didn't know how to drink?

"What a fabulous idea!" Vivi said. "Who is going to take care of bringing the alcohol?"

"Let's have a draw to determine who will bring the drinks," Ale suggested.

We grabbed little pieces of white paper and wrote "B" as in "bottle" on two of them. Everyone took a piece of paper, and, of course, I got the paper with the "B" on it. B for bottle and bruta. Pia got the other B paper. I honestly do not remember if we went to buy the alcohol at the supermarket or stole it from my parents' bar, but either way, it was a super easy endeavor.

We were off to the retreat in a yellow school bus, singing and eating Doritos, and arrived at a beautiful hacienda with lush gardens decorated with statues of the Virgin and the *Santitos*, a small chapel for prayer, and a prominent house in the middle.

We began the retreat, and the UROs delivered a couple of inspiring talks. I admit, I found myself entering a spiritual vibe. After dinner, I went to the small chapel with a friend and stayed there for about 40 minutes. The others went to sleep in a huge dormitory with multiple bunk beds aligned. After we finished in the chapel, we headed to the dormitory through the vast, dark garden.

As soon as we walked through the door, my Nirvana faded away when we found a chaotic jungle. One of my best friends was crying uncontrollably, others ran, others laughed, and others were cleaning vomit. So many classmates vomited in the sink that it clogged. Someone even grabbed an empty Sprite bottle and used it as a plunger. It was utterly disgusting! I went to ask Gaby, my friend who was acting as a plumber, what happened.

"Well, they started drinking, but I guess they didn't know how much vodka was reasonable, and they ended up with too much vodka and very little Sprite in their glasses," Gaby explained while she kept unclogging the sink.

"Crap!!! We need to clean up and keep them quiet; the UROs

are going to catch us," I said, realizing the trouble we were in.

The UROs came from different countries worldwide because the Legionaries of Christ had been opening schools everywhere. The URO in charge of the retreat (bless her heart), the one who encouraged me to bring my friends closer to Jesus, was from Spain.

Some of us tried calming things down to divert the disaster coming our way. The word got out and almost everyone in the class, nearly 40 girls, were in on it—a huge, literally holy, fiesta. Suddenly, the door opened violently, and a tall figure stood frozen at the door frame and shouted in a Spanish accent, YOU HAVE BEEN DRINKING!"

Holy Shiiit! They caught us!!!!

I was sitting on the bed next to Gigi, who was wasted, waiting to hear our fate. After assessing the damage, the URO told us to calm down.

"We know that this has happened in other schools, but we want to know who is responsible—who brought the bottles. Be honest. I tell you there won't be any retaliation; trust me."

I raised my hand, and Pia did too. I didn't drink a drop of alcohol, and I spent the night cleaning up my friends' vomit. I brought a bottle; I thought it was the honorable thing to do. But I wasn't the only one who volunteered to bring alcohol to this party.

Poor Gigi was lying practically unconscious on the bed and was one of the most intoxicated. She had horrible luck because she was in the bunk bed at the entrance of the dormitory, and she was hard to miss, unlike the other drunks who hid in the back beds.

The Spanish URO approached Gigi and started smoothing her hair, holding her hand, whispering, "Oh, but how dumb you are, how dumb..."

Gigi came alive and, like the exorcist, vomited all over her. The URO reiterated to us several times that there would be no retaliation.

"Do not worry. You have told the truth, and there will be no reprisals."

I remember it clearly because the word "reprisal" sounded so unusual to me, having never heard it before. We tried to go to sleep, in the middle of the smell of vomit, surrounded by semi-unpacked weekend bags, and filled with unbearable remorse. I was so tired from the trip and all the commotion that I was only able to sleep for a couple of hours.

When we woke up, another URO came in and told us to gather our bags because we were returning to school immediately. At that moment, I knew we were screwed. Our parents were going to kill us.

We had a religion teacher that we adored. She arrived enthusiastically with a cake to celebrate my birthday. Instead of finding a group of girls praying in silence, she found us crying, with our bags packed and unprepared to face the consequences of our actions. A retreat that should have lasted a weekend didn't last twenty-four hours.

Happy birthday to me!

We went back to school, where the headmaster was waiting for us. By now, everyone in school, including my sister Isabel, knew what had happened. They divided us into groups based on our behavior. Poor Gigi was in a group of her own. There were four girls in my group: Pia, me, and two exchange students from Spain who gleefully indulged in our Mexican traditions. They had been quite drunk—not a great sign to be in that group.

Gigi went first into the meeting room with the headmaster, the discipline prefects, and two UROs.

"Gigi, you are going down the wrong path. First, you started smoking, and now you are drinking. All these decisions will end up leading you to an abortion," affirmed the headmaster, who also happened to be a URO.

Abortion? How did she get to abortion? Gigi hasn't even been kissed yet, I thought after Gigi told us the story.

"Therefore," the headmaster continued, "I think it is important to be an example to your classmates and the school. You are expelled until further notice. Pick up your books and go home. You will not graduate next year with your classmates."

She had been put on trial and sentenced.

Gigi came out of the meeting room crying inconsolably. Then, it was our turn.

"Girls, I don't know if you understand the damage you are doing to our institution. You are to be expelled, effective immediately. Please grab your things and go. You may come to school to take your exams until the school year ends, and if you have good grades, you will be allowed to come back and graduate next year," the headmaster announced. When she stopped talking, I realized how furious I was. I did not drink a drop of alcohol, and now I was expelled in the middle of the school year.

"Expelling you gives me no pleasure," she said as we were standing up to leave the office. "I know that you are good girls, and for that reason, I am going to give you the option to come back next year to graduate with your friends. There are five months until the end of the school year. Come back in your senior year, and you can graduate with them."

Of the five of us who were expelled, the two Spanish students went back to Spain; their Mexican experience cut short. Gigi's parents were very well-connected with the Legionaries, so she was quickly accepted into a similar school. As for the two who brought the alcohol, Pia and I, we had no school to go to. My parents did not go ballistic on me because I told the truth and I hadn't drunk. They thought it was enough punishment that I was being expelled. My dad even tried to defend me with the headmaster.

"You are being unreasonable!" I heard my father shouting from outside her office, but nothing worked. Even though I didn't drink and told the truth, I got expelled. So much for honesty. While waiting to find a new school, Pia and I would wake up early every morning and go to Blockbuster. We were living the life. But we wanted to find a new school so that we wouldn't feel so useless and guilty.

Finally, we found a school that accepted us in the middle of the school year, even with such bad references. This school was the exact opposite of our old school. Although it was still a Catholic private school for girls, it was much more modest than my previous school. It was on a crowded avenue in the center of the city, where you could hear and see all the buses polluting the air, in contrast to my school, which was literally in the middle of a forest. The new school was in a big old house with a badminton court used for recess. My classroom was a room made from a metal sheet on the roof of the house; getting up there was a hazard. Five girls were the entire junior class. This school accepted girls with disabilities, economic problems, and special needs.

At first, Pia and I were shocked by the stark contrast in environments, but in the end, it was an invaluable experience. We met the most generous teachers that we had ever encountered. They offered us classes on weekends at their homes without charging us, as the curriculum was quite different. All the school staff wanted to help us without any interest or judgment. For me, this philosophy was mind-blowing because we came from a school where even the principals evaluated you based on your family background and how much you could donate. If your dad were a prominent entrepreneur, you would get the main role in the Father's Day play even if you sang like a crying wolf.

Even though this school was rundown in appearance, it had the most unselfish and generous people I had ever met. It opened my eyes to how small and limited my reality was and how lucky we were.

We finished our junior year with solid grades, having become much more mature, and were able to return to our old school to graduate with our friends. I don't know with whom Gigi's parents spoke, but she was also able to come back for her senior year. Luckily, we all returned to graduate, except for the Spanish girls, who, I bet, were happily eating tapas and serrano ham back in Spain. We were elated to be together again with our friends, enjoying our last year of high school. This was the first experience in my life that taught me that growth and good things can come from huge, big, sloppy mistakes.

CHAPTER 4

The Seed of Fear

The greatness of a man is not in how much wealth he acquires, but his integrity and his ability to affect those around him positively.

—Bob Marley

In the nineties, Mexico was transforming rapidly; politics, economy, and society evolved, and some aspects began to deteriorate. In these years, the presidential candidate Luis Donaldo Colosio was assassinated at a campaign rally, and an armed movement started in Chiapas. Insecurity, corruption, and impunity flourished.

A single political party, the Revolutionary Party (PRI), had governed Mexico for many years since the Mexican Revolution in 1910. There was no democracy; it was a one-party dictatorship. The president in power decided who their successor would be, and we, the people, watched and applauded, distracted by soccer and telenovelas.

Mexico developed significantly economically, but the Mexican political class was, with very, very few exceptions, corrupt and opportunistic. One influential Mexican politician shamelessly declared, "A poor politician is a useless politician."

How could politicians make these massive fortunes while in power? It seemed they went into politics to make money, not to serve the people. The business class and entrepreneurs had mostly been critical of the political class because there was so much to improve, criticize, and oppose. But, they had to comply, because without permits (which are generally given with a bribe), a business could not survive or grow. My dad was a fierce critic of the ruling political party and always stood with the opposition party. I always heard my dad support the few honest candidates who tried to make a positive change for our country.

My dad, with the backing of my grandfather Eduardo, developed successful businesses. He worked very hard and would arrive late at night, often worried, disheartened, or in a bad mood.

"Another devaluation of the *peso* against the dollar is coming," he would foretell. "Once again, these corrupt PRI thieves are stealing the country. Look, girls, that guy on TV is going to be our future president."

Before the presidential campaigns began, it was known who would win the elections; they were completely rigged, a practice called *el dedazo*.

Every couple of years, a major economic crisis would hit the country hard, and the *peso* would inevitably be devalued against the dollar. That meant you would wake up one day, and if you had 100 *pesos* in the bank, in comparison to the dollar, you would now have 50. Naturally, inflation went through the roof. Mexico suffered, and the differences between the upper and lower classes became greater and greater. The middle class was disappearing, and the people's discontent was growing.

While all this was happening, I grew up oblivious to the political and financial tensions. My day-to-day reality was not affected even in the worst devaluation or crisis. Of course, my dad would see his business struggle and be sick with worry, but we were some of the few lucky ones who were able to thrive. While the middle and lower classes were gasping for air, we would carry on with lavish trips and shopping sprees.

Resentment started to brew, and things rapidly deteriorated. Armed robberies in the street were becoming more common, and jewelry or cash was taken by force. They started stealing stereos from cars, and then the cars themselves. A typical Sunday at my grandparents' house would not be complete without hearing the alarm of a car set off. One day, we heard the alarm uncomfortably close, and all the adults rushed to the street to see what was happening. Someone had broken the glass of my uncle's car, and his brand-new stereo had been stolen.

"Shit, they even took the speakers," said my Tío Rodrigo, fuming.

"Let's call the police. I heard there is a band stealing stereos and cars in the neighborhood," somebody suggested.

"Are you crazy? Call the police? It is a waste of time. The police usually protect criminals. They are one and the same," said my Tío Rodrigo, pissed and powerless.

That is how it all started, with stereos. Most of the time, the police were in cahoots with the criminals. The crimes went unpunished, and the criminals were loose in the streets with no one to stop them. After realizing that there were no consequences, they started to steal cars, then rob houses, and eventually, the kidnapping began.

I remember when they told us about the kidnapping of Pablo Fernandez. Pablito, as we fondly called him, was the oldest brother of one of my school friends, Camila. The Fernandez family lived in a red-brick house three blocks away from my home. When we went to high school, we were not allowed to walk anywhere, but sometimes we sneaked out of my house and walked to the Fernandez's without our parents knowing we had gone on foot.

Pablo was five years older than us, and sometimes, if his plans allowed it, he would take us partying or give us a ride back home if we decided to ditch our date at the club. He was very responsible and reliable, your typical big brother.

At 27 years old, Pablo was already a professor at one of the most prestigious universities in Mexico City. He worked in his family's company, which had large coffee plantations. One morning on his way to work, a couple of armed men took him near the Central Market of Mexico City.

There had been a pair of high-profile kidnappings in the news, but this was too close to home. When a kidnapping happens, the family is immediately isolated. They aren't allowed to talk to anybody outside their inner circle. In a certain way, they are also kidnapped from the world.

The Fernandez family hired international specialists to deal with the gruesome negotiations. Pablo's kidnappers were a band led by a man called *El Mochaorejas* (the ear-cutter). They were ruthless kidnappers who sent ears or body parts of the victim as proof of life. We could not believe that this was happening to someone as young, as loved, and as unique as Pablo. Long days became short weeks, and nobody knew about the whereabouts of Pablito. Finally, the family received proof of life.

However, after a couple of horrific months, Camila's parents stopped hearing from the kidnappers. It seemed that after a difficult call between the negotiators and the kidnappers, communications halted. The silence was deafening, the waiting eternal, and as time passed, the hope of getting Pablo back was fading.

But the Fernandez family never lost faith; they spent their waiting days attending daily Mass. We knew the time they'd attend Mass mid-week, so sometimes we'd go and sit at the back benches of the empty church. We would not approach them, so as not to disturb them, but rather accompany them in faith.

After waiting in anguish and overwhelming impatience, Pablo's brother started looking for him in the city's morgues. He eventually found Pablito's lifeless body in a common morgue like an ordinary John Doe. How much is a human life worth? How much money can you ask for the life of a fellow human being? Of a son? Of a brother? Of a friend?

When and how did human life become a commodity?

The fact that Pablito's brother found his body was some sort of a miracle. In a city as big as Mexico City, finding him was like finding a needle in a haystack. Pablo's body had been unidentified in that morgue for months. A few more weeks and, by procedure, they would have thrown him into a collective grave. If he had been transported to the collective grave, the family would have never known his fate. Heartbroken and devastated, at least the family could give him a heartfelt farewell.

I remember the funeral mass; the church was packed with mourning souls, and a sea of white candles inundated the *solea*. I could breathe a sigh of sad resignation. Although Pablo had passed away, at least in a way, he came back to his family. I wondered why someone with so much promise had to be taken away in such a harrowing manner.

Pablo's family remained standing with an unshakeable faith during his captivity and after his death. The testimony of the Fernandez family's grace and integrity had a profound impact on the entire community and the entire country.

Following the death of Pablo, a march was organized where more than 100,000 people walked shoulder to shoulder, dressed in white, demanding justice, peace, and security from the Mexican government.

Entire families flooded the streets of Mexico City. You could see the images in newspapers. Reforma, one of Mexico City's main avenues, was painted in white with the Angel of Independence witnessing from above the silent shouts for justice. They pleaded for Pablo and for all those victims who, unfortunately, were increasing daily.

After the pressure of civil society weighed on the government, they captured *El Mochaorejas* and his band. The band was formed by Daniel Arizmendi, a former police officer, his brother, and a few other men. They had committed several kidnappings and murders, making a fortune in the process. With this money, they bribed the police so they could continue operating with blatant immunity.

After the kidnappers were arrested, Pablito's mother visited the prison where they were held. She asked to speak with the murderers of her son, with several rosaries in hand. The band's leader, Daniel Arizmendi, refused to see her, but the other members agreed. She gave them each a rosary and told them that she forgave them, that they should pray and be closer to God.

This act of generosity, humility, and greatness of spirit took my breath away. To be able to forgive the people who took away her son leaves me speechless to this day.

After Pablo's death, his mother created an important organization that continues to help victims and families who have suffered a violent crime. The organization also demands that the government help provide a safe environment for every Mexican, which sometimes seems to be an unsolvable problem.

Without a doubt, Pablo's mother is one of the most admirable women I know. She has continued dedicating her life to fighting for a safer and better country. I don't know where she finds her courage and strength. For me, Pablo's family is an example of one of the most valuable families in Mexico.

This event affected me in a way I didn't realize at the time. It planted a seed, a seed of fear. As time passed, that seed grew, feeding off similar tragedies and crimes happening around me and in the country. The feeling of helplessness, vulnerability, and hopelessness grew, prompting me to take significant leaps in the future. With Pablito's death, my dear country's innocence died, and the seed of fear was planted within me.

CHAPTER 5

Choosing a Lane

You're off to Great Places!
Today is your day!
Your mountain is waiting, So... Get on your way! Oh, the
places you'll go.

—Dr. Seuss

I was completely clueless about what I wanted to study in college. As a mediocre student with no clear ambitions, I initially chose architecture, influenced by my dad's dreams. However, after just one semester, I realized this path wasn't for me.

"Dad, I hate architecture," I admitted tearfully in the kitchen, afraid of disappointing him. "I want to study fashion design."

"Fashion design? Fashion design is not a career. You need a real degree. Why don't you study business administration? Get your degree and then do whatever you want," he said.

I thought about it for less than a second; business administration sounded like a safe option. I changed my major to business and went with the flow. But as the semesters passed, I spiraled into a crisis. I didn't like my career, my love life was in the gutter, but most importantly, I felt empty and without purpose.

I bumped into a book that changed how I looked at life—*The Alchemist* by Paulo Coelho. It motivated me to find my passion and remember my love of creating and imagining dresses.

In life, you are fortunate if you find your passion early on. For me, it has taken a lot of twists and turns to get there. Every Wednesday, we went to have lunch at my Abuela Carmen's house. At the table, my abuela, my mom, and *tías* would talk about everything, but inevitably, the latest styles of it-girls were discussed, as if they were the fashion police.

"Did you see Lady Di's dress? She looked flawless."

"Yes, but Fergie is a mess, and that hair doesn't do her any favors." They would discuss these characters as if they were best friends and had dinner with them the night before.

For my mom, fashion and personal appearance were essential. She told us that when she was younger, she would travel to Barcelona and shop in one of the most exclusive boutiques of the time, called Santa Eulalia.

The store would hold private fashion shows for them so they could choose pieces from the new collections. Once they had chosen their new closet, they would custom-make all the pieces they had chosen especially for them.

I remember drawing paper dresses as a little girl. Once I drew a dress with a blue horizontal stripe. After a while, Lady Di happened to wear one that was very similar.

"Look, I designed a dress like Lady Di's. I imagined it and drew it before she wore it," I told my nanny very excitedly.

Maybe I'm not so lost.

Determined to pursue fashion, I split my time between business classes and a fashion school in Polanco. However, the workload became overwhelming, forcing me to drop out of fashion school. Ultimately, I completed my business degree but struggled to find a job because I didn't have any experience. How was I supposed to have experience if nobody gave me a chance? To be fair, I don't think I would have hired myself. I looked like I had no idea what I was doing, and I didn't.

During that time, I had a couple of boyfriends, but no one special. My family wanted me to marry a certain type of guy who belonged to the Spanish community in Mexico, or at the minimum, to have some acceptable references. My sister and cousins were already paired with great guys who were their high school sweethearts; their families knew their parents and even grandparents. They were all happily acquainted with each other. Although those young men were nice, to me, it all seemed predictable and boring.

It seemed that my parents and society had carved a path for me without asking me. It didn't matter what my dreams were or what I wanted to accomplish. What was expected of me was to marry well and create a family. I was drowning; I didn't know who I was or what I wanted. The expectations suffocated me. I felt unanchored, like a sailboat wandering adrift where the current or wind took me.

"Why don't you go to Boston to study the same program as my boyfriend, Santiago? You just need your bachelor's degree to apply," my friend Renata suggested.

It sounded like a plan. I felt stuck in Mexico; there was no place for me anymore. Leaving for Boston was perfect. I told my parents, and they were impressed. I could go to Harvard, even if it was the Extension School. Harvard is Harvard!

I clearly remember that early morning when I took my suitcase, and, like a whisper, I went into my parents' bedroom to say goodbye. The bedroom was pitch black, and my mom and dad were still sleeping peacefully in their bed.

I didn't want to wake them up, so I gave them both a kiss on their foreheads. As I left their room and closed the door carefully, I realized that my life was about to change. When I returned to Mexico, I wasn't going to be the same.

As I was walking down Commonwealth Avenue heading back to my new apartment on the corner of Massachusetts Avenue, I couldn't believe that this was my new life. I rented an apartment with Julie, my friend from high school. She enrolled in photography courses at Boston University, and I attended the Certificate of Special Studies in Business Administration at the Harvard Extension School. I could breathe with a new sense of freedom and reinvention in my new city.

It was late summer, and we were getting settled. We spent time walking to the Boston Common, the central public park downtown, or watching the boats sail away on the Charles River. I had to pinch myself when I went to buy my books at The Coop at Harvard Square, in front of the bench where Matt Damon played chess in the movie *Good Will Hunting*.

I was able to take classes all around the Harvard campus. For the first time in my life, I discovered what it felt like to study in a stimulating and exciting environment. I was captivated by what the teachers had to say; they made the classes interesting and enjoyable.

Now, I was able to make my own decisions and fly on my own. I was excited to learn, do better, and be better. A whole world opened for me, and I was not going to waste this opportunity and experience.

Growing up, I never had to pay a bill or balance a checkbook because everything was done for me. In Boston, I learned how to take care of myself and to do everyday things like figuring out which bus to take to get to class or how to do laundry in the nearest laundromat. I began to recognize the value of being my own person. Nobody asked or cared about my last name, and I loved it. I was another anonymous student in a sea of young people from every corner of the world.

As Julie and I settled in with our schedules, we needed to find a crew. Mexicans, when living abroad, tend to gravitate to other Mexicans. It was September 15th, the day Mexico celebrates its Independence, and we got word that the Mexican Consulate was organizing a party with mariachis included. We were especially excited because many Mexican students, like us, would attend.

While standing there sipping our margaritas and enjoying "*Cielito Lindo*," we noticed a small group of friends talking animatedly.

There was Alejandro, the son of a Mexican politician. His roommate, called Mini-Me because Alejandro was so tall, and Ricki was so very short. Liz, who was very friendly and funny. She started calling me *La Chiquis* from a Mexican book called *Las Niñas Bien*, written by Guadalupe Loaeza, in which upper-class Mexican women from the late 80s are portrayed. I think she saw me as an airhead at first, but with time, we became close friends.

In Mexico, there is a practice of calling everyone NOT by their given name. Let me explain, we are big on nicknames. If you make a funny comment, have a favorite food or even a favorite animal, you are in danger of being called that for the rest of your life. So, in our group, there was also *El Cubas, El Niño,* and *La Quesadilla*, a fun and picturesque bunch. They all came from different Mexican states and backgrounds.

We enjoyed camping trips in the fall, when we drove through New England's foliage and breathed fresh air surrounded by trees with red, orange, and yellow leaves. We would go on fishing trips or ski in New Hampshire. I felt like I was in an episode of the sitcom *Friends*.

The year ended, and if I didn't find a job in Boston, I knew I would have to go back to Mexico. I couldn't live on my father's dime; I needed to start making my own money. I applied for a job at the Mexican Consulate, the only place that would give me a visa and a chance to stay. It was a long shot, but I gave it a try. In the middle of summer, I received a call from the new Consul in Boston. They offered me a job.

OMG!!!

I couldn't believe it. I called the gang. While some were gone, we had two new and fabulous additions to our group of friends: Vanne and Mariana. Mariana was the daughter of my dad's best friend. As soon as we reunited in Boston, we started what has become a long-standing friendship, just like our dads. Vanne was smart and confident; she didn't take crap from anybody.

One night, we met Alejandro for drinks. He also had new additions to the gang. He introduced us to *El Mada*, remarkably tall, skinny, with dark black hair, glasses, and an intellectual look.

They called him *El Mada* because his schoolmates thought he looked like a famous Mexican television character, *El Madaleno*, who had spiky black hair and a sarape. I didn't get the resemblance at all; he looked more like a skinny adult Harry Potter.

"Hi, Chiquis," El Mada said.

"Do I know you? Why do you call me Chiquis? My name is Monica," I said, all bitchy, high and mighty, with Vanne by my side. El Mada was with his roommate, El Mato. They were both pursuing their MBAs at MIT's Sloan Business School. The MIT gang was down-to-earth, funny, and interesting.

I had a new job and a new roommate from Costa Rica, Melissa, a freshman at Boston College. I was five years older, but we hit it off right off the bat. Between barbecues and nights out, we were having the time of our lives. We all decided to go to New York City to watch the New York Marathon. We met for some drinks at a trendy New York bar. I had a crush on Alejandro, and Liz, my friend, could tell.

"Be careful. He went out with my college friend, and he left her utterly broken-hearted. I don't think he is for you," she cautioned.

Nevertheless, that night in New York, we started going out.

"I can't believe I am going out with a girl like you; you are so different from the girls I used to date," he said.

"I feel exactly the same way," I answered.

I don't think any of our friends took us seriously; we were total opposites. I came in without expectations and knew deep inside that Alejandro wasn't for me. We talked frequently but didn't see much of each other. He always had an excuse, whether it was schoolwork or crewing with the team. I played it cool, but I waited by the phone for his call. Eventually, all these games took a toll on me.

My girlfriends and I organized a trip to Spain. Vanne, Liz, Mariana, and I flew to Barcelona and had a blast. When we returned, a friend told me that Alejandro had been making out with another girl while I was away. I confronted him when I got home.

"I swear it is a lie. Give me the phone; I'll call right now the girl that I supposedly made out with, so she can tell you the truth," Alejandro said. He was distraught and so adamant in his denial that I believed him.

"Thanks, Chiquis. I don't want to break up," he said.

"I prefer breaking up over you going behind my back," I said. "No, Chiquis, don't worry. I'll let you know before that happens."

As things cooled down after our argument and I believed his story, we started discussing different topics, and he suddenly became quite serious.

"You know, I genuinely respect El Mada. He's brilliant and a good friend. Three years ago, he had cancer and almost died."

"What do you mean, he almost died?" I said.

"Yes, he had chemotherapy and radiation; he almost died," he explained. He was visibly upset.

"Don't feel bad for El Mada. He seems happy, enjoying his life.

He is rocking his MBA and in love with his doctor-girlfriend," I tried to console him.

"I know, but it's mind-blowing he had to go through that."

"Yeah, I know, it must be a life-changing experience," I responded.

Life continued, and the year flew by. I enjoyed working at the Consulate, helping Mexicans in Boston process their passports or addressing any other issues they may have had. I was quickly promoted to be the Consul's personal assistant. It wasn't my dream job, but finally, I was supporting myself. It was ironic that I wound up working for the Mexican government, considering how critical I had been of it my entire life. The Consul, my boss, was committed to helping Mexicans abroad. I soon understood that not everything was so black and white.

Alejandro was his usual self, making excuses, and I was becoming more frustrated. In January, Boston was immersed in winter; everything was black, white or grey. It was freezing cold. I went to work in the dark and came home again in the dark. The people on the bus were quiet, gloomy, and lifeless. I didn't enjoy my job of organizing someone else's life. As each day passed, a little light inside me died. My girlfriends were worried because I didn't eat much, and I was losing weight surprisingly fast. With the spring air, I gained a little bit of strength and felt better.

"Hey, do you want to go for a run?" Alejandro asked me.

"Why don't you run while I skate beside you?" I suggested.

We started running and skating; he was so fast. I saw his long legs lunge in front of me. Even though I was skating the fastest I could, I couldn't catch up with him. We went from Cambridge through Harvard Square and crossed the

Charles River. I was struggling and suddenly fell. He stopped, looked back,

and helped me up. We headed back to his apartment, but before we did, we stopped in a park nearby.

"I can't do this anymore," I said.

I realized he was always going to be running in front of me, and I was always going to be trying to catch up. I would never catch up. I didn't want that. I wanted someone to be running beside me. He agreed it was time to let go, and we parted ways.

I worried about what the future looked like. We had the same friends. He was the leader of the gang, and I would eventually be sidelined. But my girlfriends were there for me; they helped me find my way back to myself. I slowly started to recognize myself again. My friends would check on me daily. They made me laugh, let me cry, and helped make fun plans; they were literally lifesavers.

My parents came to visit. When I went to the airport to pick them up, they didn't recognize me because I had lost so much weight. I stayed with them at a nice hotel. We saw movies on pay-per-view and had room service.

"Come back home," my mom pleaded. "I am very worried; what are you doing here? You don't even like your job."

She had a point. I hated my job.

"You can come back and work with me," my dad suggested. "I am excited that you can apply everything you learned here in my business."

It was very tempting. I was drained, exhausted, and emotionally destroyed. Maybe it was time to go home.

My girlfriends were sad but understood. I told the Consul that I was leaving and thanked him for the opportunity. My friends threw me a farewell party; everyone came to say goodbye. Alejandro called the day before I was leaving.

"You're leaving tomorrow, right?"

"Yes," I replied.

"El Mada is going back to Mexico to do an internship for the summer. He's going on your flight; I told him to please take good care of you for me."

"Oh, ok. Great." I said.

My girlfriends drove me to the airport. We were crying and distraught, going our separate ways. El Mada arrived at the airport, and he had a look on his face of, "Shit, what did I let myself get into?" But he was a good sport; I was so upset. He took my passport, carried my laptop, and brought me home. On the airplane, I kept crying, feeling disappointed for having to run back to my parents. I also thought about Alejandro and was sad that it was over for good. I gazed outside the window.

"Don't look back, Chiquis. Don't look back," El Mada said. What a nice guy, I thought.

"Are you still dating the doctor?"

"No, we broke up. She's now going out with one of my classmates."

"Oh, I'm sorry," I said. "So, there is going to be this huge welcoming party for me at the airport; my Mexican friends, who are all super gorgeous, are bringing mariachis. I will introduce you to Pia, one of my best friends. I think you two will hit it off. I think you are really going to like her."

"Perfect," he said. We landed at Mexico City airport. I saw a driver dressed in a suit and a tie waving at El Mada.

"Welcome back, Mr. Perez. Your father just landed from New York; he is waiting for you in the car," the driver said.

"Chiquis, where is your welcoming party?" El Mada asked. In a panic, I didn't spot any of my friends.

"I don't know where they are; they swore they were going to be here," I said, embarrassed as I looked around.

"Where are the mariachis?" He was laughing.

"I don't know." Knowing full well the mariachis were an exaggeration on my part.

"Do you want me to give you a ride?" he asked.

"Sorry to interrupt, but your father is waiting in the car," the driver said again. I had five suitcases, and it was late, and my friends were MIA.

"If it is no trouble, I would love it if you took me home," I said.

We walked with El Mada's driver as they helped me with my luggage, and we got into the car.

"Hello, Dad, how are you? This is Monica, a friend of mine," El Mada said. His dad turned slowly from the front seat and looked at me, amused.

"Hello, Monica," he said.

"Very nice to meet you, Mr. Perez," I said, feeling slightly embarrassed. He just nodded, and then he smiled.

Later, I asked my friends what happened. Why did they forget to pick me up?

"Oh, we did go to pick you up, but while waiting, we had some Margaritas at the airport's TJ Friday's, and I guess we weren't paying attention at the exit, we just missed you," Gigi said nonchalantly.

I never understood how we could have missed each other. At that time, cellphones weren't a thing. Maybe my life would have turned out differently if I had found my friends that day!

CHAPTER 6

Stepping on Crap Can Lead You to Love

As I landed in Mexico in time for Ale's wedding, one of my high school friends. Julie, my first Boston roommate, was engaged to the guy she met while living in Boston. It was the year 2000, and everybody was moving forward. I felt left behind and heartbroken.

Thankfully, I received news from my Boston girlfriends, who were planning a trip to Costa Rica for the summer with my roommate, Melissa. They invited the whole gang: the girls, Mini-Me, Miguel, and El Mada. The trip was upcoming, and Miguel and Mini-Me canceled, so El Mada was left hanging. By that point, we were becoming good friends, going out dancing and having fun. He would tell me about his dates, and I would tell him about mine.

"Are you sure you want to come along with crazy ladies like us to Costa Rica?"

"Sure, it will be fun! I am not afraid to deal with you guys."

From the get-go, El Mada sensed that we were going to be a handful. On the airplane, we were laughing, trashing all his friends, and men in general. But he was a good sport, driving a group of loud-mouthed females through Costa Rica in a white van.

"Shotgun!" I claimed, riding in the front of the car.

In Costa Rica, it takes six hours to drive everywhere, so we would have deep conversations on the steep, dirt roads.

We arrived at El Arenal, which is a huge volcano surrounded by thermal waters. El Mada was a tall, shaggy guy escorted by six cute, young girls. By now, he was one of us.

"After this trip, I hate men, too. They are the worst," he joked.

We enjoyed the thermal waters of El Arenal, which are hot springs warmed by the volcano, creating a natural jacuzzi. El Mada was in the middle of the pool, with three girls on each side. An American guy approached and asked him, "Dude, what is up with all those girls hanging out with you?"

"They are all my girlfriends, the six of them," El Mada replied.

"No, I don't believe you," the guy said.

"Go ahead and ask them," El Mada challenged him.

"Hi, girls! This guy says that you are all his girlfriends. Is that true?"

"Of course, he is our boyfriend, and we absolutely love him," we said as we hugged him. El Mada was in heaven.

When we returned to Mexico City, I felt better. A big shift occurred inside me. I decided that I didn't care anymore about Mexican society's expectations for young women like me. I realized in Boston that there were more options for women beyond marriage and children. I decided that I wanted to work on something I loved. I had learned that if you don't love, enjoy, or find purpose in your work, your soul dies a little bit each day, and eventually, you'll feel dead inside. I had to figure out what I loved. I was not going to follow anyone's rules anymore. Even if I didn't marry and was alone for eternity, I was going to do something that fulfilled me—something that I loved, that I could dedicate my life to.

Liz's wedding was approaching. Everyone was going to be there. In Mexico, every life event is an excuse for a massive celebration, and women often require dresses for these special occasions.

Since I was a young girl, I would design my own dresses, and a seamstress would sew them for me. This time, my mom told me about a young woman designing dresses who was making a killing. I made an appointment so she could help me with the dress for Liz's wedding. She worked out of a small house in the upscale residential area of *Las Lomas de Chapultepec*. In the waiting room, I found pieces of fabric piled all around me: silks, taffetas, chiffon, prints, and tulle. It was a new world!

"Maria will be here in a minute; please wait in her study," a lady said.

A lovely woman in her thirties came in. She had brown curly hair and a welcoming smile.

"Hi, nice to meet you, Monica! You need a dress, right? What do you have in mind?"

I described the dress as I imagined it: something sexy but not too revealing. As I talked, she drew what I was describing, a one-shoulder crop top with the back open, paired with a pencil skirt. I chose the fabric and color, and came out of her office ecstatic.

I had done this process before, but this time was different. I don't know why, but I knew that this was what I wanted to do with the rest of my life. She inspired me. A light inside me turned on. I had an appetite for learning, an ambition for creating. I had never felt this way about anything before in my life.

After a few fittings, I picked up my dress. It was gorgeous! I felt confident, ready, and empowered to face anything. I wanted to show everybody that I was doing great and was happy.

Liz's wedding was in Cuernavaca, which is two hours away from Mexico City. Friends flew from all over the world to the wedding. El Mada offered to drive us, and, once again, I was seated in the front passenger seat. We arrived at the wedding venue and parked the car in an adjacent lot. I opened the car door and carefully took a step down to the grass with my six-inch heels. As I took a second step, I marched into a big old pile of mushy dog crap.

"SHIIIIIIT NOOOO!!!" I shouted.

"What happened?" El Mada asked.

"I stepped on dog crap." I was feeling like a million bucks until I put my foot in a load of poop.

El Mada walked toward me and said, "Give me your shoe."

I untied my ankle strap and slowly gave him my shoe; the sole of my stilettos was dripping in poo. He grabbed the shoe and started cleaning it, scrubbing it against a tree and the grass. All the crap was gone, and the shoe was as good as new.

I could fall in love with this guy, I thought, as I watched El Mada struggle to remove the shit from my shoe. We had spent most of the summer together and had a blast, whether in a Volcano in Costa Rica or dancing and laughing in a Bar in La Colonia Roma. I realized that my feelings for him had changed somewhere along the way. What started out as a friendship was slowly becoming something else.

Wedding season was in full throttle by then, so I went to Maria for another dress, but this time I drew the design and brought my own fabric. It was a cream-colored, silk degradé, ending in shades of red. I designed a strapless dress with a little train on the back. It came out beautifully. Maria asked if she could use it for a fashion show she was putting together.

"Of course, you can use it!" I was honored she wanted to use my dress.

In one of the multiple weddings I attended, I bumped into Maria and her husband.

"How are you?" she asked.

"Great," I said. "I loved the dresses you did for me. They made me feel beautiful and confident. I want to be like you someday."

She laughed. I was serious.

By that time, all my Boston friends, including El Mada, who I was getting particularly close to, had already gone back to their studies in Boston, and reality hit me. I was working at my dad's company, but I couldn't care less; I was going to disappoint my dad again. I think he wanted me eventually to take over his business.

"Dad, I've got to talk to you," I said as I entered his office.

"What do you need?" he asked, keeping his eyes on the desk.

"Remember in college, I tried to study fashion design but couldn't handle the workload?"

"Yeees. . ."

"Well, I was wondering if I could work here half-time and in the evening attend fashion school. I will pay for it with the money that I make here."

He covered his face with his hand, exasperated.

"Is that what you want? After you went to Harvard and worked for the Consul, now you want to be a seamstress?"

"I'm sorry, Dad, I really want to do it. I don't like my job here as much as you do. This has been your path. I need to follow mine."

"Do whatever you want," he answered. I could see the disappointment and heartbreak on his face.

I felt horrible, but I was determined to show my parents that I was serious this time. Even though he didn't seem thrilled, he accepted my plan. I enrolled in the same small school in Polanco that I attended years ago and started classes. I was excited and couldn't learn fast enough. I bought myself a sewing machine and started practicing in my room. In Mexico, young people normally live with their parents until they get married. I still lived at home, so when my dad heard my sewing machine, he would cringe.

"I can't deal with it; she went to Harvard, and now she is sewing in her room," I could hear him say to my mom.

The pace of fashion school was slow for me. I started practicing, making dresses for my friends. What I loved about it was the art of transforming a simple piece of fabric into something beautiful. I was excited to learn and eager to execute my ideas on the fabric.

As I found new clarity in what I wanted to do with my life, my self-confidence grew. I decided that if I didn't find someone incredible to marry, I would move to New York and work in fashion. I wasn't scared anymore of being single or alone. I wasn't afraid of disappointing anyone. I was empowered to follow my dreams and make them a reality. When you are fully engaged in what you are doing and have clear goals for yourself, you radiate a special glow, a unique kind of beauty and self-confidence.

I would go out with my two single Mexican girlfriends. One of them was Regina, whom I had met in kindergarten. She had expressive, green eyes and was full of life. She had always been drawn to show business, and at this time, she was dating Luis, a member of a famous Mexican boy band. Her family was naturally opposed, but she wasn't deterred. We became party girls, going out every Thursday through Saturday night, while still working and studying. I started meeting many guys, but now I felt in control and was having the time of my life.

Regina, Gelo, and I would drive to Acapulco for some weekend fun. One night, Regina's boy band boyfriend took us to meet some "friends." The mysterious friends ended up being in a Mexican regional band *(gruperos)*, *Los Temerarios*. We wound up in a huge house with an amazing pool and garden overlooking Acapulco Bay. It was a pre-concert party with many big hombres with sombreros. I felt like I was in a *Scarface* scene, Mexican-style.

We boarded the Los Temerarios tour bus and went to their concert, enjoying it from backstage. Afterward, we went to the most exclusive club in Acapulco, the *Baby'O*. We arrived in the tour bus of the grupero band, which for us was very exuberant. We were nervously laughing that somebody we knew might see us.

Usually, we would travel alone to my apartment in Acapulco, but this time, my parents stayed in the apartment with us. We came home to the apartment laughing, with the first rays of sun coming up, about the crazy adventure we had just had to find my mom, who was furious, waiting for us.

"It is dawn, are you crazy? We were getting ready to go looking for you; we were worried sick." Regina and Gelo, staring at the floor, ran to my bedroom while my mom blasted me.

"Mom, you don't have to worry, I'm a grown-up," I said.

"As long as you live under our roof, you have to follow our rules. The worst thing that has happened to you is going to Boston; you have changed so much. I regret the day you left," she said bitterly.

"Well, Mom, for me, it is the exact opposite. It is the best thing that has ever happened," I retorted.

"Go to your room; I can't see you anymore."

I was twenty-five years old, living under my parents' roof and still a little bit lost. But at least now I was clear that fashion was my future.

When I entered a fabric store, my heart started pounding out of my chest. I would go crazy thinking of all the unlimited possibilities. I was amazed at how many different styles, personalities, and even realities you could create for yourself with a simple piece of fabric. I would see fabric rolls aligned and organized by silks, chiffon, crepes, tulle, printed, and solid colors—the options were infinite. I also began learning which fabrics suit each style best and how to handle them effectively. I wanted to understand what silhouette was best for each body type to create the best style that would enhance the bodies of everyday women. I wanted to help women of all ages and body types look and feel their best.

I had battled insecurities about my appearance and knew how it could affect the way a woman perceives herself. I was never the prettiest in the room, but I had worked on feeling better on the inside. Self-esteem and self-worth are hard work, but they don't come from clothes; instead, they come from working deep within yourself. I loved creating clothes for women because I could make them feel confident and beautiful in a small way. If you are happy with how you feel and look, you can take over the world. I loved being able to make women happy and confident in themselves.

I started making my own clothes. Once, when I was going out, I wore something that I'd made: a metallic grey miniskirt with a lateral slit. I was talking to a guy, and he said to me, "I love your skirt."

"That is the best compliment you could have given me," I replied.

After a while, the party scene started getting old. I was dating a lot, but when I came home, I would call El Mada to tell him about my dates and the guys I was going out with. Something started to change; if I didn't talk to him, I would miss him. If something exciting happened, I wanted to tell him right away. Eventually, I stopped telling him about my dates.

El Mada was coming home from his last year of his MBA for the weekend and invited me to his cousin's wedding. That week, the Popocatepetl, an active volcano near Mexico City, was fuming and heaving ash. I watched the news and started to freak out because they were closing the airport due to the ash in the air and the non-visibility. I almost started crying because his airplane was coming in soon, and I thought it might crash. Isabel, my sister, started to make fun of me, saying I must really like this guy if I got upset over such nonsense.

Despite my fears, he arrived safely, and we went to the wedding together. It was then that I realized I had started having feelings for him. Still, he was one of Alejandro's closest friends, and I was the ex-girlfriend, so it was not going to be that simple. I drank a shot of tequila to give me courage.

"What about all the guys you were dating? Do you like somebody?" El Mada asked me.

"Well, there is someone, but he is not around right now," I said.

"Everything comes at the right time," he said.

In the meantime, Isabel wanted to learn Italian during the summer months. I found an intensive course in fashion design at the Marangoni Fashion Institute, which is one of the top schools for fashion design. We asked our dad if we could go to Milan, and he started to fume again.

"Girls, you can't go to Italy alone; the men in Italy are very sexually aggressive. They will pinch your butts!" he said, alarmed.

My mom calmed him down and told him that we knew how to take care of ourselves. So, we planned to go to Italy for the summer. I was thrilled because Italian fashion was, by far, my favorite, and Milan was the epicenter of it all. I had returned to Mexico from Boston a year prior, and I was amazed at how my life had changed in such a short amount of time.

My friend Pia was dating an American guy whom she met through work. Everybody was freaked out that Pia was going out with Tommy, the American. Her friends and family told her that she didn't know anything about this guy. I met Tommy, and he was intelligent, handsome, and so nice; most importantly, he was in love with Pia.

"Pia, don't listen to them and go for it," I said. I was so over the Mexican limitations.

It was the summer of 2001, and El Mada had finished his MBA and returned to Mexico City for good. He invited me to watch a movie at his parents' house. He knew I was leaving for Milan very soon.

We started watching the movie, and out of nowhere he asked me: "I really like you, do you want to be my girlfriend?" I was both ecstatic and surprised that he asked; everything was moving so fast.

"Of course, but I'm leaving for Italy, and you've just arrived. I know for sure that I want to be with you, but don't you want to explore the Mexican scene? I want you to be confident in your decision to be with me. Maybe you want to date other girls until I come back from Milan."

"I don't need to date anyone else; you waited for me while I was in Boston; I will wait for you to come back from Milan," he said. I was blown away by his feelings for me and his willingness to wait for me.

Isabel and I flew to Milan, and it was breathtaking. The Marangoni Institute exceeded my expectations. At the end of the course, I presented a collection, and the Italian teacher told me that I should seriously consider enrolling full-time. However, I needed to return to work and face my reality. I couldn't be a student forever.

I talked to El Mada every day. I missed him. He got a job at a consulting firm in Mexico City, and before I knew it, I was back in Mexico with El Mada, working with my dad and making dresses for my friends and family. Pia called me with great news.

"Moni, I got engaged to Tommy. I am so excited. I am moving to the Virgin Islands after we get married in Guadalajara. I thought maybe you could make the bridesmaids' dresses?"

"It's so exciting, Pia! Of course, it is an honor to make your bridesmaids' dresses, thank you, thank you!"

I bought a soft pink crepe and started designing the dresses for six of my best friends. I designed them according to their personality. I made the patterns and started sewing the dresses. My sewing skills were still limited, but the fittings went well, and I was determined to make an impression on the wedding attendees.

The wedding was approaching, and sewing six dresses alone was not an easy task. I remember sewing day and night, but with all the mistakes I kept making, I would unsew and sew again and again.

My friends started to get nervous, and I started to panic.

My whole family flew to Guadalajara for Pia's wedding. She had been a sister to me since they kicked us out of high school. I delivered the dresses hastily, but my dress wasn't done. I finished it very late at night in my hotel room the night before the wedding.

As I joined the church's bridesmaids, I saw how great they all looked in their dresses. The finishes were awful, but in general, they appeared to be happy with them. The bride, Pia, arrived at the church; she looked beautiful as ever. Her sister Pau arrived with her and joined the bridesmaids. I also made her dress, but couldn't have a fitting because she was living in London. We started walking into the church, and I noticed Pau crossing her arms, holding the dress's cleavage. The dress was literally falling apart, and if she let go, you could see her breasts. As I walked down the aisle, I watched my dad notice what poor Pau was battling with, and he nodded his head in panic, covering his eyes.

As soon as Pau sat down in church, she covered her dress with a shawl, and when the ceremony was over, she changed into a different dress. I was so overwhelmed and emotional about Pia moving to the Virgin Islands that I wasn't so mortified by Pau's mess of a dress.

"Pau, I am so sorry about your dress. I saw you having some trouble in mass," I said.

"Don't worry, Moni, I get that you are new at this; let's forget about it and celebrate."

Wow, what a trouper I would have been pissed if I was her, I thought. *I am so lucky to have such understanding and amazing friends*. I danced the night away with El Mada, wishing the new couple happiness forever.

Recipe to share with friends at a tropical location, if possible

Acapulco Shrimp Cocktail

- 1/3 cup purple onion, chopped
- 1/3 cup white onion, finely diced
- 1/3 cup cilantro chopped, plus more for garnish
- 1/3 cup freshly squeezed lime juice
- 1/3 cup freshly squeezed orange juice
- 1 pound chilled small, cooked shrimp – peeled and deveined.
- 2 Roma (plum) tomatoes, chopped
- 2 serrano chiles, seeded and finely chopped
- ½ mango chopped into cubes
- 2 teaspoons salt
- 2 teaspoons ground black pepper
- 1 cup chilled ketchup (such as Heinz®)
- 2 tablespoons hot pepper sauce (such as Valentina®)
- 2 tablespoons of Maggi Seasoning
- 2 tablespoons of Worcestershire sauce seasoning
- 2 avocados - peeled, pitted, and chopped

Instructions:

1. Mix the onions, lime, and orange juice in a small bowl.
2. In a large, separate bowl, whisk together the ketchup, tomatoes, cilantro, mangoes, Maggi seasoning, Worcestershire sauce, hot sauce, salt, and pepper. After it is incorporated, add the lime juice mixture and stir into the dressing.
3. Add the cooked shrimp and toss until thoroughly combined.
4. Gently fold in avocado cubes. Cover and chill at least 1 hour.
5. Serve with salty crackers or tostadas.

CHAPTER 7

The Face of Fear

As we walked through Guadalajara's airport, ready to board our flight back to Mexico City, I was still feeling a hangover sting from Pia's wedding and Pau's dress debacle. While walking to our gate, my dad received a phone call. He stopped abruptly and, pale as a ghost, said: "When? How? It can't be. We will be right there." He hung up.

"What happened, Dad?"

"Your Abuelo Eduardo was kidnapped," he replied. These five words changed my life forever.

My parents had a difficult time in their marriage when I was younger. During that period, my Abuelo Eduardo would often invite us on family trips and was always very caring.

"Moni, when I am having a tough time, I pray to Saint Jude. He always has my back," he said once as he handed me a little printed image of Saint Jude. Saint Jude is the patron saint of desperate and lost causes; he was perfect for the task.

"Pray to him, I am sure he will help your parents get back on track."

I prayed and prayed to Saint Jude, like my life depended on it. I can guarantee that Saint Jude is very effective because he did perform a small miracle. Since then, Saint Jude has become one of my favorite saints, but I don't bother him with small nuisances, as he is a very popular saint.

"What do you mean they kidnapped him?" I asked, scared.

"I just got a call from your Tío Ricardo. He told me that they kidnapped him, that they are watching all of us, and to be careful and head straight back home."

El Mada called his dad with the news. At the time, his dad was working as a high-level executive, and for his security, he was given an armored SUV. He kindly sent his driver with the vehicle to pick us up at the airport, so we could safely return home. As soon as we arrived home, my dad left for my Abuelo's house, and he warned us:

"You can't tell anyone what is happening; the life of your Abuelo depends on it. From now on, you're in charge of your Abuela. Take her to mass in the morning, but immediately after, go back to the house, stay there, and don't talk to anybody," he commanded.

It was the early days of December, and it was already cold. The city started painting itself with red, green, and white, celebrating the holidays, but for us, it was painful to see the Christmas decorations and festivity all around. For us, time stopped.

Where is he? Is he cold? Are they treating him well? Will he suffer the same fate as Pablito? My mind was reeling.

The days passed, one the same as the other. We were on automatic, like lifeless robots following the motions. We didn't have any news and didn't ask. We went to mass, and then to my Abuelos'. My Abuela was incredibly composed. We would sit in silence in the living room, waiting for the news. Two weeks passed, and Christmas Eve was approaching like a black hole. I felt a knot in my stomach, an omen that he was going to be in captivity at Christmas.

We just wanted him back alive so that we could celebrate many future Christmases together. Christmas Eve arrived. There were no decorations, no tree, no presents, no Christmas carols. We had dinner at the kitchen table with heavy hearts. We knew the negotiations were progressing, but there was no specific update. I wondered if anything would ever be the same.

After three weeks of the most terrifying nightmare, my Abuelo Eduardo safely returned home to his wife, daughters, and grandchildren. The next day, we were all summoned to my abuelos' house. He wanted to see us. I remember clearly how we all stood waiting for him in the foyer. He appeared at the top of the stairs and came down in a black pantsuit.

I was so relieved!

We hugged and cried, and I thanked God for his return. My family was complete again.

This event changed me on a cellular level. I remember driving my car and seeing random people in the streets as incoming threats. I had never seen people as threats before; I just saw them as people. I started living in constant fear, paranoid about the whereabouts of El Mada or my family. My dad decided to armor my car, and I hated that it had come to this. My family slowly recovered, but I couldn't. I remembered my sense of freedom in Boston, and I missed that safe and carefree environment.

Through it all, El Mada was my anchor. He became my source of comfort, of strength. I loved him deeply, and so did my family. He was funny, intelligent, and supportive. He laughed at my jokes. He believed in me more than I believed in myself. He was my best friend—and, for the first time in my life, I felt seen. Loving him felt like watching puzzle pieces fall into place. Everything in my life, all the chaos and growth and pain, had led me to him. After all that we had been through together, he asked me to marry him, and I said yes with all my heart.

CHAPTER 8

Cancer 101

The months leading up to the wedding for the soon-to-be couple are a time of hopeful anticipation, filled with dreams and plans for a new life together. But for us, we needed to confront difficult subjects, the consequences of El Mada's past cancer treatment.

He had cancer in his lymph nodes, Hodgkin's disease, when he was 24 years old. It was an aggressive type of cancer, but he got better after chemotherapy and radiation. He didn't talk much about it, but often said it was the best thing that had happened to him. Before cancer, he was anxious and overthought everything. Afterward, he felt grateful, ready to live fully, and credited Our Lady of Guadalupe with his healing.

"Why do you say that?" I was surprised because he wasn't particularly religious.

"I don't know, I just felt it," he responded.

After courageously fighting cancer for a year, El Mada was given a clean bill of health on December 12, the day of *La Virgen de Guadalupe*.

"Flaquita, because I had radiation when I was treated, there is a pos- possibility that maybe I can't have children. I saved some sperm for the time I would like to have children of my own, but nothing is certain. What do you think about adoption?" he asked.

Honestly, it was a subject not on my radar.

"My five-year checkup is coming up; you can come if you want, if you have any questions," he said.

"Yes, I would love to come."

We arrived with El Mada's dad at the hospital's cancer pavilion. It was the first time I came close to the cancer world— people in wheelchairs, bald and weakened by the disease. My heart shrank. It was hard to see people so sick and to think that El Mada had gone through it, too. We greeted the doctor as he came into the exam room.

"Hi, everyone. Nice to see you, how have you been?"

"Very good. This is my girlfriend, Monica, and you remember my dad."

"Yes, of course. How are you, Mr. Perez? I am glad to meet you, Monica," he said. "How are you feeling? Your exams are great. It is five years now, so most likely it's not coming back."

"That is great news," El Mada answered.

"Are you hanging around anyone who smokes? Remember, you can't; it damages your lungs."

"No," El Mada said.

Phew! I thought. I just quit smoking a couple of months ago. El Mada hated to be around people who smoked, but he never asked me to quit. I was so relieved that I had quit. Even though I gained six pounds, it was worth it!

"Are you exercising?" the doctor asked.

"Yes, I ride my bike every chance I get," he answered.

"Well, everything looks good," the doctor said. "Do any of you have any questions?"

"I do," I jumped. "What is the chance of the cancer coming back?"

"It's been five years since his diagnosis, so he is technically cured. The chances of him getting cancer are the same as yours or mine." "Can he have children?" I asked.

"We can't say how the treatment affected his body. There is a possibility he might not be able to have children, but we don't know," he said.

"Is his cancer hereditary?" I asked.

"No, his cancer is not hereditary."

"Thank you, Doctor."

I was embarrassed to ask these questions of the doctor and, moreover, in front of El Mada's dad. Nothing would change my decision to marry him, but I needed to acknowledge our reality.

When we left, El Mada's dad turned to me and said, "It was very appropriate that you asked those questions of the doctor. It is important to be informed."

Thank God, he didn't think I was being too nosy!

"Are you sure you want to marry him? Aren't you scared that he might get sick again? Maybe you need to think this over. Marry someone who hasn't been so seriously ill," a friend later said.

"You know, sometimes it does scare me that his cancer might come back, but I love him. I prefer to be with him, whatever time we have together, rather than spend my whole life with anyone else. Besides, nobody has tomorrow guaranteed."

We got married at sunset in a beautiful garden overlooking Acapulco's bay. As the priest led the ceremony, seagulls flew above us, crossing the painted skies.

CHAPTER 9

Miami Fashion Week

We settled into newlywed life. I loved El Mada but found it difficult to adapt to the gym, coffee with friends, cooking, and cleaning for my husband's lifestyle. Having kids was mandatory; my life was all mapped out.

Is this it? Is anything exciting going to happen again? Was I just another overprivileged Mexican housewife, destined to swap stories about nannies or my kids over brunch? I knew I had to return to what made me feel alive—designing dresses.

Even if I had a lot to learn, I could transform a piece of fabric into something wearable and, at times, beautiful. My family remained skeptical, but El Mada was supportive and enthusiastic as always, even when I messed up more times than I can remember.

I converted a small storage room in our apartment into my first studio. I bought a full-length mirror and filled the space with bolts of fabric in every color and texture, and pinned my old fashion school sketches on the walls. I hired a seamstress, who taught me many things, far more than I learned in fashion school. There is no better school than experience. I first hired her for a couple of days a week, but after a while, she worked full-time. As I made more dresses, the word got out, and my clientele grew.

While all this was happening, we had our first baby boy, Ignacio. The moment I saw him, I fell completely, irreversibly in love. It was the kind of love I had never known before. I couldn't believe this perfect mini human being was formed inside me; my existence was altered forever on so many levels. What didn't change was my will to keep making dresses, learning and growing. Soon after Ignacio's birth, I decided to open my first shop. By then, I had enough clients to afford rent, so I moved to an office on the first floor of a small building on a popular street close to my apartment. The street wasn't fancy. It was surrounded by taquerias and dry cleaners, but it was very well-located. I had already hired another seamstress because we had a lot of work. I would make dresses for weddings, graduations, and christenings. We had a party or event almost every weekend, and people wanted something exclusive that nobody else had.

My work was very well priced, but I had my hits and misses. My clients were generally happy, but when they didn't like what I made, I felt devastated. I taught myself not to be very affected if things didn't work out because it could take a toll on me. But I listened attentively when they had complaints, tried to fix them, and learned from my mistakes.

I started getting some press for the dresses I was making. One day, out of the blue, I got an unexpected call.

"Hello, is this Monica? Hi, I'm Gabriel. I saw your feature in ELITE magazine. I work with the organizers of Miami Fashion Week. It takes place in three weeks, and I think you are a good fit. Are you interested in presenting?" he asked.

My heart raced, and my mind exploded.

"Of course, I am interested! What do I have to do?"

He explained all the requirements to me, and I discussed them with El Mada. My in-laws had a vacation apartment in Miami that I could use for the preparations. I had to pay a fee to be in the event, which would cover everything, including the models. I had never done a fashion show; it was a dream come true, and moreover, in Miami.

Miami had already become one of my happy places. Every time I visited, I didn't want to leave. I felt free, like I did in Boston, but with much better weather!

Challenge accepted.

I had no idea how to do it, but I was determined to figure it out... in three weeks. I had no time to lose. I started drawing day and night, and with the fabrics I had in my office, I created my first collection: AIRE. The collection consisted of short and long dresses with clean, airy lines. The colors were mostly neutral and had beading in very light tones. I accompanied the dresses with tulle to give them a whimsical feel.

I flew with Gelo to Miami in disbelief. The organizers sent me a schedule of all the events. The first event was casting the models for my show. We arrived at a Miami Beach club at midday, and we were seated with the other designers at a long table. All the aspiring models were given a small sign with a number on it, and they started walking, showing us their best smile or asset.

At that moment, I felt horrible for them, me, and women in general. It felt so demeaning to judge them on the length of their legs or narrow hips. I felt like I was choosing cattle for a livestock show and found myself smiling so much at them, compensating for the fact that perhaps they found me weird. The fashion industry has been very unfair towards women in the past, imposing unrealistic beauty standards that can be devastating. We decided to cast the girls based on their walking attitude, energy, and how well the dresses suited their body types and personalities.

After the fittings, the collection started to take shape and looked amazing. I was going to be featured in an evening dress showcase alongside other Latin American designers. The event was in Miami Beach, under a huge white tarp. My parents came to the event with El Mada. I went to say "hi" to my mom, who was seated in the first row.

"I don't understand what you are doing here. I can't believe it!" She was flabbergasted.

"Me neither," I answered. Then, it was time for my show.

Everything was in place. Lights. Music. Action. The girls, one by one, took the runway. I was backstage, mesmerized, looking at the monitor. They were gorgeous. My heart started pounding really fast; tears began to fall. I didn't want anyone to see that I was crying, but I couldn't contain my emotions. I saw all these beautiful women walking down the catwalk with my dresses flowing. A picture I had in my head was now a reality. It was surreal.

The show ended, and the audience started clapping; it was time for me to walk onstage. I took a big breath and stepped toward the catwalk. Crowded flashes were going off. Press photographers from around the world gathered in front of me at the end of the catwalk. In the audience, I found my mom with Ignacio in her lap, who was just a few months old. I sent them a huge smile.

Afterwards, I went to meet my family. While I was looking for them, people approached me to congratulate me. A man came to me and said, "I loved your show, but most importantly, I am proud that you are Mexican. I am Mexican also, and you just put the name of our country very high. Thank you." I honestly think that was the best compliment I have ever received.

The next day, I was beat. I just wanted to relax on the beach with my family. Instead, I received a call from the organizers saying that there were buyers interested in my collection. I hurried back, and the buyers started asking me questions about prices, sizes, export, etc. I thanked them for their interest, but told them that we weren't currently selling to the States.

Then a light went on in my head. Selling to the USA? My Spidey senses turned on!

We welcomed our second child, Alex, into the world —a gorgeous and chubby baby. I needed someone to help me; the workload and stress were growing, and I wanted to raise and enjoy my kids. I invited a talented girl named Mai to join me. The business continued to grow. We were showcased in magazines and did multiple fashion shows in Mexico City and other cities in Mexico. We began dressing Mexican celebrities, and we even had the opportunity to dress the actress Liv Tyler for a fashion magazine.

Six years had already passed since we got married, and I kept dreaming about moving to the States. Since my Abuelo's kidnapping, I had grown paranoid. I would always ask El Mada where he was, and at what time he was coming home. I didn't venture far myself in Mexico City. I stayed close to home, and a driver would accompany me everywhere I went. By now, I had two kids, and the idea of something happening to them seemed unfathomable. I kept telling El Mada, "Let's leave, please; I don't feel safe."

In the mid-2000s, the war against drugs began, and we started to hear about horrible things happening all around the country. They would say that Mexico City was safe from the drug dealers, but I wasn't so sure. A dismembered head appeared two blocks behind our gated community.

What sort of environment was this? We were fine; my family was fine. It is known that drug dealers don't mess with people who are not involved in their business, but we were all trying to ignore a reality of violence, impunity, and corruption that was growing around us. I still don't know why it affected me so profoundly. Every other member of my family seemed fine and enjoying their lives, but I felt in my heart that we had to get out of there.

After attending Miami Fashion Week, I realized the immense potential of the fashion industry in the U.S. Unlike in Mexico, where shows are mostly for marketing, American fashion weeks are focused on sales—buyers attend to place orders.

I also learned about Coterie, a major trade show in New York following Fashion Week, where global buyers discover both established and emerging brands. I asked El Mada if we could visit—stay at our favorite hotel, take a break from the kids, and explore the opportunity.

We attended as guests, curious and inspired. The energy was electric— buyers in heels rushing between booths, models showcasing fresh collections. I was in awe, especially seeing pieces from my favorite designers. I asked our host what it would take to participate.

"Your collection must be approved by a panel," she explained. "It's highly competitive, and yes, expensive—but it puts your brand in front of top global buyers." I couldn't even imagine getting into that world.

Also, my friend Regina told me about a prominent Mexican fashion Public Relations expert in New York, named Gabriel Rivera-Barraza. He was friends with Carolina Herrera and Oscar de la Renta, and was working with a Mexican designer who won prestigious awards and was selling in Saks Fifth Avenue. Regina called Gabriel to make an introduction, and we scheduled a call.

"Hi, Gabriel, this is Monica, Regina's friend," I said.

"Hi, Monica," he coldly responded.

"I was thinking about moving to the States and wanted to get your feel for new Mexican designers."

"Mexican designers have no idea what they're getting into. This is not Mexico. They come with big egos and don't have a clue about what it takes to succeed. It is very hard. Honestly, I don't think you get it," he said.

His response left me frozen. I didn't expect him to be this tough. I was frank and told him about my plans. I don't know if I said something funny, but he eventually agreed to meet me.

"I have five minutes; I can see you at the Starbucks that is in the corner of my office. I can't bring you up, but bring your lookbook and some samples of your work. See you there, and be punctual. Don't be the typical Mexican," he said.

"I will be on time, don't worry. Thank you so much for agreeing to meet me."

The meeting took place during our next visit to New York. We arrived promptly at Starbucks. El Mada was in for the ride. Gabriel arrived, very well put together and elegant. He started to talk about how the fashion industry works in the United States and how hard it is to break into.

"Mexicans come to New York thinking that they are the big shit, and don't have a clue how to do it. In Mexico, maybe they are slightly famous. Here, they are nobody. Let me see your designs," he said and started looking at the pictures of my dresses, the shows, and celebrities I had dressed.

"I like it," he calmly said. "Your work is elegant and clean. I think if you prepare, organize yourself, and hire a good team, you can make it. But still, it is going to be extremely hard."

It was music to my ears; I was even surprised he liked my designs. His demeanor changed, and he invited us up to his office. We were there for more than an hour. The five minutes he reluctantly gave us turned into an hour and a half. He was so sweet and generous with his time; I was so grateful.

"Call me when you are settled, and we will talk. I will introduce you to the right people," he promised.

I didn't sleep that night.

By 2006, El Mada had a good job as Marketing Director of a bank and made a good living. I kept hearing horror stories around me in Mexico. I dreamed about taking my family to a safe haven.

I begged and pleaded with El Mada to move to Miami, where his parents had an apartment.

"Please, let's get out of here!" I would beg him from time to time.

"Who is going to hire me? We don't have work visas. And considering how bad the economy is right now, nobody is going to give me a job."

"I just can't bear our kids growing up here. They are surrounded by family and love, but they are growing up in a cage. I don't want anything bad happening to them." I argued.

"Nothing is going to happen; we are safe, and they are safe."

"Can you guarantee that?" I asked

"Let's not talk about it, I am happy here in Mexico," El Mada pleaded. "Please, let's find a way to leave," I begged.

"It is not that easy; we don't know anybody. Where am I going to work?"

"You have an MBA from MIT. I have a solid education. If so many Mexicans leave with nothing-no degrees, no connections— and still make it in the U.S. through hard work and perseverance, why can't we?"

"I have a career here. We have a great life. They leave because they have no opportunities. We stay because we have ours."

For years, we would revisit the same conversation. Me, always trying to convince him that our future was waiting north of the border.

CHAPTER 10

Anna Wintour at Gate 33

My biggest dream was to make it in the United States as a fashion designer. It was a very lofty dream; I was in my thirties, a mom raising young children, and Mexican. I didn't know anyone in the American fashion industry or how it worked, but I knew who some of the key players were.

Anna Wintour was one of them. She was the editor of *Vogue* magazine and could make or break designers with a glance. *The Devil Wears Prada* movie had come out a couple of months before, loosely based on her, but she was still not that well-known to the general public.

Pia and Tommy had invited us to ski at their vacation home in Aspen. We flew with the kids from Mexico City to Los Angeles, and from there we would take a direct flight to Aspen. El Mada and the kids were seated in the waiting room for our assigned gate, while I went to buy some water and snacks for everyone at the airport stores. When I came back, I saw Anna Wintour just a couple of seats away. I obviously did a double-take.

Is that her? It can't be, she is too tiny, I thought. She had her signature bob haircut, sunglasses, and skinny jeans. She was quite petite, much more so than she looks in pictures. She was reading something very intently. After a quick internet search, I was sure it was her. I was so excited about this celebrity sighting.

"Hey, do you remember that movie *The Devil Wears Prada*?" I asked El Mada discreetly.

"Yes, the one you made me watch three times?" he replied.

"Yes, that one. That is Anna Wintour; she inspired the movie. She is the editor-in-chief of *Vogue* magazine, the nasty boss. I can't believe it is her. I am having a mini panic attack!" I said, barely containing myself.

"If you admire her so much, why don't you go and introduce yourself?" he said, unimpressed.

"Are you crazy? And what am I going to say? Hi, I am a middle-aged Mexican fashion designer with three kids? Didn't you see the movie? Besides, I don't want to bother her; it would be tacky to interrupt her," I replied.

I wrestled with the idea of approaching her. I thought that I would never be in the same room as her again in my life. Maybe I could show her my work; maybe she would like my work. I immediately imagined myself in New York, in her office. *No, best not to bother her*, I thought.

I got up and bought a copy of Vogue magazine at an airport store, and started happily reading it nearby, as if to say, "Hey, I know who you are." Now that I think about it, that move was cringeworthy.

The gate for our flight was announced. Most of the people in the waiting area stood up and started walking to the designated gate. We grabbed our things and collected all the baby stuff you carry when you have kids under the age of four. We started walking towards Gate 33 in the wide halls of LAX. El Mada was pushing the baby stroller, and I was walking beside him.

Suddenly, as I walked to our gate, I watched El Mada run into someone with the baby stroller. I turned to see who it was, and to my horror and disbelief, it was Anna Wintour. I wanted to die!

"I'm sorry!" Anna said apologetically to the air, completely distracted, as if El Mada brought her back from whatever place she was daydreaming.

"Oh, please, excuse me," El Mada said as he calmly walked away and didn't realize who he had just run over.

"Do you have any idea who you just ran over?" I semi-yelled.

"No, who?" he said, startled.

"It was Anna Wintour!!! The *Vogue* lady!!!"

"No clue who she is. She crossed in my way," he said, unaffected.

"I can't believe you!! You don't even realize what you did!!"

"Would you calm down? Nothing happened, she seemed fine," he insisted.

"No, I just can't believe you just ran Anna Wintour over with our stroller, of all people," I said, panicking.

"Would you relax? It was just a tiny bump. She survived."

I saw her boarding the small plane that would take us to Aspen. Now, forget about approaching her. I never had the nerve to do it, anyway. No loss there, we have never been invited to the Met Gala, probably never will, so I don't think it made a big difference altogether. I must say, she was pretty calm about the whole incident. Let's face it, people with strollers can be annoying, and she even apologized when she could have been pissed about the incident. This close encounter of the third kind was both a motivation and a sign to keep going. We often place people we admire—especially those in the public eye—on pedestals. But at the end of the day, we are all human. With a little luck, hard work, and faith in our journey, dreams can come true—sometimes in the most unexpected ways and in a single, life-changing moment, our fates turn around for the better. I would think about this chance meeting often when I was building my business, imagining the day I would see my designs in the pages of Vogue, chosen by Anna Wintour herself.

CHAPTER 11

"Let's Get Out of Here."
"OK, But You in Front."

One night, El Mada came home distraught. A coworker and friend was killed in the middle of the street while walking with his date. Two guys at night approached them and shot him; the girl was spared. The victim's mother tried to report the crime, but the police didn't want to pursue it. Someone even threatened the shattered mother to leave the matter alone. Devastated and terrified, she moved to Spain, leaving behind her dead son and any likelihood of justice.

"It's just the place we were destined to live," my mom lamented when she heard this kind of story. I didn't think so.

"It is time. We need to leave," El Mada said, finally convinced. "I can't believe his death is going to go unpunished. He was a good guy. We need to find a way to move to the States legally."

It was the beginning of 2010, and Juan, our third child, arrived healthy and happy, making our family complete. As our family grew, so did my anxiety.

Finally, he agreed to leave everything behind in the hope of a safer and better future for our kids and ourselves. I was excited and scared at the same time.

The question now was: how could we move legally to the United States? It wasn't going to be easy, but we had to find a way.

Mexico had just elected a new president, Enrique Peña Nieto—hair Jimmy Neutron style, a wannabe telenovela actor, unqualified, corrupt, and self-serving. Peña and his inner circle would go on to drain public funds, leaving the country in complete disarray.

Our first choice for a fresh start was Miami. We could stay in my in-laws' vacation apartment for a few months while figuring things out. During spring break, we flew there to meet with an immigration lawyer and explore our options.

"What about an investor visa?" El Mada asked.

"You'll need to invest a significant amount, start a business, and employ at least two full-time people," the lawyer explained. "That visa would allow your spouse to work as well, but there's no path to citizenship. You'll also have to return to Mexico each year to renew it and prove your business is still active and successful."

El Mada didn't hesitate. "That could work for us. We can establish Monica's business here in Miami."

I was paying attention, but at that moment, I jumped out of my seat.

"What are you talking about? What business?" I asked him, shocked.

"Your fashion business. We can get the visa through your business," he said proudly.

"I don't have a clue about how to do business here. It's too much responsibility with our visas depending on my success."

"Well, do you want to leave Mexico or not? I don't see any other way," El Mada said. "You establish your business first, then they'll grant me a work permit. Once I have that, I'll look for a job in finance. Besides, after what I saw in New York, I believe you can make it in the U.S. That's your dream, right?"

I appreciated his confidence—he believed in me more than I

believed in myself. But I was freaked out. It felt like he had thrown me to the wolves. Yes, it had been my idea to leave—but I hadn't expected everything to depend on me!

We had to create a detailed business plan, explaining exactly how the investment would be used, proving the source of the funds (our personal savings), and submit my resume and work portfolio. If the Consul deemed my business viable, we'd receive the investor visa.

Our immigration lawyer helped us prepare everything—a ten-pound binder full of documents. It was so heavy, like a brick, that it could be used as a murder weapon. But really, our entire future was in that binder. We were making an enormous bet: risking our savings, El Mada's stable job, and our comfortable life. We were burning the ships. Leaving behind family, friends, and certainty, everything, for a promise of nothing.

Once we filed, we waited, paralyzed, for our interview with the American Consul. It was our one shot—and we were all in.

The day arrived. I put on my best professional yet chic outfit, as if to say, "Hey, I'm cool for it, I can totally be an outstanding investment visa holder."

Nervous and hopeful, we headed to the American Embassy in Mexico City—El Mada, our three kids, and me.

The Embassy is a massive compound and heavily guarded by Mexican and American police alike. We entered after an intensive security check and a long line full of petrified Mexican applicants. I was the main applicant, and my family members were my dependents. This role was new for me. El Mada had always been in charge. Now the roles were reversed.

They called my name. My hands were sweating. I approached the window cautiously, where the consul was. She started to ask me questions about the business plan. I perceived she was a little bit intrigued and even excited about my work in fashion. Maybe if we were selling tortillas, she wouldn't be as interested.

"So, you know you have to hire at least two people, right?" she asked. "Yes, I know," I said.

"So, have you hired them?"

"No, because we haven't left. We need the visa to get to Miami and settle the business." I replied.

"No, you have it backward," she said. "You need to settle the business, and afterwards, we will grant you the visa. Go to Miami with your tourist visa, invest the money, open up the office, hire the employees, begin to sell your line, and then we will give you the visa."

"But what if you deny the visa after I settle the business?"

"If you do everything right, there is no reason for us to deny you the visa, but I can't guarantee you anything. Here is an email where you can update us on your progress. Good luck!" She handed me a .gov email on a card.

Seriously? That's it?

Everyone in our family and all of our friends thought we were out of our minds about this whole idea. I also questioned my sanity. Why walk away from a life of comfort? In Mexico, we were someone; in Miami, we were no one; nobody knew us. But at least we had a plan, sort of.

My father-in-law offered us his Miami apartment for a year until we got settled. We could rent our Mexico City apartment, and with that income, we could live until El Mada got a job and my business was established.

It was time to tell my dad we were leaving.

"Dad, we are going to go to Miami to live for a couple of years. We are leaving this summer," I said.

"I don't understand why you want to leave. Why do you have this crazy idea?" He said.

"Because I want to give my kids a better life, a better future," I said.

"What are you talking about, a better life? There is nowhere in the world where they are going to have a better life than here in Mexico," he insisted. "They are surrounded by love and family and every opportunity ."

"I know that, but we live like prisoners. We only go to the same safe places, and the children are not allowed to be out of our sight." I answered.

"That is because you are traumatized. Go to therapy if you are so worried. Don't leave the country and take the kids with you," he argued.

"Sorry, Dad. Believe me, it is very difficult for me also," I said with tears in my eyes. "I wouldn't leave if things were different."

"And with what visa are you going to live in the States?"

"With an investment visa. We are going to settle my business in Miami," I answered, trying to show him that I had everything *"under control."*

"Your business?? What business?" He seemed terrified.

"The dresses! We are going to launch a fashion label."

"Now you have gone mad. Doing business in the USA is a whole different ball game!" he warned me.

"Well, that is the plan. We will try for a year, and if it doesn't work, we will come back." As I said this, I knew that I was lying. I didn't want to come back in a year.

"And what is El Mada going to do with his job?" he asked, exasperated.

"He's quitting his job, and after we get the visa, he'll get a work permit and look for a job there."

"What do you want me to say? I think it is crazy; you are risking everything," he said, almost mad about our decision.

"Dad, here we are prisoners of our own privilege. There is nothing you can say. But I love you so much and will miss you guys." I knew deep in my heart that leaving was the right thing to do.

"We love you, too. We will miss you and will be waiting for you to come back," he said.

We had everything figured out, but we still had a difficult conversation pending. Ignacio, our son, was now seven years old. He was a happy-go-lucky kid. He had started school and was thriving in Mexico. At a family dinner, we started telling Ignacio about our plans to move. Alex and Juan were too small to understand fully.

"So, honey, do you know how you love going to Miami for vacation?" I started the conversation.

"Yes, Mom."

"What do you think if we went for an adventure and lived there for a year?" I asked.

"What do you mean?" his demeanor changed.

"Well, your dad and I were thinking that it would be fun if we moved to Miami," I finally said.

"I would have to go to school there and leave my friends and cousins?" he asked, as I feared.

"Yes, darling, like an adventure!" I said, trying to sugarcoat the fact that it wouldn't be easy for us to leave our loved ones behind.

"No, Mom, no! I don't want to go! That's not an adventure; I don't want to leave. I am not leaving!"

I could feel his heart breaking. I could feel the pain and see the anguish in his face, in his eyes. For the first time in his short life, I could see he was actually physically hurting. In that moment, I took his innocence away. I broke his heart into a million pieces. He had, until then, such a perfect childhood, surrounded by cousins, uncles, and extended family. We lived in a beautiful, gated community with a golf course, clubhouse, and bike trails. A small paradise captured in a seemingly unburstable bubble. I was popping his bubble, taking everything he knew and loved away, and exchanging it for uncertainty and a cold, unknown, new beginning.

"You'll see; you will love it. If you don't like it, we will come back. I promise." I said.

"No, Mom, I want to stay. I will stay with *los abuelos*, please, let's stay, promise me, Mom," he said with tears in his eyes. "I don't want to leave Mexico."

"Settle down, honey, calm down, we'll see..." I felt a pit in my stomach.

We were extremely worried about Ignacio's reaction to our move, but we were hopeful that, once settled in Miami, he would love the new lifestyle. It was going to be a tough change.

"Are you nervous about leaving?" El Mada asked me.

"I'm not nervous. I'm pretty excited. I can't believe we are doing this. Are we crazy?" I asked.

"Yes, I think we are."

"I know. The only thing that really scares me is thinking that our relationship could deteriorate as a result of all the pressure. Everything else, I don't care. We can always come back. But what if this move takes a toll on our marriage? I don't want things to change between us." I said.

"Don't worry, flaquita," he assured me. "Nothing can come between us. Nothing will change."

"I hope so," I told him.

CHAPTER 12

Welcome to Miami
Bienvenidos a Miami

Arriving in Miami from the airport, our taxi drove over a majestic bridge that connects the city to the beautiful Caribbean waters. I could smell the sea, the air of freedom. I opened the cab window a little bit, closed my eyes, and let the wind splash my face. It was the first time in years that I had absolutely no clue what our future looked like. It was a giant gamble, daunting yet thrilling. I felt freedom, the freedom I had yearned for so long and a new, exciting future lying on the horizon. I was bringing my family to safety, as if we were escaping a war zone.

I had a lot of work to do. I had to build a business to finalize the visa process. We bought an office that was in foreclosure, located in a tall modern skyscraper just off Brickell, near the bustling business center of Miami, as part of our investment. All our savings went into it. My office was near where we were going to live, so I could come running home to take care of the kids.

El Mada had promised to help more with the kids, housework, and everything in between. Back in Mexico, he left early for work and came home late. This was going to be a big change for all of us. I had to figure out how to build a fashion brand in the United States—a completely different game. I didn't even know where to begin hiring. I figured a small team would do: a seamstress and an assistant. I would handle the patterns, the seamstress would cut and sew, and the assistant could help with sourcing suppliers and managing logistics.

I ran around like a crazy person trying to set everything up. I hired both the seamstress and the assistant, but the office still wasn't ready. I kept sending progress updates to the American Embassy. They were pleased, but insisted the office had to be completed.

The contractor and the construction permit process in Miami were an absolute nightmare. It seemed it would never get done. If they didn't grant us the visa, we would have been shipped back to Mexico with our heads hanging low. What a failure this adventure would have turned out to be! The kids had already sacrificed so much. We had rented out our apartment in Mexico—we didn't even have a home to go back to. Finally, the office was done, and a few days later, we received a simple email: our investment visa had been granted.

The empty space was now a showroom and atelier. Everything was white—very Miami. Clean, modern, furnished with Ikea. In the foyer, a large white glass wall doubled as a projection screen for my fashion shows and new collections. Past that was an open workspace for two assistants. My office sat at the back with walls covered in sketches and drawings from my kids. In the adjoining room, we set up the mannequins, sewing machines, and a massive cutting table— shipped all the way from my old workshop in Mexico City.

I began reaching out to boutiques in search of clients. The first thing they asked for was my line sheet. I had no idea what that was. I quickly learned that it's a catalog of your current collection, which includes wholesale and retail prices, along with product details. We needed a photoshoot to create one.

I hired a model and found Justin, a talented photographer. He wanted to understand my vision and had a thousand questions:

Indoors or outdoors? Urban or beach setting? Modern or feminine aesthetic? What kind of lighting? Where would the model change? Who would do hair and makeup? My head was spinning, no idea.

Justin recommended Claudia, an amazing and talented makeup artist, and we eventually decided on a contemporary outdoor shoot. We chose a location under the bridges of Miami—concrete walls with glimpses of the sea in the background. The model looked incredible, but I struggled with the unrealistic image we were selling. The message was: "If you buy this dress, you'll look like this." But that wasn't true. Not even the model looked like her photos.

I saw firsthand the illusion—the makeup, the lighting, the editing. The model had a normal skin breakout that day, which Claudia, covered flawlessly. She also avoided smiling in every shot because she had crooked teeth. Even the most beautiful models have imperfections. It felt wrong to contribute to this illusion of perfection. We're taught to aspire to impossible standards of beauty, and I felt complicit in reinforcing them.

Thankfully, the fashion industry has evolved somewhat since then, and now we see more women from diverse backgrounds, including all types of bodies and ethnicities, represented in high-fashion campaigns. I am sure fashion can be more friendly and attainable without losing its magic and power of transformation.

I was happy with the results of the shoot. I used the images for the web page, the line sheet, and to promote the new collection. This was a different universe from what I did back in Mexico. It was like comparing dancing salsa in Calle Ocho with a full-blown production of the Swan Lake ballet at Lincoln Center in New York City. I figured out how to set up a small production in Hialeah, near Miami. Hialeah was formed by Cubans and Central Americans who worked in the manufacturing industry.

For my kids, everything was new—new language, new school, new friends, and a new lifestyle. When El Mada dropped Alex at the school gate, Alex turned and started running behind the car, crying, "Please don't leave me here, come back!" The teacher ran behind trying to catch up.

With three kids and a new business, we needed help with childcare and household tasks. We hired Tita to help us settle in. Tita was born in Nicaragua and instantly became part of the family; the kids adored her. I was running around like a crazy person, getting the kids settled in their new environment, making a new home for them, and discovering a new way of life. I had a to-do list that was about five pages long.

I was overwhelmed with the new responsibility. I was now the family breadwinner and felt pressured to make the business work; our whole American adventure depended on it. I was responsible for every single step of the clothing manufacturing process. I was designing, buying the materials, making the patterns, and helping with the sewing. If a thread was missing, I would drop everything and make a run for it. It was safe to say I bit more than I could chew.

With my kids on different schedules, my days were a logistical nightmare. I'd drop off Juan at kindergarten, come back to take Alex, and later go again for Ignacio. I was making three trips to school every day, running around like a chicken without a head. On top of the chaos, I was battling impostor syndrome, and the worst part was knowing I'd dragged my whole family into this. They had left everything for my hopeful, perhaps naïve, dream.

I felt a deep responsibility to make it up to them. I loved the freedom and ease of Miami; my children were safe and healthy. I just needed to make this work.

Meanwhile, El Mada seemed to be enjoying life. He'd ride his bike daily through Miami's scenic paths like a retired birdwatcher. He took on occasional consulting work outside the U.S.—nothing too demanding. He was networking, hoping a bank might sponsor him for a work visa.

I started to resent him. I was carrying the full weight of our move: the business, the visa, the kids. In Mexico, we had lots of help. Here, not so much. And he behaved like nothing had changed—still king of the castle, expecting to be looked after, while I was juggling so much. And he was out there happily riding his bike.

At night, I couldn't sleep. My mind raced with a million things I still had to do. I kept tossing and turning, knowing morning would come soon. I rolled over and looked at El Mada—peacefully, deeply asleep, blissfully unaware of the storm I'd be walking into tomorrow.

UGHHH! I hated him.

Something came over me, and I kicked him in the legs. He woke up not knowing what had happened.

"What happened? Did you feel that?" he asked me with eyes half open.

"No, I don't know what you are talking about," I replied.

He went back to sleep, and I regretted resorting to violence, but realized he had to help me more or I was going to crash. The next morning, I asked him if we could have dinner just the two of us.

"Do you realize I'm killing myself, running around like a crazy woman, and you are like a retired granddad on your bike enjoying life," I said.

"Well, you wanted to come to the United States, didn't you? You knew it would be hard. I told you," he answered, reminding me of his past words.

"Of course I did, but I am working my ass off, and you don't help at all."

"I'm looking for work, and that in itself is a full-time job."

"I watch you in your biking shorts, and I hate them. I hate the sight of you in your tight shorts, with your little helmet and your biking shoes, going around, enjoying Miami, while I am literally sweating bullets," I said bitterly.

"I told you this was going to be tough. I talked to George, and he is going to hire me the moment they issue my work permit, but that process takes months."

"Please, I need you; I need your help. I am serious, if you don't start helping me with the kids and the business, I want to go back to Mexico. I'm killing myself; it's not worth it. And what I feared the most is happening; our relationship is deteriorating. I am starting to resent you. Please help me more, promise me," I said, teary-eyed.

"Sorry, flaquita, I promise you. I am going to help you more with the kids, and I will support you more at the office," he said.

"Please do. If this doesn't change, I want to go back to Mexico. Everything is on my shoulders, and I feel completely disconnected from you. This is no life for me; it isn't what I dreamed of. I am tired all the time, and life is not what I thought it was going to be."

"It never is," he answered.

It's funny; once we achieve our goals, something we dream of for so long, we tend not to enjoy it fully, and we focus on a new goal to achieve, dismissing the hard work it took us to get there. Obviously, I was happy that we were finally living in Miami. I couldn't contain my gratitude in my heart when I saw the Caribbean Ocean or thought about the world of opportunities I was giving my kids, but I didn't expect it to be so rough. We had the visa; we were now safe, and although the kids had a rough landing, they were adapting. I started making friends with other school moms and neighbors. But I had to stop and make an effort to enjoy our new reality.

At work, we finally received a few orders from a couple of boutiques, but it was extremely hard to get them. The owners were hesitant to buy a new line from a stranger. Nevertheless, a gold dress with an open back, the main piece of the collection, was a big hit and sold itself, but I had to find new ways to start selling more, and pronto!

CHAPTER 13

Tacos y Salsa

My grandfather made pots and pans that found their way into kitchens across Mexico. Both of my abuelas were incredible cooks. With their Spanish heritage, they mastered traditional dishes like *croquetas* and *tortilla de papa*, and they learned the art of combining those elements with the deliciousness of Mexican flavors, creating mouthwatering and vibrant flavors.

Christmases were a big deal. The turkey was the main dish, and my Abuela Carmen would make a gravy that, to this day, is a secret family recipe hidden in a safe box. Family was reunited at the table, and the exquisite food that my grandmothers and their mothers cooked was the thread that brought us together. To this day, Mexican food is part of my identity, my heritage. When I hear that Taco Bell is Mexican food, I get offended. That is not real Mexican food. Chimichangas do not even exist in Mexico, or not that I know of, anyway.

My mom inherited that love for cooking, and I would watch her try new recipes. Delicious smells would always emanate from the kitchen.

La Tía Chata was well known for her love of cooking; she gave homemade cooking classes to all my tías. To all her nieces, she gave as a wedding gift a recipe book that I had brought to Miami. I treasure this recipe book as if it is worth gold. It had the basics for tasty home-cooked meals, from simple home recipes like party noodles to Aztec cake and tortilla soup.

Tita, the amazing lady making my life and survival possible, was just pure sunshine. She loved my children as her own, took care of everything in the house, and cooked as if she were Mexican.

I started teaching Tita, who is from Nicaragua, all the secrets of my family's seasonings. She learned all the family recipes, but I have to admit that Tita is a much better cook than I am. She didn't just learn the family recipes; she improved them. She learned how to make my mom's famous chicken taquitos, salsa verde, and guacamole. Fideos and homemade chicken soup were also staples of our kitchen. Tita made our landing in Miami so much easier. While she cooked the food we love, she brought us back home with the smells and flavors of our dear country.

My kids were so grateful that they could recognize their favorite tacos, rice, and frijoles in their lunch. El Mada was ecstatic that we found such a gifted cook in Tita. She was always very thoughtful, making him food that he loved. She made *molletes, chilaquiles, or enchiladas* especially for him.

I would give her pointers or tips on how I remembered my mom and my abuela's cooking, but Tita had a passion for the kitchen, and it showed. In Miami, every ingredient for a nice Mexican dinner can be easily found, but one of the most important ingredients was impossible to get: good corn tortillas. Corn tortillas are the base of the Mexican diet. We use tortillas like the rest of the world uses bread.

In Mexico, there is a *tortillería* on every corner and inside every supermarket. We eat fresh tortillas on the daily; two pounds will fly in less than a week in a family household. The smell of fresh tortillas can hypnotize and bring me back home in a millisecond. Those delicious, fresh, natural tortillas were nowhere to be found in Miami. The only tortillas available were packaged tortillas at the supermarket. They are super sweet and full of preservatives. When heated, they break like glass. I stopped eating tortillas altogether. However, Tita managed, I don't know how, to make the chicken taquitos with the tortillas found at the supermarket.

Every birthday party for the kids, Tita would make the famous chicken tacquitos and the salsa verde. The tacos and the salsa were always a big hit. Once, we caught the Canadian dad of one of Juan's friends grabbing a spoon and drinking the salsa as soup, without a taco.

"Wow, these tacos are something special," a party-goer said.

"Delicious and crunchy. Monica, stop serving these tacos; my diet is going down the drain," Cris, my friend, would say while having her fourth taco.

If the dresses don't work out, maybe we could start selling tacos, I thought.

Mexican Chicken Fried Taquitos (Chicken Taquitos)

Ingredients (Makes about 12 taquitos):

- 4 chicken breasts
- 4 garlic cloves
- Half an onion
- 1 teaspoon garlic powder
- Salt and pepper to taste
- 12 corn tortillas
- Toothpicks (to hold them closed while frying)
- Vegetable oil

Optional:

- Cotija Cheese
- Salsa roja o verde
- Mexican cream or sour cream

Instructions:

1. In a saucepan, combine chicken, 2 cups of water, onion, garlic, salt, and pepper. Boil until the chicken is fully cooked (about 15–20 minutes).
2. Remove the chicken and shred with two forks. Please take out the boiled onion and garlic and blend them with 2 tablespoons of the broth until smooth.
3. Mix the blended paste into the shredded chicken. Taste and adjust seasoning.
4. Slightly warm the corn tortillas so they don't crack when rolled. Place about 2 tablespoons of the chicken mixture in each tortilla. Roll tightly and secure each with a toothpick.

5. Heat about 1 inch of vegetable oil in a deep pan. Fry 3–4 taquitos at a time, seam side down, until golden and crispy (about 2–3 minutes per side).

6. Transfer to a paper towel-lined plate to drain excess oil. Remove toothpicks.

7. Serve with your favorite toppings: salsa, sour cream, and crumbled Cotija cheese.

CHAPTER 14

Hustle, Mamacita!

One way to market a clothing line is through fashion trade shows. There are big ones like Coterie in New York, and smaller local ones. I decided to take a shot and applied to Coterie.

The application asked things like how long I'd been in business, past trade shows, and my buyers. I tried to sound seasoned, but truthfully, I had zero experience outside Mexico. Nevertheless, I sent the form with a couple of sample dresses and hoped for the best. A few weeks later, the dresses came back with a kind rejection letter. It was a letdown, but honestly, I wasn't ready. If a big store like Neiman Marcus had ordered 200 golden dresses, I might've had a massive panic attack.

I looked for manufacturers in Mexico but couldn't find any that focused on women's fine apparel. In the U.S., I'd learned that most big brands had partners in China. Maybe going that route would actually make things easier.

I'd seen the superior quality, amazing fabrics, and low prices that China offered for manufacturing. With that, I could make a line profitable. A dress that costs $100 in Miami could be made for $20 in China. I visited New York manufacturers who outsourced to China; if a big order came in, I knew where to run.

Another path to selling more was getting into a showroom—a space where brands are shown to retail buyers. A good showroom could put my line in front of serious retailers, so I focused on that, letting them handle sales while I focused on design and production.

I had done everything Gabriel suggested: moved to Miami, launched the business, built a team. Now, it was time to head back to New York—and reconnect with Gabriel. I called him and he told me he had been working with a high-end New York showroom that typically featured European designers. The owner's name was Tim Valle, a Mexican-American. Gabriel offered to introduce us, suggesting I bring samples in case Tim was interested. We scheduled a meeting in New York. Slowly, the dream I'd been chasing was starting to take shape. El Mada and I arrived at the Tim Valle Showroom in the Meatpacking District. Gabriel was already waiting for us in the back of the showroom.

"Hi, Gabriel, how lovely to see you again!"

"Hi, darling, I must say I didn't think you were going to make the jump," he said.

"I know! We left Mexico. It has been hard, but we have been enjoying the ride," I said.

"Let's hope your ride goes well," he said. "Let me see what you brought." He was anxious to see if I met the standards. He opened the garment bag and examined my new collection. "I like it. They are sellable, you have good quality and finishes."

Tim Valle entered the room. He was a tall, well-built guy whose family immigrated from Mexico to Chicago before he was born. He spoke half in English and half in Spanish, a mix of Spanglish, which we all do regularly.

"Hello, Monica. Let's see what we have here," he said, coldly.

Gabriel began presenting the clothes, pitching them as if they were their own. He watched Tim closely, trying to read his reaction—his own reputation clearly at stake for bringing in work that might not meet their standard.

"See this detail here," Gabriel said. Tim nodded, expressionless, and took a seat.

"So, what is your situation? Where are you located, and, most importantly, what do you want?" Tim asked me without hesitation.

"We just moved from Mexico to Miami, and I want to sell my clothes to retailers and boutiques," I said.

"It takes a lot of money to make money, and this industry is cut-throat."

"If I get the orders, I can look for investors. It has been extremely hard to break into the industry," I said.

"Tell me about it!" Tim responded and looked at Gabriel. "We have been busting our asses for years in New York. You have to pay your dues. If you are ready to kill yourself working and make the investment, I can take you as a client."

Gabriel smiled and excitedly said. "Monica, if you want to make it, you have to go to the right events and meet the right people. I can take care of that. You will have to attend a lot of social events, flying back and forth from Miami to New York, maybe two times a month."

"Don't worry; she will be here. She can fly every other week to New York for whatever events she gets invited to," El Mada answered, seemingly excited.

Hold on! Travel every other week, parties, and social events? What about my kids? Alex had needed extra help for a while now, and my kids weren't settled. I kept quiet as the three men continued talking and planning. Then, I spoke up.

"First of all, I thank you both, so, so much for this opportunity, and for opening this door for us. It is a dream for me just talking with you guys," I said. "I understand what is involved to make it big, and the investment it takes. I will talk to the people who may be interested in investing in my brand, and I will get back to you as soon as I can," I said, appreciative of their willingness to take my brand.

"Don't worry, *Mija*; we are here for you," said Tim.

He was a funny mix between a cosmopolitan, modern guy and a Mexican-American from the barrio. I was super impressed with what he had accomplished. We left ecstatic; we had an opening.

"We can raise the money from different sources, you can travel to New York, and I will help you more with the kids," El Mada said excitedly.

"Did you hear everything they said? I am freaking out. I don't want to sacrifice so much time with the kids. As it is, I don't spend enough time with them, and you know how they struggle with some issues. I have to take them to doctors' appointments, therapy, and be there for them. The kids have always been my priority. I don't think I am ready for this level of commitment. They are so young: two, five, and eight. I don't want to scale it so big right now."

"But this is what you have been waiting for your whole life!?" El Mada said, confused.

"I understand, but I am not ready. I haven't secured the production side of the business, and I only get one shot. If the buyers place an order and I can't deliver, I am done. I want to do it, but I want to do it right. We are rushing, and I still have so much to learn. We just landed in Miami. The kids need me, and I need them."

"Ok, so what do you want to do?" he asked, exasperated that I brought him here and now I was chickening out.

"Let's look for local showrooms in Miami, then we can grow organically and test the market. If everything goes well, we can come back looking for them."

"Ok, but either way, I am super proud that we have made it so far."

"I know. It was so cool just getting into the showroom." I called Gabriel a couple of days later. "Hi, Gabriel. I was speaking with my husband, and to be honest, I think I want to grow organically and start with small productions, so we don't mess it up. I am sorry if you feel that we wasted your time or Tim's, but I take my work very seriously and I don't want to let you guys down."

"You know, Monica, I prefer for you telling me this now than to agree with everything and leave us hanging. When you're ready, we'll be here. New York is not going anywhere," he kindly said.

"Thank you again, you are amazing. I hope to call you soon."

We needed to sell more, and fast. We were going through all our savings like water. I explored the route of being in a small local showroom in Miami. The only one that answered my call was the Jac Belzer Showroom. Jac Belzer was a character. He was the son of the owner of a well-known shoe brand, and since he had already attended trade shows to sell his dad's shoes, his side hustle became his own showroom.

We arrived at his warehouse-slash-office with some samples. I had brought pieces that were all hand-beaded, evening dresses, and a couple of miniskirts with modern embroidery designs, perfect pieces to wear for a fun night out in Miami Beach.

We sat down in the meeting room and waited for Jac. He came into the room abruptly—a middle-aged bald guy with a manicured mustache and beard. He was wearing a tank top that showed his well-toned muscles, covered with a huge eagle and a flower tattoo on his shoulder. Imagine a biker with a leather vest and spikes, but fashionista.

He started going through the rack. "Oh my god, these skirts are gorgeous. How much is your wholesale price?"

"I was thinking about two hundred dollars so that the store could sell them at five hundred dollars. They are hand-beaded by Mexican artisans," I said proudly.

"Are you crazy? The price is outrageous, and, honey, news-flash: nobody cares that they are hand-beaded," he said.

I was insulted by that comment, but I had heard it before from Gabriel. For me, hand-beading is an art form—the technique, patience, and precision that Mexican artisans use. In the US, what mattered was the bottom line, the price.

"I like your clothes, but you need to make them more Miami, less wedding, and you need to bring prices down. If you do that, I can get you in at least forty boutiques," Jac said.

"Let me think about it, and I will give you a call. Thank you for your time." I got up super quickly, packed all the samples, and left the warehouse.

"No," I told El Mada. "I don't want to give my collection to him; he doesn't get me. I don't think it is a good fit. He doesn't value the Mexican artisans' hand-beaded work. He wants to sell Lycra-type dresses, not my style. Why don't we go to the trade shows and try to sell it by ourselves?" I suggested.

"Are you sure?" El Mada said patiently.

"Positive. Let's look for local trade shows. I am not handing my dresses to just anyone. They're like my babies."

We went to a couple of trade shows. The first one was at a massive convention center in Dallas, Texas. The place was like a small city, filled with showrooms showcasing everything under the sun. We set up a small booth and dressed two mannequins. I couldn't believe I was there. When the show started, buyers stopped by, glanced at the clothes, said something polite, and moved on. Our booth was tucked away in the section for small, unknown brands. I wandered over to where the big names were, with fabulous clothes and exclusive labels, and somehow, I was showcasing my own designs there too. Well… in the kids' area. The thrill didn't last. By the second day, reality hit hard—I had made just one sale. The competition was brutal, and I felt like a tiny, sucky bacteria in the vast Atlantic Ocean of fashion.

We came back to Miami feeling crushed. We had only moved to Miami ten months ago, but at this rate, we'd be broke in a few more months. I was exhausted, overwhelmed, and under pressure. I had sent our line sheet to what felt like a million showrooms and stores across the country, and the answer was always the same: a no-go. Stress and anxiety started building up. *Maybe I am not good enough? Who did I think I was to believe I could make it in the United States?* The only word I kept hearing was no, and it was bearing me down.

I had uprooted my family; the kids were still adjusting, and El Mada's work permit was still pending. I had traded a world of comfort and familiarity for the unknown, for a place where we were nobodies. Back in Mexico, we were settled. We had a network, a rhythm, a sense of belonging. We missed the Sunday gatherings at my parents' house and the warmth of family and friends. Here, I had no support system. I was scrambling to make new connections, trying to build something from scratch. Bottom line: I was lonely.

One afternoon, I was watching the kids play in the park, feeling guilty that I had dragged them to the USA. *Please, God, give me a sign*, I thought. *I made a mistake in coming here. Maybe we were better off with our family in Mexico. Please send me a sign.* I felt depleted.

I continued watching the kids, and suddenly, in front of me, a pair of little green parrots landed happily on a tree. Vivid green parrots who didn't care about visas, jobs, or belonging. A bolt of hope struck me. *We are going to be fine, I know it, we just have to stick with it*, I thought.

We decided to do another trade show in Miami. Again, we bought a booth and set up shop. I sat in the booth and again received lots of compliments, but no sales. My eyes began to tear up as the second day was ending, and I had just a couple of orders. El Mada came in, saw my face, and said, "Go home, I will take over. Don't worry." My face was full of hurt, disappointment, and failure. It was humiliating just to sit there and taste failure.

I grabbed my things and said, "I don't know what I am going to do."

He didn't respond. I started walking out of the trade show, making my way through the booths, and saw a huge booth, jam-packed with buyers. Boutique owners were buying like crazy. I came a little bit closer to see what all the fuss was about and saw Jac Belzer in the middle of all the commotion.

"Hi, Jac," I said.

"Monica! What are you doing here?" he said, excited to see me.

"Well, we have a booth over there," I answered, a little bit embarrassed.

"And how are you doing? We are doing amazing!! What a good show. We are killing it!"

"I could be doing better," I said.

"I told you, you need to join me. I am doing a show in Las Vegas and New York in a couple of weeks. Let me sell your stuff. Did you make more casual things?"

"Yes, I did," I responded. At that point, I just had to let go. "Jac, you are right. I will hand my collection to you. Take everything, and please sell as much as you can."

"I will. We will discuss details later, but this will work out, you'll see."

"I hope so." I sighed. I had to leave behind any preconceptions or expectations I had and take the opportunities as they came.

To attract more customers and increase my name recognition, I reached out to a prominent PR representative who appeared on the Bravo reality TV show, *Real Housewives of Miami*. Marysol Patton owned a PR firm in Miami and had a huge portfolio of high-end brands. It was worth sending her an email to see if she would take me as a client. I always thought that if you dress celebrities as a fashion designer, the sales would naturally improve. She agreed to meet us at my office.

I had seen a couple of the *Housewives* episodes. They were kind of big at that time, and she was preparing for filming the next season. We met and she liked my work. I agreed to dress her for the season and all her social commitments, and in return, she would represent me as a client for a lower fee. She wore a lot of my pieces on the show. For me, it was exciting to watch something I had created on American TV. I couldn't believe she was wearing my dresses!

Millions of people were seeing them. Marysol, unlike Jac, appreciated the delicate hand-beaded work of some of my pieces. She looked amazing on screen. Unfortunately, *Miami Housewives* was canceled that season. Still, thanks to Marysol Patton, I had been able to showcase some of my work in the media. I thought that having a celebrity wear my designs would automatically boost my sales, but it didn't. However, she did a good job getting me into different TV shows for interviews and placing my dresses in magazines. I was slowly making a name for myself. I did an interview for *¡Despierta America!* and showcased a couple of dresses. The next day, I went to Nordstrom's to buy some makeup and asked the sales associate for some recommendations.

"You are Monica Ocejo, the designer, right?" she asked. I was stunned and freaked out. *How did she know me?*

"Yes, hi. Have we met?" I asked her.

"I saw you on a television show. I liked your dresses."

"Thank you so, so much. You are too kind," I said.

I was baffled. In what world would the Nordstrom makeup counter lady recognize me? The PR was working on name recognition, but again, I had impostor syndrome, always thinking that I wasn't good enough or that I was improvising. That's why giving Jac the collection was an excellent decision. In time, we were selling to more than 40 to 50 boutiques around the Caribbean, Puerto Rico, and Florida. He sold shoes, but I was one of his best-selling clothing lines.

I was happy with the newfound success, but the business's finances were not adding up. We had to hire more people as we grew, but we weren't selling enough to make a profit. By now, El Mada had gotten his work permit and started working for a consulting firm from the Midwest. Before, I was upset because he was not working; now, he was working too much and away from home. I missed him. He had really stepped up and helped me with the business and the kids.

I hired an assistant, Victoria, fresh out of college, to help me with all that was going on. Meanwhile, Jac was signing more fashion lines to his showroom. Previously, I was his only contemporary line, but now, with the competition, I was getting fewer orders. At the same time, Alex, my middle child, was having issues at school, and I was already struggling with all the different developmental therapies we were attending. With El Mada's new job, I was practically alone the whole week. He would basically come home for the weekends. I was stretching myself thin.

In Miami, I had Cris and Amelita, two friends who were family, but I still struggled to find people to hang out with on weekends. I barely had a support system. I started doubting if it was all worth it. The time of the year to renew our business visa was approaching again. Every year, we had to return to the US Embassy in Mexico City and demonstrate that my business was thriving. From my point of view, having arrived just three years before, I thought I was doing pretty good. El Mada was doing well in his new job, and his generous American bosses offered to help with the Green Card process. This was great news for us; a huge pressure came off my shoulders.

We had finally moved into our own place. We felt free, safe. The kids were happy, making friends. In December, we went to renew our visa, leaving behind the brick at the American Embassy. Then we waited. Because it was December and most of the Embassy staff were on vacation, the process dragged. We ended up stuck in Mexico City for a couple of weeks, uncertain, waiting to find out whether we could return to our lives or not. We spent Christmas with my parents in Mexico City, waiting for news. For New Year's Eve, my *tíos* invited everyone over, but El Mada and I chose a quiet night at home, sitting by the fireplace with a glass of wine.

"We need to enjoy life more," I told him. "Lately, it feels like we're just trying to keep our heads above the water."

"I know," he said. "Let's start making time, just dinner and a movie now. We've been too focused on surviving."

"It's been a tough transition," I admitted.

At midnight, we hugged, exchanged New Year's wishes, and went to bed. We were sound asleep when the phone rang. El Mada answered.

"Yes, oh, OK, I understand. Yes, I think that is correct, thank you." And he hung up and went back to sleep.

"Who was that?" I asked him.

"It was your Abuelo Eduardo's nurse. She said that he wasn't breathing and if she could call in for an extra oxygen tank," he said nonchalantly with his eyes closed.

"What do you mean he isn't breathing? He is literally one hundred years old. If he isn't breathing, he is dying," I said to him, alarmed, and immediately called back the nurse. It was around 1:30 am, and my parents were still out celebrating New Year's.

"Hello, Elvira, what do you mean he isn't breathing?" I asked.

"Well, he is not breathing," she said, sounding scared.

"You mean he is dying?" I asked.

"I would appreciate it if you could come and help me," she said.

OH, SHIT! I have to call my parents, I thought. Thankfully, my dad answered his cellphone.

"Dad, Elvira just called and told me Abuelo Eduardo is not breathing," I said.

"What do you mean he is not breathing?" he responded.

"I don't know, Dad, I think he is dying," I said.

"Ok, we are heading to his house right now. We will meet you there," he said.

We left the kids at my parents' house with the nanny and arrived at my grandparents' in a flash. Everything was dark and quiet. My Abuela Carmen slept in a different room from my Abuelo, so she had no idea what was happening outside. Marital life at 100 years is like boarding with your bestie, if you are lucky.

I went into my abuelo's room. My mom and dad were already there. My mom was holding his hand on the other side of the bed. Elvira, the nurse, sat quietly in a chair, crying. I sat on the bed and kissed my abuelo. He was still warm. He looked like he was sleeping, so handsome, with so much peace. I waited in silence.

For me, it was a privilege and a gift to be there and see him go.

My Abuelo had been such an important part of my life and an example for me in so many ways. Since I left for Miami, every time I said goodbye, I thought it was the last time I would see him. I was sure I would get a call to go back to Mexico because he had passed away. The fact that I was there to accompany him in his passing was a privilege and a gift. It was so peaceful. We stayed there for a while, and suddenly I felt like his spirit had left his body, exiting through his feet and flying away. I know it sounds crazy. I can't explain it, but I felt the exact moment he left.

"We need to wake up your mom and tell her. I think it would be best if we called Dr. Portos to tell your mom. We need to make sure that she'll be ok," Dad said to my Mom.

Dr. Portos arrived at 3:30 a.m. He is a cardiologist and a family friend. We woke my abuela up, and she looked scared. The poor thing didn't know why everyone had invaded her house at that time of night. When Dr. Portos told her the news, she didn't quite understand what was happening, but she went inside the room where my abuelo was resting peacefully. She sat on the side of the bed, praying the rosary, with the love of her life for the last time. I sat quietly beside her, praying.

Mom came in and told my abuela, "It is time for them to take Dad; you need to say goodbye now." Everyone left the room to give her privacy, but I didn't want to leave her alone. I stayed behind her chair, making sure she was alright, and then she started speaking to him.

"Thank you for all did for me; thank you for all your love. If I did something to hurt you, please, forgive me. I never meant to hurt you. Please, take me with you as soon as you can. I want to be with you. I don't want to stay here without you," she said tenderly. This was the most amazing legacy that my grandparents have given me:

the example of their love for each other. I am grateful to have witnessed their love firsthand.

She kissed him and gave him her blessing, and then two men came into the room and took him away.

CHAPTER 15

Midlife Crisis Calling

My fortieth birthday was around the corner. I was astounded that I was reaching middle age, the fourth floor. I saw my first grey hair and studied it for hours, wondering, How could this happen? How did I get so old so quickly? I still felt like I was 20 years old—maybe not early twenties, but definitely late twenties. Obviously, this wasn't the case anymore.

I was extremely burned out. Leaving everything behind in Mexico, running around like a piñata at a kids' party, setting up the shop in Miami, and the kids' issues were taking a toll. I wasn't well. My sister Isabel was much more excited about my birthday than I was, and she called to announce that she had organized a party for my 40th birthday in Mexico City at her house with all my friends. I was excited to go; I hadn't seen anybody since we had come to Miami three years before.

With the fashion line gaining traction in the U.S., I took a leap and scheduled a meeting with Londres, the biggest department store in Mexico, with 90 locations. It was a long shot, but landing that account would be a game-changer. They scheduled an appointment for me on the morning of my birthday party. A good omen, I thought. I could celebrate afterward. I marked the date and time on my phone's calendar and crossed my fingers.

I arrived in Mexico with the new collection samples to show to Londres and was ready to celebrate afterwards. I steamed and organized the clothes on a rack. I had the lookbook; I was ready to go.

The day before my appointment, I sent an email to the head buyer's assistant just to confirm, and what she replied floored me.

"Miss Monica, we were wondering what happened to you. Your appointment is not tomorrow. Your appointment was today at eleven am. All the buyers were waiting for you and were disappointed that you missed it."

WHAAAT???? THE APPOINTMENT WAS TODAY? I DON'T UNDERSTAND. IT IS TOMORROW!!! I thought. I called the assistant right away.

"Hi, this is Monica Ocejo. What do you mean the appointment was today? I have it in my calendar for tomorrow," I said, panicking.

"Hi Monica, there must be some confusion. Please look at the previous emails. You can clearly see the date for the appointment was today."

I furiously looked for the email, and she was right. I registered for the appointment for the wrong day.

"I am so, so sorry. I don't know what I was thinking. I am so embarrassed. Is there any way I can reschedule? I have everything ready. Can I go tomorrow?" I said.

"Sorry, the buyers' schedule is packed. They don't have anything available for the next couple of months," she apologized.

"Please, I flew from Miami just to come to see you guys. I am so very sorry. It was an honest mistake," I begged.

"I understand. If there is an opening, I will contact you. I have to go." And she hung up.

Never in my whole life have I felt like such an idiot. I couldn't believe I had screwed up like that; I was officially going crazy. I had so many things going on, but there was no excuse. I was never going to forgive myself.

I went back to check the original email. She was right; it was over. I had blown my big chance, and now they would never take me seriously.

"How was your appointment with Londres?" Julie asked when I arrived for my 40th birthday party.

"I got the date wrong. It was yesterday, not today," I answered, looking down, ashamed. I saw her face transform into a look of panic.

"I don't want to talk about it," I said, and she let it go.

My sister did an amazing job of organizing the party. The tables were decorated with little mannequins made out of mini roses. My two grandmothers, along with all my aunts, my mother-in-law, my cousins, and my friends, arrived. All the women who have had a significant impact on my life in Mexico were there. I was able to block the Londres disaster for a couple of hours and enjoyed myself.

"Monica, how were you able to get into so many stores in the US? How did you do it?" Gelo asked.

"I have no idea," I answered, unmotivated. I only remembered what had just happened with Londres. *I am such an idiot*, I thought.

I returned to Miami drained, with very low energy. Something was not right. One day, soon after, I stopped on my way to work and went into a church to pray. The church was empty—only two other people were praying with candles burning.

"Please, God, help me," I prayed, not knowing what was already growing silently inside my body.

CHAPTER 16

Meet My New Best Friend

I believe that I am guided by chance encounters. I believe in the miracle of chance encounters.

—Paulo Coelho

I went to the trade show to check out the display of my new collection, and my eye caught a fashion line that was also being represented by Jac. The line was called Solei.

The fabrics were amazing. They were stretchy silks, delicate prints, and feminine laces that I had only seen on runways. The lines were clean and modern. The clothes were amazing, and to my detriment, the prices were lower than some of my prices. I looked at the label to see where they were manufactured, and it said, "Made in China with Love."

Of course it was made in China, at those prices, I thought.

I was so into the clothes that I didn't notice a woman behind me looking at how I probed the line.

"Hi, can I help you with something?" she politely asked. "I am Sofia, and Solei is my line."

"Oh, sorry! I was just admiring your clothing line. It is amazing, congratulations," I said, a little bit self-conscious. "I am Monica. I'm the designer of that line." I pointed, embarrassed and sheepishly to my line.

There is no way in hell I can compete with this line, I thought. Her silk dresses were cheaper and better made than my polyester dresses.

"I saw your line. It is nice. I like the dress you have on the mannequin," Sofia said.

"Thank you. I love what you are doing. Where are you from?" I asked her.

"I am from Panama, but my parents were from Italy."

"Nice to meet you, Sofia. I am Monica, and I am from Mexico," I said. "I am very impressed by your line. Congratulations. Where do you produce it?"

"In China," she shyly responded. She seemed a little bit ashamed by it, and she quickly added. "But we make it with lots of love."

"Well, I think it is fabulous that you produce in China. Well done! I feel that it takes you to another level," I complimented her.

"I know," she replied. "The construction and the textiles are of the best quality. I co-own a factory in China with my partner, Adi. I go back and forth every two to three months, from Miami to Hong Kong, because to produce in China, you need to be there. If not, it is a disaster."

I was blown away by her. *How did a young Panamanian woman get to co-own a factory in China?* She seemed so young, maybe in her mid-30s? And flying back and forth as if it were around the corner. I thought about how I have always dreaded flying, and more so, transatlantic flights. Everything in her line was perfect, even the way the labels were hanging. I had so much to learn, and so far to go.

"It is impressive that you can fly to China so often," I continued, complimenting her.

"Yes, and I source unique fabrics because I can supply them from other huge factories in China," she explained. "Where do you make your production?"

"I produce here, in South Florida. I wanted to produce in

Mexico, but it just wasn't an option. I struggle with the production side of the business," I said, bummed out.

"Yes, I know what you mean. It's a drag," she said empathetically.

Sofia was of medium height and medium build. She was wearing one of her dresses, with a white and grey snake print that was very delicate. She had a very structured high ponytail, and from the ponytail, a long braid extended down to her waist, touching her lower back. She had blonde hair and brown eyes, pretty in an unpretentious kind of way. She wasn't wearing a lot of makeup, but I noticed she was wearing the new Valentino studs that were all the rage.

She seemed so nice and helpful after I had raided her with my questions. I felt that I already knew her.

"Maybe we could have a coffee or something someday. I would love to talk to you more about all this stuff," I said.

"Of course, I would love to sit with you. I am so busy because I have to go back to China soon, but let's do it, for sure." And she handed me her business card, as elegant as her line.

I called Sofia a week after the show, and we decided to meet at a coffee shop near my house after work. Sofia entered the coffee shop, and I waved at her. We sat down, ordered two cappuccinos, and a *tres leches* cake that was to die for. We started talking as old friends do, laughing and sharing the cake, savoring every bite.

"I have this theory about work: you do what you need to do, you give it your all, you need to give one hundred and twenty percent of yourself. Even if I worked at McDonald's, I would strive to be the Employee of the Month every month. That is just the way I am," Sofia told me.

"It's so inspiring that you think that way. I sometimes find it difficult to juggle my family and career. For me, the priority will always be my kids and husband, and honestly, the fashion world is so fast-paced, competitive, and demanding that I sometimes struggle," I confessed.

"You know, I am married, but I don't have kids. For me, my baby is Solei. That is why I am totally invested, and my husband understands it, so I am lucky in that way."

"So, tell me, how in the world did you get to be the co-owner of a factory in China?"

"Well, I met my business partner a couple of years ago. His name is Adi; he is from India, and he and his family live in China, where they have been in the apparel business for years. His factory supplies big retail mostly in Europe," she explained. "We met at a fabric trade show, and he invited me to work for him for his big clients. We were so successful with those clients that we decided to launch our new brand, and that is how Solei was born. Actually, this is our first collection. We just started three months ago."

"Wow, what a story!" I said.

"Yeah, I feel so lucky and grateful," Sofia said, reflecting.

"Exactly, you have to live gratefully and fully because you never know, right?" I felt I knew Sofia from a lifetime ago. I paused for a moment, and honestly, I don't know why I told her this; I had just met her. "For me, my family is most important. See, my husband had cancer when he was twenty-five years old. I wasn't with him at the time, but it's something that I always carry in the back of my mind. Life is so fragile, and everything can change in an instant. I want to work doing what I love and enjoy my family."

"Maybe I can help you with that. I could do your production in China," she said.

"Really? That would be awesome! Could you do my designs, my dresses?" I asked her.

"I talked to Adi about you. We thought that if you could open markets, like Mexico, we could do Solei, by Monica Ocejo, and sell the same collection we have now."

I thought for a minute about the idea of Solei, by Monica Ocejo, but it wasn't appealing to me. I never designed for name recognition; it was just part of the job. With so many things going on with my kids and the monumental effort we had made by leaving Mexico, I was tired of being in charge of everything. And putting my name on something I didn't design didn't feel right to me. A crazy idea crossed my mind, and before I said it, I had to stop and gather courage, like when a teenager makes their move with their crush.

"Look, I am not interested in putting my name in a collection. I don't care about that. I want more time with my kids," I paused and looked down at what was left of the tres leches. "What would you think if I bought a small stake in Solei?"

Her eyes widened, and she threw her body back in the chair. "NO! I don't think that is a good idea," she replied. "And Adi would never go for it; he would kill me even if I mentioned it. He is exceptional in that way."

"I understand what you are saying. It is crazy. We've just met, but listen, I have all these contacts, an office, an assistant, a seamstress, and everything needed to create samples here in Miami. You have the production side of the business. The last couple of years have been challenging, and I have all this potential to grow, but I do recognize that I can't do it all alone. I want to be your co-pilot. I am interested in a small stake. You and Adi can have the two majorities, and I would only have a twenty percent stake in the company. You and Adi can have forty percent and forty percent," I said.

I thought about *Shark Tank* and how they asked for 20 percent of the company. I couldn't continue like this. I was working my ass off and couldn't grow, and my kids have been facing challenges that I needed to attend to. If I had 20 percent of a big company with a factory in China, I would be more than happy.

"I don't think that would work. Adi and I are a super tight team. Nothing can come between us. We are like family, brother and sister," Sofia said.

"Think about it. I can help you secure big accounts and access capital. These companies need a lot of investment. If you want to grow, we can grow faster together than each of us on our own, and I can open the Mexican market for you."

"Adi has always told me that he would love to go to Mexico," Sofia revealed.

"Of course! Mexico is a huge market, and I have contacts with people in Londres, which is the largest retail chain in the country. I could set up a meeting with them," I said, exaggerating that claim.

"Let me think about it. Let me talk to Adi."

"Of course, talk to him. Why don't you come to my office next week and see how we work, meet the staff, and see all the equipment? I am sure you will like the showroom. You've already met Victoria, my assistant at the trade show. She is the nicest."

"Yes, I loved her. We clicked, like with you, as if we met years ago," Sofia said.

"It is crazy, right? I feel the same, as if I know you from a lifetime ago. Come to the office, and we will take it from there," I urged her.

Sofia agreed, and we said our goodbyes. I went back home to find a little disaster with the kids and El Mada.

"Where have you been? Everyone is going crazy with homework and dinner," he said.

"Remember the lady I met on the trade show that I told you about the other day? I had a very long and unexpected meeting." I explained what went down in the meeting and the proposal I made to Sofia.

"Have you lost your mind? You don't even know who they are," he said, dead serious.

"Listen, with so much going on with the kids, I can't do everything. You travel so much for work, and I am practically alone on weekdays. You can't imagine the quality of the clothes, the fabrics. How could I ever compete with that? And the prices are ridiculous," I said. "I am producing in little shops around Hialeah, and they are producing in state-of-the-art facilities with the most beautiful fabrics available. On top of that, I am so tired all the time. I have no energy. I need to go to the doctor. What is wrong with me?" I was almost about to cry.

"Ok, let me meet her, and we will talk to her," he said.

"I can't continue like this anymore," I confessed.

"The good news is we are in the process of getting the Green Card, so that is one less thing we need to worry about," he said.

"That is great news, *Flaco*. But I am still exhausted," I told him.

"I understand, Moni, take it easy. We will figure it out. We'll meet with her and see how it goes."

Recipe to share with friends, old and new.

Tres leches cake

For the Cake

Ingredients:

- 6 egg whites
- 6 egg yolks
- 100 g white sugar
- 200 g flour
- 5g baking powder

Tres Leches Sauce

- 2 280 ml cans of condensed milk
- 2 340 ml cans of evaporated milk
- 2 cups heavy whipping cream

Instructions

1. Preheat oven to 350°F. Grease and flour a chosen cake mold (I make mine in a glass Pyrex).
2. Beat the egg yolks with half the sugar until fluffy.
3. In another bowl, beat the egg whites with the other half of the sugar until soft peaks form.
4. Fold in the yolks with the egg whites.
5. In a separate bowl, sift the flour and baking powder. Fold the egg mixture into the flour with a spatula.
6. Fill the previously greased and floured mold, and bake for 30 minutes. Check that the cake is cooked through with a toothpick. Let cool for 10 minutes.
7. Make little holes with a fork so the sauce can be absorbed.

8. Prepare the tres leches sauce: mix condensed milk, evaporated milk and whipping cream. Moisten the cake with the tres leches sauce by pouring it over the cake, and refrigerate for at least two hours before serving. Serves cold.

CHAPTER 17

You Give Me Hope

After getting that dreadful call confirming my breast cancer diagnosis, El Mada and I drove in silence to my office for the meeting with Sofia. I was numb, staring mindlessly out the window. The news that I had breast cancer didn't sink in. It just didn't seem real. But I had to put that aside and prepare for the business meeting.

Sofia arrived at my office and seemed impressed. The seamstress worked silently, nonstop, making samples. After I showed her around and introduced her to everyone, we went into my office. I was still in a stupor and mainly kept to myself. I even told El Mada to take my seat at the desk and to lead the meeting. I sat quietly on his side as Sofia sat in front of him. Sofia and El Mada hit it off. She was quite charming and knew what she was talking about. I don't remember exactly the conversation; I was in a haze with the cancer news. I started getting text messages from my mom, who was in Mexico, asking if I had any word yet about the biopsy result.

Shit! I have to tell my parents, this is going to break them, I thought.

Back in the office, the meeting with Sofia was going well. It seemed that she was interested in having me join Solei.

"We have gotten such an amazing response from the stores. Just in last week's trade show, we sold twenty-five thousand dollars of merchandise," she said. "The problem is I don't have an office here in Miami. I work from home, and I will be overwhelmed when I have to start sending out the orders. Honestly, I think that it would also be great for me to bring you guys into the mix."

I smiled.

"Adi is not fully on board yet, but don't worry. I will convince him. I need help here in the US," Sofia said.

"I understand," El Mada said, "but if we were to merge, we need the seamstress because we have deliveries from Monica's line this season," he continued talking and hashing details.

The meeting started to drag on, and I noticed my mom's texts becoming increasingly desperate.

"Excuse me for a second," I said. "I need to go to the bathroom."

I stepped out of the office, and I sat on the floor in a corner of the long hallway. I called my mom, who quickly picked up.

"Moni, what happened? Do you have any news?" she asked in an anxious voice.

"Yes, Mom, they called us. It looks like I do have it," I sadly said.

"No, please don't tell me that. What did they say?" She started to cry.

"Oh, Mom, don't cry! Don't worry, so many women get diagnosed with this thing. They said the tumor was only two centimeters, and the other bump they found was not cancerous. Everything is going to be fine."

"But how can it be? We have no history of cancer in our family. Just your Abuela Tere, but that was when she was much older. It can't be," she continued, crying.

"Please, Mom, let's try to keep calm. It is a lot, but I'll figure it out. I have to go, but I'll call back as soon as I can. I love you so much, and don't worry, it is going to be fine." As I hung up, I wiped a tear from my cheek.

One of the most difficult aspects of getting cancer is telling your loved ones the news. When you utter those words, you feel you are tearing their hearts into a million pieces.

I gathered myself and went back to the meeting. El Mada and Sofia were still at it. I had told him previously how much I was willing to pay for 20 percent of the company. The sales that Solei had in the few months that it had been on the market were impressive. With the backing of Adi and the factory in China, the sky was the limit.

Sofia was explaining her background in the fashion industry. "My background in fashion is very vast. I worked for Bloomingdale's. I entered as an intern after school, and because I was the best intern, they hired me full-time. They had never hired an intern before, but I was the first to come in the morning and the last to leave. I broke records in sales. They were so impressed that they made me vice president of operations for the Southeast. I would travel worldwide in a private jet, checking the stores. I would go to the headquarters to see my boss, Jimmy Hannover, who took me under his wing. I thank God every day for the opportunities that he gave me, and I will always work as hard as anyone, even if I work sweeping a gas station," Sofia said.

El Mada was impressed. He negotiated the price of what we would have to pay to be in Solei with Sofia. Finally, they reached an amount I thought fair.

"Are you sure you want to do this now?" El Mada asked me, staring directly into my eyes.

"Absolutely sure."

Suddenly, Sofia said, "I want to tell you guys something that I don't tell many people. A couple of years ago, I had cancer. I had a tumor in my spleen that grew so much that it burst the spleen. I was very ill in the hospital for a couple of months."

El Mada and I listened with our mouths open. We couldn't believe what she was saying.

"Since then," she continued. "I am so grateful for every moment I get. With all of this, how it is happening, I just feel we are going to become family," she said. By now, I was already crying. I stood up and hugged her.

"I don't think you realize what your words mean to me. You have given me hope," I said.

Sofia didn't know what I was going through. I had just found out about my cancer. Her words were like a crack in a dark room where a ray of sunshine illuminated the darkness. How was it possible that I received such devastating news just three hours earlier, and now I was en route to building something that I had dreamed of for so long? It was like that saying, "When God closes a door, He opens a window." The fact that everything happened in a matter of hours made me think that everything was going to be okay. It was a sign that I had to trust that everything in life is perfectly designed, even if you don't understand it at that time.

We agreed with Sofia to draw up the contracts, as she would be returning to China in a few weeks. There was so much to be done, but first, I had to figure out what was going on with my cancer. I needed information on my prognosis and treatment, and to tell Sofia before we signed anything. She had the right to know what I was facing, and most importantly, I had to get on top of it as soon as possible to achieve the best possible outcome.

CHAPTER 18

Fabulous Dr. Wang

Life isn't about waiting for the storm to pass. It's about learning how to dance in the rain.

—Vivian Greene

When you are diagnosed with cancer, there is a lot to do and a lot to learn. Before my diagnosis, I thought of breast cancer as a "lightweight" type of cancer. *Worry if you get pancreatic cancer*, I ignorantly thought.

It seemed that so many more and younger women were being diagnosed. "I am sure they will be fine in no time," I said when I heard about someone young being diagnosed with breast cancer. But lately, my perception was changing. A classmate of Isabel, my sister, died of breast cancer after giving birth to her third child.

Doctors didn't find out she had breast cancer while pregnant. I was friends with her on Facebook, and she would often share how she would take her "infusion," always looking very hopeful and optimistic. She would also share pictures of her kids, family, and friends wearing custom t-shirts with her name inscribed on them, cheering her on. It seemed that everything was going fine. Then, she stopped sharing pictures, and a couple of months later, we received word that she hadn't made it. The oversized tumor never shrank with chemo; she never even got the chance to have surgery. Eventually, her cancer metastasized, and she passed away, leaving behind three young children and a devastated husband. She was 35 years old when she died. Her story haunted me.

Even though most breast cancer patients do very, very well, it is something that you need to take extremely seriously. I had heard about a lot of women around me having breast cancer. The standard procedure was radiation, surgery, and taking a pill for five years.

Sounds reasonable, it is doable, I thought. I was not going to panic.

To my surprise, there are a lot of types of breast cancer. The most common types are hormonal, which comprise 80 percent of the bulk. When we got the results of my type of cancer, I was stunned to learn that I had an aggressive and rare type. It fell into the other 20 percent of breast cancers. It is called triple-negative breast cancer. Even the name is scary, like a TV game show; if you get three *X*s, you are out, gone.

I started to ask around. Luckily, when you get sick, many people come out of the woodwork to help you. You realize how many women have had breast cancer; you just weren't aware of it. The sister of a friend of mine had just gone through it. She lived in Miami and generously called me, providing the names of the doctors who had treated her. It was evident that I didn't want a Debbie Downer doctor. I wanted a good doctor, but I wanted to be supported. Even in a bad situation, I wanted a doctor with positive energy, which I can imagine is a hard thing to find in oncology.

"You are going to need three doctors. An oncologist, a surgeon, and a radiologist," she told me sweetly. There was so much information that my head was spinning.

"It is a lot to take in, but just take a breath. Here is the name and phone number of my oncologist. Her name is Dr. Wang. She is awesome; see her. Also, here is the name of my surgeon. I adore him; he was amazing. He is one of the best in Miami. But you need to go first to the oncologist. She will make a plan of treatment and supervise it," she said.

"Thank you so much. You can't imagine how much you helped me. I had no idea where to start."

I called Dr. Wang's office, and luckily, she had an opening for the next week. I later learned that this was a rare occasion; she was a highly sought-after doctor. Normally, a patient may have to wait months to get a first appointment. Thank God I got lucky! I would have freaked out waiting for the appointment with that thing growing in my boob.

I went to the appointment with El Mada and my mom, who flew in from Mexico. While we were waiting for Dr. Wang in her office, I noticed that she had many figurines and pictures of hearts scattered throughout her office. Big hearts, small hearts, pink hearts, smiling hearts, and heart frames. I liked her already. A petite, stylish woman entered the office.

"Hello, I am Dr. Wang," she said with a smile. The three of us were seated on the other side of her desk with a cluster of hearts between us. "Hi, Monica," she said, talking to me warmly. "I want to show you a small presentation about the disease, but first, let me ask you three questions. Do you drink alcohol?" she asked.

"No," I answered. My days as a party girl were long gone. "Do you eat red meat?" she asked.

"No. I don't like to eat meat; I like the occasional taco when I go to Mexico, but in general, I do not eat meat," I said.

"Do you drink milk?" she asked.

"No, I don't. I eat cheese, but I don't drink milk."

Perfect, I thought, *I don't drink, I eat healthy, I don't smoke. I am basically the most boring human being alive, and somehow, I still got this thing.*

"Ok," she said. "I will show you a presentation, and then you can ask me all your questions."

She turned the oversized screen of her computer to face us, and a PowerPoint presentation began. It started to explain the types of cancer: invasive, in situ, so many unknown words that I started to panic. I understood zilch. My mom and El Mada were focused on the presentation. I knew my mom wasn't understanding anything, although she was nodding at everything. But when I heard the words 'invasive' and 'lymph nodes,' I interrupted her presentation and asked her.

"Sorry, Dr. Wang, could you pause for a minute? Is my cancer invasive?" I asked her.

"Yes, but let's finish the presentation so that you can understand better."

"To be honest with you, I'm not understanding anything you are saying. I am extremely scared. I just turned forty years old, have three small kids, and, from what I understand my type of cancer is pretty rare and aggressive," I said, almost crying.

"Yes, the type of cancer you have is not that common, but the good news is that we found it pretty early. You are stage two. In general, that type of cancer responds very well to chemotherapy. We need to start treating you with chemo first and then surgery. We do the chemo first to see how the tumor reacts. But try to stay calm. I think you are going to be OK."

"Will I lose my hair?" I started to feel dizzy.

"Yes, I am afraid so. You will need eight rounds of chemo. It will be once every two weeks. If all goes well, you will be done in four months. It will be a tough year, but your chances of doing well are very good."

"But I don't understand why I got this? I do have a sweet tooth;

did I eat a lot of sugar? I work very hard, was it stress?" I asked, still trying to contain myself.

"I get where you are coming from, but you didn't do anything to get this. When I was your age, I had a heart problem. I also had small children at the time and worked extremely hard when I got sick. Even though you may not realize it yet, this could be an opportunity for you to live a better life after you're done. It can be an opportunity for growth, like it was for me," she said wisely.

I now know that she was right, but at the time, I didn't understand how this was an opportunity for growth. I know many cancer survivors say it is the best thing that has happened to them, but at that time, it felt far from it. I prefer to attend self-help workshops, meditate, and binge Super-soul Sunday with Oprah. *I don't need cancer to grow as a human being*, I thought.

"Ok, when do I start?" I said, resigned to my fate.

"We need to put a port inside you, so it's easier for us to give you the chemo. It will go directly to your heart, so we don't hurt your arm's veins with a catheter. Have you met with any surgeon?" she asked.

"I was referred to Dr. Costa by a friend," I responded.

"Perfect. Meet him and arrange for your port to be inserted. It is an outpatient procedure, and afterward, we will start with the chemo." Dr. Wang said.

We never got to see the rest of her presentation, but she gave me exactly what I needed. As we were driving back home, I was dumbfounded. I didn't expect chemo.

"Do you want me to take you to the chapel to pray?" El Mada asked.

I sometimes would go to a small chapel near our house. They have the *Santísimo*. I would sense a special kind of peace and comfort in that chapel. I don't go to Mass every Sunday. If I had to take a test of all the rules and regulations that I follow in the Catholic church, I would fail spectacularly. I am a sucky catholic. But, I believe in a higher being bigger than all of us, who loves us.

"No, I will go to the chapel later. Could you take me to the hair salon, please? If I am going to lose my hair, I want it to be on my terms," I said.

I had grown my hair almost to my elbows. It was the longest I ever had it, and it took an insane amount of time, effort, conditioner, and Kerastase treatments to get it there. Now, I just wanted to chop it off, take the bull by the horns, and start processing what was coming. Losing my hair was a small price to pay for being alive.

"Ok, I will take you there." He said.

At the hair salon, in a flash, my long locks became a short bob. But this simple act of cutting my hair gave me a slight sense of control. I was going to do things my way.

To say I was scared would be an understatement. I was drowning in fear and anxiety, unable to see how I could possibly take the next step, let alone face the battle ahead. El Mada and I were driving down the block, feeling completely overwhelmed. And then, out of nowhere, I saw them—a flock of small green parrots scattered across a neighbor's lawn. In an instant, light pierced the darkness, and a surge of hope shot through me like lightning. I was going to be OK.

At the beginning of our move to Miami, I had struggled deeply with much change and uncertainty, and I had prayed for a sign. I asked God to show me something—anything—that would let me know I was on the right path. And now, in my hour of greatest need, He answered again. That unexpected family of little parrots wasn't random. It was a reminder, a whisper: *I see you. I am with you. You will be okay.*

Now that I had a clear idea of what to expect from my treatment and diagnosis, I called Sofia and told her what was going on. We hadn't signed anything yet. I called her on the phone.

"Sofia, I have some news that might make you rethink our partnership. If, after you hear what I am about to say, you decide to bail out of the deal, I understand," I said in all seriousness.

"Monica, you're scaring me. What is going on?" she asked.

"Well, the thing is, I have breast cancer. It is an aggressive type, but the good news is that we caught it early. I will need chemotherapy, then surgery and radiation. I have a positive prognosis, but it is going to be a tough year, and I won't be able to work as hard as I would like," I said sadly.

"OMG, Monica, please... You scared me. I thought you were going to tell me that you were a Mexican drug dealer or something horrible. Don't worry about it. So many women go through what you are going through, and I will be there beside you, supporting you every step of the way. Don't worry about it. I am still in this partnership, and we are going to make it big together. You will see," she said.

I can't explain the immense gratitude that overcame me about how she responded to the news. She was so amazing and hardworking, I was blown away by her. It was too good to be true.

My sister Isabel was in Miami, and I told her about my agreement with Sofia. When I told her that I would invest in Sofia's company, merge the companies and open the door into our lives, Isabel was concerned.

"Have you done any background research on her? Have you asked for references? How are you going to give the key to your business to someone you don't even know? Have you done your due diligence?" she asked.

"Well, everything happened so fast, and with the diagnosis, it was a Godsend. What are the chances that she has what I need, and I have exactly what she needs? And what are the chances that she also had cancer? She understands me so well. Her company just started four months ago, and she has sold an amount larger than what I am paying her for the percentage. It's a no-brainer," I said confidently. "Besides, the best testament is the quality of the clothes; it is incredible," I said, trying to convince her.

"Well, it's nice seeing women like her, full-time, full-throttle, working women. I hope everything turns out well for you. It is a little bit rushed, though. You should ask your friend Rebeca from Panama for references," she suggested.

"You're right. I will ask Rebeca about her," I said, but the reality was that I had no intention of asking anyone about her. I was too scared to find out something that might derail our plans. I wanted this merger to work out, now more than ever.

I scheduled an appointment with the oncologist surgeon, Dr. Costa. He would first insert my port and, after my chemo, would do my surgery. My first instinct was that I wanted a mastectomy. I wanted my breasts out. I didn't want to deal with them anymore. My whole relationship with my boobs had changed. They had always been nice to me, and I liked them. Although I only got to breastfeed my three children for a week because I didn't have a lot of milk, but hey! At least I tried.

Of course, after three kids, they could use a makeover. But I was happy with them. I was grateful to them. But now they had become something else. They had become a threat, a weapon of mass destruction. I wanted them gone.

Dr. Costa came into the examining room. He was very tall. Imagine a Latin Dwayne "The Rock" Johnson in scrubs, with long, black, curly hair flowing down his shoulders. He looked like a doctor in the soap opera *The Bold and the Beautiful*.

"Hi, Monica, I am going to be your surgeon. First, we are going to insert a port so you can start your chemo. After your chemo, we will talk about your options for your surgery. You can have a lumpectomy or a mastectomy," he said.

"I want them off," I told him.

"OK, we will figure it out when we get there. Let's go step by step," he said gently.

"I am super freaked out," I confessed.

"Don't worry; it is normal. It's going to be a difficult year, but I think you are going to be OK."

That was the second time I heard "You are going to be ok." Those six words meant so much, the difference between life and death.

As he left the office, I was not convinced. He seemed nice but a little bit impersonal. But surgeons do have the reputation of being colder. He had a stellar reputation; I wasn't going to be picky.

We arrived at the hospital to get my port inserted. The port is a small pump that is inserted four inches under your skin, just below your shoulder. It connects directly to your heart, so when they insert a needle into your port, the chemo goes through to your body, so the veins in your arm don't get damaged. They do it without general anesthesia, and I was allowed to go home the same day.

We checked in on time at the hospital, and Dr. Costa was nowhere to be found. The nurses got everything ready for the procedure, and while we waited, they all gushed about Dr. Costa.

"He is one of the best surgeons in the hospital," one nurse said.

"He operated on my mother, and she did great," another nurse said, with starry eyes.

"He is so amazing and handsome," the first nurse replied.

"Don't worry, sweetie; he is one of the best in Miami. You can't go wrong."

I was happy that Dr. Costa had a fan club at the hospital, but he was already one hour late, and it wasn't sitting well with me.

"We are ready for you, love; we are now going to sedate you," a rushed nurse said to me. "Dr. Costa is already waiting for you in the operating room."

"Am I not going to see him before the surgery? I have some questions," I asked the nurse.

"Don't worry, love; you can ask him after the procedure," the nurse replied.

UGHHHH! I am sorry, but I need my doctor to see me before surgery. It's the least he can do if he is going to cut me open.

Then, they started wheeling me to the operating room, and everything became dark. The next thing I remember is hearing some voices and laughter around me. I couldn't open my eyes; my eyelids were very heavy. I tried to, but I couldn't open them. There were many light figures around me; I felt them, and they were very luminous, glowing, and all very friendly. They were chatting and laughing amongst themselves, around me.

"You did great; you are going to be fine!" somebody said.

I was flying in the clouds, surrounded by heavenly creatures, white spirits rejoicing around me. All the fear and anxiety I had been feeling during those past weeks was melting away. I felt so loved, so happy, completely at peace, as if all my spiritual friends, whom I had prayed to all my life, were surrounding me in my moment of need. The Virgin Mary, my guardian angel, and *los Santitos* (St. Jude and Saint Monica) were around me, cheering me on. It was such an amazing experience. Still, Jesus wasn't there for some reason. I was in the middle of a huddle, and they were showering me with love, assuring me that the journey ahead, although difficult, was one I would overcome, and they would be with me every step of the way. It was beautiful, a little heavenly party to cheer me up.

After what I considered a couple of minutes, I slowly opened my eyes, my eyelids puffy and heavy. What had just happened? Had I had a wonderful mystic experience? Or, maybe, I was just high from the drugs I was given. I don't know, but I prefer to think that I had a heavenly fiesta from up above.

It took a while for me to wake up fully. The nurses sat me in a recliner and kindly sent me home, still drowsy and nauseated.

"Isn't Dr. Costa coming?" I asked the nurse.

"Sorry, Babe. He waited for you to wake up, but he had to leave. But you did awesome," she replied.

I had acquired a new bump under my skin, the port, and right then and there, I decided to dump Dr. Costa. I needed to find a new surgeon, and pronto.

CHAPTER 19

Free as My Hair

I hadn't lost my hair yet; the doctors tell you exactly when you will lose it. I can't pinpoint why hair is so important for most people, but for me, my hair has always been a part of my identity. I had been trying to let it grow for ages. I loved running, letting the wind play through my hair, and trotting to the rhythm of whatever song.

I felt free, alive. Hair is part of your makeup; it can be a form of expression. The teenager who dyes her hair purple and pink to make a statement, a woman who chops her hair hoping for a new start, or summing it up in two words, Britney Spears. Maybe it's the crown that we all play with in our heads. But now, I didn't want to go to the supermarket and let people know I was sick, nor did I want my kids to notice. I wanted them to continue their lives as normally as possible.

I greatly admire women who are in these circumstances and come out bald, as they are. They rock the look with their inner beauty shining through, total acceptance of themselves, and the situation they are going through. I didn't have that strength and confidence; I decided I would hide under a wig. There is no right or wrong way to do this. Everyone manages and survives as best they can, and this is how I did it. I don't even like the word wig, but it was a lifesaver.

A cancer survivor recommended Gilberto, a larger-than-life Cuban hairdresser. Gilberto developed a method of gluing a wig to your head with a wig identical to your own hair. You could sleep with the wig, swim with the wig, tango with the wig. I had to meet him before I lost my hair so that he could see my haircut and color, and then he could make a wig identical to my natural hair. I was told that my children wouldn't even notice that I was wearing it. This was a huge win. What a thrill! My hair was an element in this cancer mess that worried me. With Gilberto's help, I had one less issue to deal with.

We arrived at his place, a few streets away from La Calle Ocho. It was a two-story brown building. My mom and I went inside, and there were pictures of Gilberto himself, in which he appeared totally bald. In the photo next to it, he was Fabio, the book model, with similar hair. He was the best endorsement for his product; good for him!

On the floor below, we first passed several little rooms, like a beauty salon, but we finally went upstairs, where Gilberto was. The walls were full of famous Latin American artists with hair extensions from Gilberto. Latin American stars—like Paulina Rubio, Sofia Vergara, and even Shakira in her early years. In his cubicle, Gilberto had pictures of more artists and women who were sick. They had their photos taken both with and without the wig. You couldn't have imagined that those women were bald. He also had a picture next to his desk that really impressed me. It was Gilberto hugging Angelina Jolie. *This Gilberto is on another level!* I thought.

After a while, Gilberto came in. He ended up being one of the nicest people I have ever met.

"What happened to my girl that brings you here today?" he asked. We told him about my cancer situation.

"But, my girl, what you have is nothing. We're going to make you look beautiful. The only thing you have to worry about is getting better," he said. "We'll put your wig on, and you need to come every four weeks. We'll take it off, wash and dry it as if you were going to the salon. You'll see that everything will be fine."

He showed me several wigs, and I chose one with a similar color and length to my own hair.

"You need to come before the chemo that makes your hair fall out. It's very unpleasant to feel how strands of hair stay in your hand and experience them falling out in the shower. I can shave off all your hair before that happens and stick the wig on. You don't even have to look at yourself in the mirror while I am shaving it off," Gilberto said.

"Great, thank you! You don't know what this means to me," I said, as I got up from my chair and hugged him.

While Gilberto explained his process, I felt a gigantic relief. I was taking control and getting ahead of one of the things that scared me the most. I wasn't going to let it traumatize me. I would get ahead of it and live it in the best way possible.

CHAPTER 20

My First Chemo

I t was time for my first chemo. I was ready to go. Bring it on! I wanted to start and kick the butt of this thing. I then received an unsettling call from Dr. Wang informing me that we would have to postpone the first chemo because my heart exam didn't come back as they expected.

To receive such strong chemo, I had to have a healthy heart, because the chemo itself will weaken or irritate the heart. They didn't want to take any risks.

"Don't worry. If I can't give you Adriamycin, there are other medications I can administer. But I need you to go to the cardiologist first, so they can do a more thorough exam to see exactly what is going on," she said.

Are you kidding me!! I thought. I had been such a good sport until then. *What the hell, there is nothing wrong with my heart! I know it!* On the day of the heart test, I saw the technician working hastily because I was the last patient, and she probably wanted to go home. It can't be right.

My mom and dad had practically moved to Miami for my treatment. They rented an apartment, and my mom was going to stay to help take care of me. My dad would fly back and forth because he had matters to attend to in Mexico. Between my sister and my parents, they would take turns coming to care for me, help with the kids, and support El Mada, although he was being a sweetheart.

After the setback of the heart exam, I saw my dad depressed and sad. I was trying to keep positive and active. I kept working, excited about the new venture, but when you have cancer, it's like you have a new full-time job, and that job is called surviving. That's why I enjoyed going to my job so much. It made me feel normal. I could even forget about my other "job."

One day, after a few hours of work, I got home and saw my dad watching TV. He was lying on the couch in a fetal position, with both of his hands tucked under his face.

"Hi, Dad, what's up?" I said. He didn't answer; he just shrugged his shoulders.

I understood that he was devastated. He never took us to the doctor because he hates all things involving hospitals, but I needed to live as normally and as positively as possible. So, I went to my mom and told her.

"Listen, Mom, I think this is too much for Dad. I understand this is horrible for him, but I need a positive space. Maybe it's best for him to go to Mexico for his work."

"Don't worry; I will talk to him about it," my mom promised.

At the appointment, the cardiologist performed a more detailed examination and concluded that my heart was perfectly fine, thank you very much. I was fine for chemo . . . HURRAY!

Then it struck me: I was cheering for the opportunity to receive one of the strongest chemotherapies available, Adriamycin, also known as the Red Devil. I wanted to have the most aggressive treatment possible. I realized then that having the opportunity to receive treatment is a gift. Some people don't get that chance.

They called my chemo, Red Devil, because it was bright red and the devil for its terrible secondary effects. Incredibly, this was the same chemo El Mada had when he got sick. I can't stop thinking about all the coincidences we share in life. Because he had gone through this same process, it made him an exceptional companion. He understood what I was going through because he had experienced it, just like me.

We triumphantly arrived at the chemo room. When I think back about that place, I can't describe the vibe. It gave me almost the same feeling I got when I went to the little chapel to pray. Everyone is gathered into themselves. It is very peaceful and quiet; the nurses and technicians could not be nicer. It seems to me that it is a place where you reflect on your life, hoping and praying that you will receive the cure. People would be knitting, reading, sleeping, or lovingly chatting with their supporters. All accepting their new reality, their new fate, with hope in their hearts that they are healing. When I think of that room, I remember a place filled with love, a place where God is present.

I sat on the recliner, and they gave me a warm blanket. With a very large needle, they punched the port I had in my navel. It didn't hurt that much.

They started with the premeds for nausea and who knows what else. Afterward, the main course arrived, the famous Red Devil, a bright red liquid in a plastic bag. They connected it to the IV. As it started pumping into my veins, I felt the same. I didn't start bursting into flames. "Take that, freaking tumor, start shrinking immediately, you asshole! The Red Devil has arrived, and it is going to kick your butt," I told my tumor.

After a couple of hours, I was done and sent home. They said that I would feel fine that day and that the effects would start approximately two days later. After I got my chemo, my family went to Hillstone's to have some burgers. *Perhaps this won't be so bad after all*, I said to myself.

When I arrived home, I received a text from Sofia. She needed the money for the buyout. She was leaving for China, and she wanted to leave with everything signed. I had a couple of hours to get her the money and wait for some symptoms to start. I was preparing for the storm and organizing the shelter. To get the agreed-upon amount, I had to draw checks from different bank accounts. I also got part of the money from my mom.

At that point, I think she would have given me everything she had in her bank account. I grabbed the car, and with the Red Devil starting a war inside my body, I drove around to the different banks to get the certified check for Sofia.

I was getting the check, and the cashier asked me, "Hi, how are you doing today?"

"Fine, thank you," I answered.

Imagine I had told her, "Great! I was just in a hospital for seven hours getting my first chemo because I have cancer, but other than that, everything is peachy, thank you."

It was surreal.

As I arrived home with the checks, I started to feel weak, just in time to let myself go. I got into my pajamas, climbed into bed, and with closed eyes, I waited for the storm.

"Sofia is here," El Mada quietly announced.

"Tell her to come up," I said.

Sofia sat on the side of the bed. The certified checks were on the table. El Mada brought the agreement, drawn by the lawyers, and I sat up to sign the papers. I gave her the checks and all my savings, investing in my dream, feeling something big coming.

"We are going to be the next Zara," Sofia said, "only better quality and fabrics."

I was starting chemo the same day that we sealed our fates

together in a company. A dream that both of us would do anything in our power to make successful. We had the support of Adi, with a factory in China, and El Mada, with his financial expertise.

"Sofia, you have no idea what you are doing for me. I have never met a person like you. Thank you so much for allowing me to be part of Solei, and even more so under these conditions. I feel that God placed you in my path, in this precise moment, to give me strength and hope that everything is going to be fine," I whispered, with my eyes half-closed, after we both signed the agreement.

Sofia started to cry.

"No, Moni, thank you; we are family now. We take care of each other. Don't you worry about anything! I will fly to China and bring the most beautiful collection ever. Adi is now on board and is excited that you are going to be our partner. I think you will like him, you'll see," she said kindly. "I'll let you rest, now. I'll start to send clothes to the office. Please take care of yourself."

She took the checks from my night table, gave me a kiss, and left. "See you in two weeks," she said, standing at my room's door.

"Bye, Sofia, take care," I replied, and drifted to sleep. Whatever happened, I had made something of myself. I could let go now and be carried into the night.

The day passed by, and I didn't feel so bad. However, the next day, a tsunami of nausea hit me. I would take the medication and sleep all day. I tried to be around the kids and hide how I was really feeling. On Monday, I woke up and went downstairs. I didn't know what time it was, but I felt a horrifying pain in my belly, an awful cramp. I went to the bathroom to see if I could relieve myself, but the pain only got worse. I started to sweat, heard a loud buzzing noise, and fell to the floor.

I called my mom for help.

"Moni, what is going on? What is wrong?" she said.

I couldn't speak; the pain was debilitating. I blacked out.

I opened my eyes on the floor of my kid's bathroom, drenched in sweat, still in pain. Cris arrived, looking terrified. She was so close to giving birth, I didn't want her to see me like this.

"Cris, please, go home, please," I said to her. I didn't want to scare her.

El Mada arrived from the office.

"We are taking you to the hospital right now. Can you walk?" my mom asked.

"I don't know. I don't think so," I said. "Please, try," she begged.

They helped me up and laid me on the car's back seat. I was in so much pain, I would doze off and be woken again by the pain. It was like a massive cramp that was tearing apart my hips. I had never felt pain like this before.

We arrived, and the nurse asked what was wrong with me.

"She has a terrible cramp, she has breast cancer, and she had her first chemo two days ago," El Mada said. As I heard this, it became surreal to me again. How had I ended up here? Tears rolled down my cheeks.

"We are going to give her some morphine for the pain until we find out what is wrong with her," the ER doctor said.

The pain wasn't going away, and I felt so weak. My blood pressure was very low, and I was dehydrated. My sister Isabel flew in from Mexico. She brought with her a delicious green tea pancake, my favorite, but I couldn't eat it. My mom stayed with me the whole day, and Isabel slept in the hospital at night. The doctors didn't tell us much except that I had low potassium, and they just kept hydrating me.

I opened my eyes and saw written on the blackboard in front of the hospital bed, my name, the name of the nurse, and my level of pain. Under *diagnosis,* it said, "My first chemo."

First Chemo. Me? No, I couldn't believe it. I always feared that cancer was going to hit my family because of El Mada's history. I was painfully aware of the fine thread from which all human beings hang. I am aware that anything can happen in an instant, and nobody is exempt from death or sickness knocking at your door when you least expect it. But I always thought that if somebody was going to get sick, it was going to be El Mada, not me. I had no history of cancer in my family. Cancer was not in my family's picture. How was this happening to me?

I closed my eyes again. I couldn't sleep and couldn't talk to Isabel. I was weak and felt nauseous. Isabel didn't sleep the whole night. She stayed on the chair watching me. She would check my vital signs and be on top of the nurses. I felt so cared for by her side. The morning came. My mom arrived, and Isabel left to shower and take a nap. I didn't feel much better. Throughout all my struggles, I had believed in and prayed to God, my guardian angel, the Holy Spirit, and Our Lady of Guadalupe. I had always trusted Him to be by my side, but now I felt completely abandoned to my fate and pain. I didn't feel hope; I was broken, surrounded by darkness.

I started to cry, and I asked my mom, "Mom, where are they? I don't feel them here with me. I feel that God has abandoned me. I pray, and I pray for faith, but I feel totally hopeless. I don't feel they are looking out for me. I don't feel their presence. Where is my guardian angel? You know I have been praying to him since I was little. He is not here with me," I told her, deep in hopelessness.

"Yes, Moni, he is here with you, taking care of you."

"No, Mom, I don't feel it. I feel abandoned. They have left me alone," I said, hopeless.

"No, honey, they haven't left you. He is here," she repeated.

I closed my eyes. It was so nice that my mom was trying to cheer me up. I just wanted to stop feeling pain. The doctor came in and said that my potassium levels were still low and that if the pain in my belly didn't stop, they would do a colonoscopy. No way, I wanted to go home! It was then that I received news that Cris had just given birth to a gorgeous baby girl.

The next day, as soon as I regained some strength and my blood numbers were up, I wanted to leave. They suggested some exams, like a colonoscopy, that I refused to take. Dr. Wang wasn't in this hospital, and I didn't trust those doctors. After a bit of convincing, they discharged me.

"Please take me to see Cris and her baby," I asked. I arrived to meet Cris's new baby girl feeling like a character from *The Walking Dead*. My body was drained, my spirit heavy—but the moment I saw her, I felt a sudden and overwhelming sense of hope. This tiny, perfect baby girl had come into the world just as I was being reborn. As she grows, I will grow with her. I hope I can be at her graduation, her wedding, and accompany her in her life's journey. The birth of Giuliana was a glimmer of light in a very dark time. I had survived the first round of chemo. It had been brutal, but Dr. Wang reassured me the next cycle wouldn't hit as hard; the body begins to adjust to the poison. "What doesn't kill you makes you stronger," I thought. Maybe, just maybe, that was true.

CHAPTER 21

Focus on Chayanne

As the chemo was underway, I would continue to work as best as I could. I was thrilled about everything happening with Solei, and since Sofia left for China, boxes and boxes of orders had started to arrive. I couldn't hold in my excitement. It was the best decision I had made in my life.

It was time to visit Gilberto. I had to do a thousand things before they gave me the next chemo. I had quite a few things on my plate with work and the kids, so I only had a small window to see Gilberto. I called El Mada and told him I was going to get my wig put on.

"Who are you going with?" he asked.

"Alone," I answered him.

"You're crazy; you can't go alone? I'll go with you," he said. "Do you mind if I don't come inside when he shaves your hair off?"

"Don't worry, you don't have to go in," I told him.

We arrived, and Gilberto received me in his office. El Mada sat outside and waited until everything was over, watching his cell.

"Naysbeli is going to shave you. When she is done, I'll apply the wig," Gilberto said. I saw the picture of Gilberto with Angelina Jolie nearby.

"Hey, Gilberto, I can't get over the idea that you made extensions for Angelina Jolie. Is she nice? I was always Team Aniston," I said.

"What are you talking about?"

"That picture, you're hugging her." I pointed at the photo.

"There? No, *mi niña*! I took that picture on a street when I went to Los Angeles, and there were doubles of celebrities everywhere, but Angelina Jolie's was exactly the same!"

We all started laughing. I had bragged to everyone who would listen that Angelina Jolie's hairdresser was doing my hair.

"I'll leave you with Naysbeli, and I'll be back in a moment."

Naysbeli arrived and began taking out all her utensils and the electric shaver.

"I don't want to see myself in the mirror."

"Don't worry, you won't see anything," she said. Naysbeli covered the mirror with a wooden board. She grabbed the electric razor and started shaving my head.

I held my breath. I watched as she grabbed my long locks of hair in her hand and threw them away in the wastepaper basket, as if they were some useless garbage she had found on the floor.

I closed my eyes and gripped the chair handles in the middle of the small room. I imagined a beam of light coming out of my head, connecting me to the light above, to the skies. I felt connected to something much bigger than me. Being in that state of connection, all I thought about was my marriage to El Mada. I asked God to please take care of him.

Our relationship had deteriorated a lot with the move from Mexico to Miami. I felt a lot of resentment toward him, and sometimes I felt totally disconnected from him. We were like two partners taking care of the company that was our family. I wanted to be connected to him again, to admire him, and to feel him as close as before. I offered my hair for that purpose.

Naysbeli finished and called Gilberto. I hadn't seen anything, but I knew I was completely bald. I felt raw, naked, and vulnerable. It was like being in an unknown dimension.

Then Gilberto put on my wig and started cutting it as if it were my normal hair. He made the wig to match the shape of my hairline and ears. After he made all the adjustments to the piece, as he called it, he glued my wig in place and started cutting it again. I noticed that he made layers and some bangs. I was so numb that I couldn't articulate a word. Then they washed my new hair and blow-dried it just as he had said, as if I had gone to the salon.

"There it is!" Gilberto said. "You can now see yourself in the mirror."

They lifted the wooden board, and I saw myself with my wig. The truth is that it looked pretty good. You couldn't tell it wasn't my hair. One minor detail was that it wasn't the wig that I had chosen. It was a dark wig, and it wasn't my haircut. Gilberto had gone wild with the scissors, cutting layers and bangs. My look was totally different, but I wasn't going to complain. At least I had hair, and I hadn't gone through the awful process of losing my hair strand by strand. This was a clean-cut, tear-off-the-band-aid kind of deal, and I was ready for the next round.

After the horrible reaction I had to my first chemo, I was not only paralyzed with fear but physically weakened by the awful side effects, and now it was time for my second round. I pleaded with Dr. Wang to reduce the dose she was giving me. But she wouldn't waver; my blood numbers were fine, so we were moving forward as is.

We arrived at the hospital. This time, it was my sister Isabel's turn to be by my side. Seated in the chemo room, bursting with the premeds that they give you before chemo, I told Isabel, "I don't know how I'm going to survive this; I don't think I can. Last time was awful. How am I going to do it? I am not strong enough."

A nurse ran toward us when she saw me crying. It wasn't a big drama. I was crying quite softly, discreetly, like a little mouse.

"Nobody cries here. You are going to disrupt the other patients; please stop crying," the nurse said.

Great, I can't even cry, I thought, but then I realized that if I start crying, I will trigger the general crying, like when a baby wakes up and cries, waking up the other babies. I imagined everyone sitting in their seats, crying with me, and I thought I'd better shut up.

Isabel, my sister, and I started laughing about the fact that I couldn't even cry anymore. The nurses in general were angels, but this one was kind of mean.

They began to give me the Red Devil as Isabel watched her iPad. The sessions were exhausting, each lasting about six or seven hours.

"Guess what?" she said excitedly. "Chayanne is coming to Miami right after you finish your chemotherapy," and showed me the image of Chayanne on the big iPad screen.

Chayanne, for those not familiar with him, is a Latin American star, like Ricki Martin or Enrique Iglesias, but he has special moves à la Elvis Presley that make a bunch of middle-aged women swoon.

"The only thing you are going to focus on is Chayanne; the only thing you can think of during these months is that you have to get to his concert. We are going to go to his concert and celebrate that you finished your treatments," she said.

I really love Chayanne. He is so handsome and dances so well, plus he is so nice to his wife. It was a great idea! What a wonderful goal, arriving triumphant in June at Chayanne's concert. That was all I was going to think about—handsome, sexy Chayanne. From that moment, when I felt the terrible chemo side effects, the debilitating nausea, the prison sentence of being thrown in my bed without being able to open my eyes or raise my hand, I asked El Mada to please play Chayanne's music.

Poor, nervous El Mada ran to his phone, made a mistake, and put something else. Without opening my eyes, I said, "Enrique Iglesias, noooo, please, Chayanne."

The truth is that I felt so bad, so weak, so debilitated. Thinking about getting to the bathroom was a journey, an impossibility. As I began to hear the notes of "Tiempo de Vals" (Time for a Waltz), a song that maybe every *Quinceañera* has danced, and which I think, maybe, is the corniest song ever, it transported me. It transported me to another time in my life. When I was younger, when I was fifteen years old, when I was single and lived with my parents, when life was simpler, when my biggest concern was any trivial matter, when I didn't have cancer.

The power of music is limitless; it heals, it helps you escape, it makes you relive wonderful moments, and it transports you to a time and place where nothing matters.

CHAPTER 22

Still Working, Still Fighting

Sofia arrived from China, bringing samples for the next collection. I couldn't believe my luck. Who could be so nice as to accept a situation where she would take all the burden and wait for me to recover? I admired Sofia so much. I felt she had what I lacked. I have always been nervous about flying in airplanes, but since I had my kids, separation anxiety became an even bigger problem. I couldn't think of going to China as Sofia did. Alone. I marveled at how Sofia would fly to China on a whim, as if it were a trip to Palm Beach.

She would fly from Miami to Dallas for 3 hours, and then from Dallas to Hong Kong, which takes 16 hours. Just thinking about being 16 hours in an airplane, I get hives. Sometimes I even thought that she didn't need to go so frequently, but she was obsessed with making this work, and she was good at it.

When I had good days on my chemo treatment, I would go to work and supervise the seamstress and Victoria. I also helped in securing the investment; El Mada was willing to act as our financial advisor. He even let us use the American Express Corporate card, which he was responsible for, because I didn't have any credit history in the US or Mexico, for that matter.

We had the first photoshoot with the new collection as Solei. Victoria and Sofia were getting close, but Sofia and I already felt like sisters. Sofia was new to the fashion scene in Miami, so I reached out to Justin and called Claudia, the stylist whom I knew well.

"Hi, Claudia, I have a photoshoot next week. I would love for you to help us out."

"Hi, Monica. I would love to, but I can't. I'm traveling around the country with Chayanne. He's on tour now, and next week I travel with him."

"You are kidding, right?" I asked, stunned.

"No, I work with Chayanne."

Claudia didn't know what I was going through. It's not like you call every contact you have and tell them you have cancer.

"Claudia, you are not going to believe it. A couple of months ago, I was diagnosed with breast cancer, and I have been going through arduous cycles of chemotherapy. I have been listening to Chayanne in the hardest moments. My sister and I bought tickets to his concert here in Miami in July to celebrate, because it is just two weeks after I finish my chemo. I can't believe you are working with him," I said, holding back tears.

"I am so sorry, Monica; I didn't have a clue," she said. "I will be there at the Miami concert. I will take you backstage and introduce you to Chayanne. He just lost his mother to cancer. I am sure he will be happy to celebrate with you," Claudia said.

"Claudia, that would be amazing. I would love to meet him," I said. "My sister is going to be so excited."

I was gobsmacked by how small the world was and how many gifts I was receiving in this process. I had my third chemo, and the photo shoot was just days afterward. My mom advised me not to go. I looked weak, but I honestly didn't care what they told me. I was going to be there during the shoot.

I arrived at the photoshoot and finally saw the collection that we had produced together. Printed silks with different strokes of color, a white romper with a cape, and much more. We arrived at the studio, and it was madness, but Sofia treated me normally, not like a sick witch, which I greatly appreciated.

"Moni, please grab me that dress and hang this on that rack." I quickly did what she needed. I ran back and forth, but I was soon getting tired.

"Hey, go easy on her, she is recovering," Isabel said to Sofia.

"Sorry, Moni. Are you feeling ok? Why don't you go home to rest? We will take it from here," Sofia said.

"No, I love helping you guys out. Everything is gorgeous." I said.

"When you feel tired, just tell us, and you can leave if you want," Sofia told me.

"Yes, Moni, don't force yourself too much," Isabel said.

"Twenty minutes more, and we can leave, ok?" I asked Isabel.

"Ok."

I was grateful to have these moments to escape my reality.

Some mornings, when I woke up, just for a moment, for the first microsecond of my day, I would forget that I had cancer. Everything was fine. Everything in the world was ok. But afterward, a sinking feeling would strike and hit me like a pile of bricks in the middle of my chest. *Crap! I have cancer*, I would remember. I tried to keep positive and made an effort to leave scary and negative thoughts out of my head. But sometimes, it snuck in on me, and it would debilitate me on different levels.

When you are diagnosed with cancer, you feel you live in a different realm from everyone else. I watched a woman walking on the street. The heaviness of my illness, the word "cancer," plummeted over me. I would remember I had cancer, and infinite dread would imprison my body. As I watched this lovely woman walking down the street, I would think, *Does she know how lucky she is?*

I didn't know her problems, but from my perspective, they seemed like tribulations from another planet. She was living, and I was trying to survive. An abyss separated us; I watched from the other side as she lived a life my body could no longer carry. I was from another species, from another planet. I was from Planet Cancer. I wish I were like her. I wish I weren't living on this planet. I wanted to be with the Cancer-free.

One night, I went to sleep and had the most vivid and lively dream. More than a dream, it was an experience.

I was in a vast, elegant dining room with round tables, filled with people I knew. It was a large family gathering event like so many I had attended before, but it had a celestial vibe. Everyone was dressed in white, with a heavenly, misty cloud flowing into the air. My whole family and friends were there. I started walking and said "hi" to my Aunt Mary, who was also there, looking beautiful. Then I saw my Abuelo Eduardo. He was all dressed in a white suit, and he was much younger than when he died at 100 years young. He was in his prime, maybe in his forties or fifties. I felt a rush of love and excitement when I saw him. I didn't expect him there. I ran to him excitedly and embraced him. I buried my face in his shoulder and started crying while hugging him.

"Abuelo, do you know what has happened to me? Just look at the shape I'm in," I said.

"Don't worry, Moni, you are going to be fine. Everything is going to be fine." He just said those simple words as we hugged, reassuring me. Everything was so vivid: his crisp young face, his prematurely white hair, his tender eyes, like Ricardo Montalban when welcoming you on Fantasy Island. I woke up that morning and called my mom immediately.

"Mom, El Abuelo Eduardo visited me last night. He said I was going to be fine," I told her, crying uncontrollably. Every time I talked about that dream, for a couple of years, I cried. I felt his presence, I was with him, and his simple words healed me. He came to tell me everything was going to be fine, and I believed him. I was in the middle of the eight chemo sessions, with still a ways to go.

Since Gilberto had glued my wig to my head, I would bathe, sleep, and do everything with my wig permanently plastered to my head. But a couple of weeks passed, and the glue started to chafe, and I had to go and get my maintenance with Gilberto. They would apply dissolvent to my head, and the wig would come off. My mom accompanied me to my wig maintenance session.

I told the nice lady who started to do the wig deluging that I wasn't ready to see myself in the mirror, bald. I was escaping reality and basically being a chicken, but I didn't want to let more lime drops fall into the wound. I was happy hiding behind the wig, and I put a towel over my head while they washed it.

"I am going to take your wig to the other room; I will wash and blow-dry it. When it is ready, I will bring it back and glue it to your scalp again."

"Perfect," I said. "My wig is having a spa day."

My mom and I chatted in the room as they left us. Of course, I took a selfie to remember this glorious moment. The lady was taking her time.

"What do you think she is doing to my poor wig?" I asked my mom.

"I don't know, but it has been a while now," she said.

Finally, the lady came back with my wig magnificently placed on a mannequin head. "OK, now let's get this beautiful wig on you," she said. She started to put the wig on my head, and I started to freak the hell out when I noticed something that wasn't there before.

"Excuse me, lady, this is not my wig. This wig has very short bangs, and my wig didn't have these bangs before," I said, alarmed.

"Of course, it is your wig. Look how nice you look."

I focused on the bangs, and they looked like a five-year-old had been left alone with scissors and a mirror and decided to cut her own bangs. I knew this because I had done exactly that as a five-year-old and had suffered the consequences.

"Please look at these mini tiny bangs at the crown of my head. It looks like a blind person cut them while they were drunk. Why did you cut bangs on it?!" I started to panic and lost my patience.

The lady started to panic; my mom, likewise. The room was panicking.

"I swear by the most sacred, I didn't cut the bangs," she said, as if it were a crime to cut bangs, which, in this case, it kind of was.

"Then you must have changed my wig. Please go back and look for my wig. Maybe there were two wigs in the sink, and you grabbed this one," I suggested.

"No, no, that is impossible. I never took my hands off the wig the entire time, I washed it and blow-dried it, I didn't separate from your wig." She was almost crying.

"It doesn't make sense! This is not my wig. It didn't have these chopped bangs, look at me," I said as I began to cry.

Again, panic in the room.

"Señorita, what can we do? She is right, the wig didn't have bangs," my mom said.

The señorita started pacing the room nervously, while my mom was consoling me.

"Please, call Gilberto. This is not my wig. I can't leave like this," I said to the lady. Suddenly, I remembered something. "Ohhhh! Wait! Don't call Gilberto. I know what happened," I said, solving the mystery of the chopped bangs. Both my mom and the stressed señorita looked at me with panicked eyes.

"I remember a couple of weeks ago, because the hair of the wig was so dry, it started to tangle with the chain of my necklace. I took the chain off, but a huge knot of hair was stuck in the chain. I thought it would take forever to untie the knot, so I grabbed some scissors and cut the chain's knot."

It is not my hair, anyway, I had thought.

"The wig is upside down. The back of the wig is in front, and so are the chopped bangs," I said, solving the mystery and making Sherlock Holmes proud. We went from panicking to nervously chuckling. A sigh of relief was felt in the room. She had to unglue it and repeat the process to place the wig properly.

"At least I have my wig back," I sighed. *Everything is right in the world now.*

CHAPTER 23

The Lady of Lourdes Knocking on My Door

A couple of weeks after my diagnosis, I cut contact with the outside world. I became selective about who I would let into my close circle. I was vulnerable and would get upset by unwelcome opinions or suggestions. Everybody asked many questions that I didn't have the answers for, and many times I found myself consoling people who called me supposedly to cheer me up. I would let people in who would give me positive energy, not those who took it away from me. One day, the doorbell rang. I opened the door and saw a friend that I wasn't very close to.

"Hi, Monica, I know you are busy, but I just wanted to give you this." She handed me a small bottle filled with clear water. "It is water from Lourdes. My mother-in-law has pancreatic cancer, and Our Lady of Lourdes is the Lady of the sick people. We went to the town of Lourdes, France, this summer. My mother-in-law is doing very well despite her diagnosis. I brought you some water from the stream that has healing power."

I took the little glass bottle with the holy water and thanked her for thinking of me. I wasn't very familiar with Our Lady of Lourdes. Since I am Mexican, Our Lady of Guadalupe was my main squeeze. But I believe that God, the Universe, the Light, or whatever name you want to call it, is greater than any religion. I respect every religion, ideology, belief, or lack thereof.

I just keep trying to look for the light in the dark, for the positive in the negative. I believe in the power of the human mind and spirit. I believe we create our own fate, and whatever energy you put into the world will be what you receive. I believe in the power of being grateful. There is nothing purer and greater than a grateful heart. A grateful heart is the key to happiness. Being grateful just as we open our eyes in the morning. Thank you, God, for letting me be alive for one more day. I believe in the power of prayer. Richness of experiences is what makes life worth living. To experience deep love, deep compassion, joy, overcome pain, and reach goals.

But now the Virgin of Lourdes kept popping up in my life like she was poking me, saying, "Hey, look this way. Here I am!" I realize that all the different apparitions are of the same Virgin Mary, the mother of Jesus. Still, I believe they have different charisma. Let's say she wears a different outfit because she goes to a different party, but it's the same person. I looked up the history of the Virgin of Lourdes to become more acquainted with her. Our Lady of Lourdes started making her appearances to a little girl named Bernadette Soubirous in 1858 in a small town in France, near the Alps, on the border with Spain.

Bernadette went to collect firewood near the river. When she approached a grotto, a vision appeared of a lovely lady praying the rosary. Bernadette told her parents what she had witnessed, and they forbade her from going back to the grotto. The lady appeared again and asked her to come back every day for the next two weeks. The rumors spread like wildfire in the little town and beyond. Crowds started gathering to watch Bernadette in a trance, and some believed that the lady before Bernadette was the Virgin Mary. While they could watch little Bernadette praying, they couldn't see the Lady.

In one apparition, the mysterious lady asked Bernadette to drink water, but Bernadette didn't notice any water; instead, she saw only muddy dirt. Bernadette dug in and started to drink the muddied waters as the crowds burst out laughing, thinking the poor child had gone mad. Her aunts and mother swiftly took her away, her face covered with mud. It was a low point for the family. But the next day, from that muddy dirt, a little stream of water started flowing. It quickly revealed itself to be blessed water with miraculous healing properties.

There have been 70 recognized miracles attributed to the Lady of Lourdes by the Catholic Church, but 7,000 miraculous recoveries have been registered at the French Shrine. Miracles such as a man stranded in a wheelchair who started walking, or cancerous tumors disappearing without explanation. For a miracle to be officially verified by the Church, it undergoes a rigorous process that lasts years and is deeply scrutinized. For me, the miracle of Lourdes is about hope and knowing that someone somewhere is watching over us, that we are not alone. The Virgin of Lourdes gives hope and solace to the millions of visitors from every corner of the world who flock to her church, praying for health. Lourdes is the second most visited city in France, only behind Paris. After I was given the clear water, before all my chemo sessions, I would put a little water of Lourdes on my boob.

A few weeks later, I was working in the office when Victoria, my assistant, told me that a friend of hers was going to Lourdes.

"She knows what you are going through and asked me if you want to write a letter so she can take it with her and place it in the Grotto."

"I would love to, thank you."

This is the letter I wrote:

Dear Lady of Lourdes,

I thank you that you have been knocking at my door calling my name. I am so grateful for your mercy and know that you are by my side in this challenge that has created so much pain for my family and me. I offer you my suffering, every tear I have shed, and all the tears I will shed caused by this ailment. I offer them to you. I will imagine that every watery round tear falling down my cheek suddenly transforms into a beautiful red rose. I offer that rose and all the roses that will come to you, my blessed lady. You, more than anyone, knows what the love of a mother to her child means. Please, Our Lady of Lourdes, all I ask from you is to let me live 10 more years, so I can see my children grow. That is all I ask from you. I want to watch them become good humans. I want to be with them in their struggles and tribulations, in their sickness, in their glories, and in their happiness. Guide them and protect them. Even though I hope to do it myself, I know in my heart that if I can't do it you will take care of them.

I now realize that they are more your children than they are mine. Whenever I can, I promise to come visit, and thank you in person with all my being. I love you with all my heart, and, please, give me the grace to live my life with dignity and strength.

Love, Monica

I gave the letter to Victoria and hoped that it would make it to the grotto, where little Bernadette witnessed Our Lady of Lourdes's apparitions.

CHAPTER 24

Eight Quimios Eight Loves

I was already a couple of months into chemo, and although concentrating on Chayanne helped, it is obviously not the solution for cancer. This journey was still excruciatingly painful. When you are in pain, time stops. The symptoms were always different: nausea, tiredness, extreme joint pain, stomach pain, mouth sores, burning stomach, diarrhea, vomiting, and horrible constipation. But it was more than that. I do not know how to describe it. I felt like a Dementor from Harry Potter, those creatures without a soul, lifeless inside. A dark and empty figure, a soul in pain. I felt life slipping away from me, slipping like water through my fingers. I was surrounded by darkness, lying in bed, a shell of my former self. I opened my eyes. I looked at the clock. It was barely one o'clock in the afternoon. Please, God, let this day end; I want it to be tomorrow. I want to make it to tomorrow and feel better.

When the terrible days were over, I had a few solid days to recover. As soon as I was feeling like a person again, it was time for my next chemo, the blow coming again. During the chemo months, I would spend the bad days in bed, but on the days I felt better, I would go to work.

Another way I got motivated was by visualizing the progress of my chemotherapy. To try to make sense of all the pain, I offered every treatment to a person I loved dearly. I bought two photo frames. Each frame had four spaces for one photo, eight frames for eight treatments. Every time I went through chemotherapy, I celebrated by putting a photo in the frame. I thought about a person who inspired me with love and gratitude, and filled me with the strength to keep fighting.

The first photo was of El Mada. No doubt. With all his love and patience, he deserved first place. The second, third, and fourth photos were my three children, my reasons for being, my unconditional love. I was halfway through the treatment.

The fifth picture is of my parents, who appear very happy and are hugging in the picture. The sixth picture was of my sister, the seventh picture was of all my friends who fill my life with joy and laughter, and for the last and eighth chemotherapy, I put a picture of myself. A picture of me, looking happy and full of life. A picture that was taken one month before learning I had cancer. A picture of my 40th birthday, just before this treatment that was saving me but destroying me at the same time. I loved putting my picture up because it was nice to think that I was going through all this for them, but I was unquestionably and finally doing it for me.

I cherished this ritual, offering my pain up for my family and friends. Having the frames filled with pictures in my room was a trophy. Offering up one's pain for others is a way to make a little sense out of pain. When the body and soul suffer, it can hurt so deeply that it is tough to make sense of it all and to survive it.

Additionally, work moved me forward; it brought excitement into my life. Things were getting better and better at Solei, and I was basically living the dream I'd had my whole life. It was bittersweet. Some days I was living a nightmare, and other days I was living an unattainable dream, with the minimum possibility of success becoming a reality. You would think that at this point, reflecting on my children would help me get through it. But for me, the thought of my children produced anguish that broke me into pieces. I didn't comprehend why such small children had to see their mother like this. What if the chemotherapy didn't work and my tumor grew back? Why did they have to face the possibility of losing their mother? What was going to happen to them if I didn't get through this? Why do my children have two parents who had cancer?

These were things I didn't want to think about. Since I became a mom, like most people, my outlook on life had changed. I couldn't be irresponsible, selfish, or self-centered anymore. A switch was turned on; my life was no longer mine, but theirs. My mission was to take care of them, to love them, to see them grow. I felt an enormous responsibility. Nobody was going to love them as I did; nobody was going to take care of them as I did. I was indispensable to these vulnerable little humans. My greatest fear was to fail them, not to be able to protect them. I had even brought them to Miami against all odds to provide them a safer home to grow up in. Now, I couldn't protect them from the suffering of knowing their mother was sick.

I had no control over whether the treatments would work or not. I wanted to protect them and isolate them from life's suffering. But the biggest and hardest lesson I learned was that I have no control over protecting my children from suffering; I can only give them the tools to learn how to handle it. I didn't have control over protecting my children from pain, nor of healing myself, nor of all the things that I thought I would be able to control all my life.

In my work, it was essential to be in control of the dress's fit. The stitches had to be perfectly straight; the cut of the silk was flawlessly shaped. All the details are synchronized in perfect harmony, not a single stitch out of place. Now, I realized that I had no control over anything, and it was tormenting me. I had to change. I had to let go. It was then that I felt a peace that flooded me, and I surrendered. I literally surrendered. I couldn't keep worrying about everyone and everything.

I surrender to God, I surrender to You. Do with me what you must. I trust you.

These words set me free. I can understand that many people who are not believers do not get it. But for me, to know that God had been and was in control of everything—my children, my illness, my husband—gave me peace. I was decimated, destroyed, without strength. I was ashes. I went and continued to fight with everything I had, but in truth, in the end, it was no longer up to me what would happen. I gave it to Him.

At work, Sofia was a force of nature; she was brazenly driven. She was completely focused and devoted. Sofia and Victoria had gone to big shows like Magic in Las Vegas, so we decided to take a big risk and apply to Coterie. After a few weeks of waiting, we received the news: We were in! I couldn't believe it. I remembered the first time El Mada and I visited. It felt like decades ago.

The only minor detail was that I was still going to be in treatment, undergoing radiation. By now, I was close to Dr. Wang. Every appointment, I would update her on everything that was happening, and she would cheer me on.

"Dr. Wang, we were accepted to Coterie! Do you think I can have my radiation on Friday, take a plane and come back Monday for the next round?" I asked her.

"You can go, but be careful. Your immune system is compromised; don't overdo it," she said.

"Thanks. I can't believe we are going."

El Mada and I walked into the huge waiting room where all the oncology patients waited their turn for treatment. We sat down, waiting to get called, so I could have my blood taken. I watched around me, looking at my fellow patients. An older man in a wheelchair, various older women, grandmas, and grandpas. Normally, I would be the youngest in the group. I felt a tsunami of compassion overflow my body. I know what these people are going through; I know their battle. I was accustomed to my new reality, walking through them full of pride, with a deep sense of belonging.

I said to my husband, "You know, these are my people."

He looked at me, terrified, and said, "No, Moni, these are not your people. You are in much better shape than they are. We are your people."

"Yes, honey, they are. I feel so connected to them. I know their suffering, and I am proud to be part of them."

Chayanne was finally here. I had finished my chemo. I gave it my all. I had visualized this day for so long, and at last it was here. I was kind of freaked out that I was going to meet Chayanne. I had been in contact with Claudia, and she told me that she had arranged the meet and greet. Isabel was more ready than I was for the concert, but I tried to look my best. Wearing heels during my treatment was not an option because of how shitty I felt, but I would meet Chayanne in heels no matter what. Isabel arrived to pick me up, but I stalled. I wasted time and procrastinated. She waited outside and pressed me to hurry up. We were already late to meet him at the time Claudia had told us.

"Hurry up!! What are you doing? Are you crazy? We are going to be late!" she told me.

Claudia called me 30 minutes before the concert.

"Where are you? He starts soon!" Claudia sounded panicked.

"Sorry! I'm coming. I am really close by," I lied. We were still on the freeway.

"Isabel, please come in with me. I can't go in alone, and you were the one with the idea to focus on Chayanne," I pleaded when we arrived.

Isabel and I ran into the Miami Arena. We ran like crazy, but it was kind of late. I called Claudia on my cell phone. "Claudia, I am out here in the audience."

"Ok, I will come out to get you," she said.

She came out on one side of the stage, saw me, and we hugged. "Are you crazy? You are late; you missed him," she told me.

To be honest, I was kind of relieved. I was so overwhelmed with everything that I didn't know if I would be able to handle meeting Chayanne in such a vulnerable state.

"Let me go in and see what he is doing; maybe there is a chance," she said as she brought us backstage. "Wait here," she said.

Isabel and I were giddy. We saw all the dancers run around and take their places. The musicians of the band also passed by, high-fiving each other. We were so happy.

"No, sorry, too late. He is now preparing his voice to go out there," she said. "I can't believe you were late!!!"

"Sorry, Claudia, I just got caught up getting ready, but don't worry. We are so happy here, just looking around. This is super exciting," I said gratefully.

Then a tall guy approached us and said hi to Claudia.

"I want to introduce you. This is Chayanne's brother," Claudia said.

"Oh, hi!! How are you?" we greeted him.

"Hi, nice to meet you. I hope you enjoy the concert," he told us. "Where are you from?"

"We are from Mexico. I live here, my sister is here visiting," I said.

"She just finished chemo," someone said.

"Wow, that is amazing news. Congratulations!!!" Chayanne's brother exclaimed.

"Thanks," I said.

"Yes, I wanted to introduce her to Chayanne, but she was late," Claudia explained.

I laughed. "There was a lot of traffic."

"Did you know Chayanne is going to be in Mexico City in October? Why don't you come to Mexico, and then we will make sure you can come in and say hello," he suggested.

"That would be amazing. I can tell all my friends in Mexico to celebrate there. October would be perfect. If I can, I will fly to Mexico. Thank you!"

"I will see you guys in October," he affirmed.

"You should come to Mexico, Monica. That is a great idea," Claudia said.

"Thank you for everything, Claudia; seriously, you are beyond amazing."

The music started, and we saw Chayanne pass by with his entire team. The concert was about to start. Chayanne met with all his dancers and musicians; they all formed a huddle, hugged each other, and pumped themselves up as they ran onto the stage. The audience roared. They placed his microphone, and he ran on stage, singing. It was incredibly exciting; the air was filled with energy. Isabel and I ran to take our seats.

That night was magical. We danced and sang with Chayanne. I didn't have much energy to dance like mad, but I was beaming inside. I celebrated life as if I had won a battle. We celebrated with the powerful music and love of Chayanne. It was a night that I will always cherish. The evening was perfect, and I promised myself to be ready in October. I wasn't ready then, in Miami. I had wholly sabotaged it. But I was going to be ready in October.

CHAPTER 25

Lovely Dr. D.

O ne of the best things that happened to me during this time was being treated by Dr. D., who is an institution in Miami for his work against breast cancer. He is not only a gifted oncologist surgeon, but also the most caring and compassionate doctor.

He gave me so much confidence, and I trusted him completely. He had helped thousands of women throughout his career with the utmost grace.

The chemo was over, and I was ready for my surgery. The good news was that the tumor was almost gone. El Mada, at my request, always inspected my boob, looking for the tumor every week, but now he said he couldn't find it anymore. The day of the surgery arrived, August 5, 2015. We were almost happy.

Dr. D. came in while I was prepped and ready for surgery. He went over all the details again. We had agreed on a lumpectomy, since I had responded so well to chemotherapy and wasn't BRCA positive. He explained that with my type of cancer, women generally have better outcomes when they begin radiation after surgery.

I was relieved that I didn't need a mastectomy. I felt so weak, so emotionally and physically depleted—I didn't know if I could handle losing my breasts. If a mastectomy had been necessary, I would have done it without question. But I was deeply grateful it wasn't.

We were all waiting in the room to see him one last time before

I went in. I was ready. He walked us through the procedure again and asked if we had any last questions. Then he took my hand, looked at me with calm reassurance, and said gently:

"You know you got this, right?"

"I know," I replied.

"I'll see you afterwards," he said.

The surgery was a success. Dr. D. told us there was barely any cancer left- just a trace, the width of a hair. The margins were wide, and there was no indication that the cancer had reached any lymph nodes. He removed one lymph node as a precaution and had it tested. I was able to go home the same day. I was incredibly fortunate—my recovery was easy, the scar minimal. I knew how lucky I was to be treated by some of the best doctors.

Had I been in Mexico, I might not have received this level of care. That's not to say there aren't exceptional doctors there, but it's well known that the U.S. is at the forefront of medical treatment and innovation. I didn't take that for granted. I thought about how fortunate we were that the consulting group where El Mada worked provided such a great insurance plan. We were able to have access to the best doctors with his insurance. His bosses were generous and supportive, considering that El Mada had just been working there for a couple of years. They let him stay with me during chemo days as well. I will always be incredibly grateful to them for how they supported us during my illness.

Even though I have been going through the most challenging and painful events that I have ever lived, I couldn't ignore all the almost magical things that had started happening around me since I was diagnosed. It included the precise timing of Sofia's arrival into my life, the outpouring of support and love I was feeling, the pull of the Virgin of Lourdes, the Chayanne connection, and my dreams coming true right before my eyes— truly magical. The hard truth is how much we fear suffering. Admitting that pain is just a part of life and embracing it can be transformed into a path of enlightenment, leading to a better you.

I was learning things in a short period that some people take a lifetime to learn or understand. I had achieved the wisdom of an older woman. Don't sweat the small stuff; we are all going to die. Make it count. Things we have all heard, but now I was experiencing them for real.

For me, the most compelling thing during this period was my closeness to God. I don't think I have ever been so close to Him, just asking HIM, pleading with Him, and finally trusting Him... trusting Him in His plan, not mine. I was offering every tear, every loss, every chemo to Him. All my suffering, I surrendered to Him. In return, I acquired a new sense of peace. I am not saying it was easy, nor that my pain and suffering went away, but I was trying to find meaning in it. I resisted the option of going the other way and thinking like a victim or pitting myself against others.

"Sofia, I can't believe all this is happening, and how it is happening."

"I know, Moni, it is incredible. For me, you are more than a partner; you are a sister. We are family. I get chills when I think about it," she said.

"You know, with all the cancer and stuff, I really felt a magical serendipity when you told me about your cancer when we agreed to merge the companies. I can't believe the timing of it. It is how they say God has perfect timing; I am just so grateful he sent you into my life."

"Me too. As I said, we are family."

As I lay in bed, resting and reflecting on the unexpected blessings that had emerged from such a grueling time, I realized something profound: at my weakest, I had become strong. Though fear had walked beside me, I had found courage. I was battle-ready.

My heart ached for my children. The thought that their mother was enduring this journey was almost unbearable. But I was fiercely determined to do everything within my power to watch them grow—to guide them, love them, and raise them into kind, strong, good human beings.

In that quiet moment, a deep sense of purpose stirred within me. I knew I had to write a book and share my story. It felt like a calling—clear and unwavering. Just as I had known, El Mada was the man I would marry. Just as I had known that I was meant to pursue a career in fashion design. Just as I had known that we had to leave Mexico to begin a new chapter.

I needed to let women know that even in the darkest moments, there is still light to be found. That even during the fight of your life, you can receive the most incredible blessings. I wanted them to know that it's possible to feel an outpouring of energy and love from friends, from family, and even from strangers whose prayers reach you across oceans.

I could feel those prayers. I felt the love sent from people I had never met, from faraway places I had never been. My heart was full—overflowing—with their kindness. Everyone I knew seemed to take the chance to tell me how much they loved me, and it was overwhelming in the most beautiful way. People I hadn't heard from in years sent messages of support. My WhatsApp was flooded with love. I couldn't even respond to everyone.

I didn't take a single message or gesture for granted. I wanted to share my story because someone, somewhere, might need to hear it. Might need a glimmer of hope. And if my journey could offer that to even one person, it would all be worth it.

CHAPTER 26

BFF?

Sofia was incredibly thoughtful throughout my treatment. She always seemed to know exactly what to say during the toughest moments. There was a quiet confidence about her, a self-assurance that was both comforting and inspiring. Her goals were clear, and she pursued them unapologetically. I loved that about her.

She wasn't interested in having children—she wanted to excel in her field, and she didn't care what anyone thought about her choices. She was going to achieve what she set out to do. While so many women still struggle to balance career and family, Sofia didn't wrestle with that. She had made her choice, and she stood by it with clarity and purpose. I admired her deeply for that.

I was in awe of her because I realized something painful: I couldn't have it all at once. I couldn't juggle the constant challenges that come with raising three children and also travel the world managing productions and collections, not at the same time, at least.

After I finished my chemo, I was completely exhausted, and it was exactly then that my friends from Mexico and Boston wanted to visit me. I didn't want to see anyone, and most importantly, I didn't want anyone to see me. I felt so naked and so vulnerable. I didn't want them to see me sick, so I told everyone who asked to come to Miami to visit that, thanks, but no, thanks. I was tired or too busy.

But my old Boston friends didn't take no for an answer. They told me that they were coming to see me, whether I liked it or not. They all lived in different cities and countries by then, and they all left their families and flew out to see me. I was so moved by their insistence that I asked El Mada if he could go with the kids to my *suegros'* apartment and leave the house for all of us ladies. El Mada, the saint he is, left on Friday when all the girls arrived.

I was so happy to see them all. We hugged, laughed, cried, and talked until there was nothing left to talk about. One of the things I remember most is a moment when I was wearing a white cap, because I had moved on to wearing a regular wig, and they wanted me to show my bald head. Even though I loved them and felt totally comfortable around them, in my own home, I just couldn't. I didn't want anybody to see me that way. I would have felt naked, even more vulnerable.

Over the weekend, I told them how excited I was about Solei and the story of Sofia. They were all eager to meet her, so I drove everyone to my office to introduce my business partner to my friends. We settled, talking and laughing, when Sofia came in. I immediately sensed that she wasn't thrilled about me bringing all my friends there. She said "hello" but was otherwise icy. My friends were excited to meet her and invited her to join us for lunch. She reluctantly said yes.

We settled into the restaurant, and Liz, who is very suspicious of everything, started questioning her, trying to find out if she knew some friends from Panama.

"Yes, I actually know that friend of yours, but he is a dirty politician," Sofia said smugly.

"Well, he is my friend; he is really nice," Liz said.

"Do you know he is gay and married a woman just to cover it up?" Sofia said.

"That is not true. I have been friends with him forever. He is not gay," Liz said.

"Well, I grew up very close to where he lives, and those are the rumors. I come from a family of multimillionaires and knew everybody in Panama," Sofia replied.

I was so embarrassed by the whole exchange. Sofia could be smug and overconfident, but to say rumors like that about someone, and all that stuff about being a multimillionaire, sounded plain wrong. I was cringing.

The lunch ended on a good note, but afterward, in the car back to the office, I said, "Sofia, I don't know Liz's friend, but what you said about rumors of him being gay is a matter that doesn't concern anyone but himself. You shouldn't say stuff like that, and you don't need to tell people how wealthy you are. Who cares about that?" I finished, annoyed.

"You are right, Moni, sometimes I get riled up," she said.

* * *

Thankfully, everything got done, and finally, Coterie was here, and we were ready. Sofia, Victoria, and Ema, a new team member, flew to New York on Wednesday to prepare everything and set up the booth with the gorgeous collection.

I went to the hospital early on Friday morning to have radiation, and after that, El Mada and I grabbed an airplane and flew to New York. I was so excited, I couldn't contain myself. We landed in New York, and we stayed in a nice hotel. Sofia and the girls had everything set up. I wanted to meet them to see if I could help with anything, but El Mada wouldn't let me.

"Remember, we are here just to see them, not for you to work," he said.

"Ok," I told him, as we had room service and saw a movie in our hotel room.

On Saturday, I put on my wig, dressed in a Solei top and high heels, which I had hardly worn in months. We took a taxi to the Javits Center. I walked in, excited to look for our booth. It was beautiful. It was very tasteful, everything was white, and the clothes were perfectly arranged by fabric. They had done an incredible job. When they saw me coming, they all received me very cheerfully.

I hugged Sofia. "OMG, I can't believe it! We're here!"

"I know! It is incredible," she answered.

"You guys did such a wonderful job. How can I help you?"

"Nothing, Moni, just enjoy the moment," Sofia said.

It was early in the morning, and buyers began arriving. El Mada and I left the booth because it was getting too crowded, and there were too many of us. I turned to El Mada.

"Thank you for everything. Thank you for taking such good care of me and loving me, even though I'm going through this. And for supporting me in everything I do. Do you remember when we came here years ago? Can you believe we are now exhibiting?"

"No, Flaca. I really can't, but you have been so brave with everything that has happened. You have pushed forward and haven't looked back."

"But I never had been able to do it without you supporting me, believing in me," I said.

I began to feel tired—I was in the middle of radiation, and the fatigue was starting to catch up with me. All I wanted was to get back to the hotel and rest. We were flying home the next day, and by Monday, I would be back to resume treatment.

But I returned home feeling happy and uplifted. Something had shifted. My relationship with El Mada had been healed. The resentment I had carried for so long had quietly melted away. Throughout my entire cancer journey, he had been my rock, steady, unwavering, and unafraid. He stood by my side through it all, with the calm and strength that only he possessed.

He had walked this road before me, and because of that, he understood me in a way no one else could. He guided me, reassured me, and helped me breathe through the fear. There's a certain comfort that can only come from someone who has lived a similar life experience, has a special connection, and has understanding.

CHAPTER 27

Ring That Bell!

The six weeks of radiation were underway. I felt tired, but this was nothing compared to after chemo. I had to go every day, five days a week, at the same time and to the same place. I would lie down in a huge machine, and they would place my boob in a very specific place. The nurse would then leave the room, and behind a glass, they would ask through a microphone.

"Ready?"

"Yes, ready...," I would answer.

A deafening and nasty noise would begin, a light that said IN USE would turn on, and the radiation would penetrate my body. I couldn't move or breathe because the radiation is targeted only at the site of your cancer, and it can damage other parts of your body, so they have to be very careful. To be honest, I didn't feel anything when the lightning struck.

There was a young nurse named Malik. He was going to be in charge of handling and accommodating my breast and body before the radiation. He was caring, polite, and careful; he never forgot to ask me how I felt. I was glad to see him every day. One day, a female nurse did the process. She grabbed my boob and slapped it into the machine, and moved me from one side to another kind of abruptly. I felt like a piece of ham.

"Where is Malik? Is he coming back?" I asked.

"Yes, he is coming back tomorrow," she told me.

Hurray for Malik!! I'm so glad I was assigned to him. It makes a big difference which healthcare workers treat you. The weeks passed, and it got harder. My skin was burned, but nothing too extreme. Imagine a Caucasian woman from Minnesota's sunburn on her first trip to a Mexican beach. By then, I was exhausted. It would cheer me up to stop, from time to time, and get cupcakes on my way back home, my consolation prize. One of my friends, when she heard of my diagnosis, started emailing me green juice recipes and names of Chinese supplements she believed would cure me. She also pleaded with me to completely stop any consumption of sugar. She argued that sugar feeds cancer cells. I was willing to take the risk with those luscious, fluffy chocolate cupcakes. Life is not worth living without cupcakes.

"Are you going to ring the bell when you're finished?" Isabel, my sister, asked me one day.

"What bell?" I asked.

"At the Anderson Cancer Center in Houston, when you finish radiation, you ring a bell as a symbol that you are done with your treatment," she continued.

"Oh, that sounds super cool. They don't have a bell in my hospital." "Look it up on YouTube. You can see how it works."

The next time I saw my doctor, I showed him the video.

"Do you think I could donate a bell so the patients could ring it when they are done with their treatment?" I asked him.

"I don't know. You need to ask the administration," he replied.

I went to the administration and showed the video to the lady in charge. She said that she was going to ask about it. After a few days, I went back, and she told me that it was fine, that I could bring the bell.

I started to look for bells online and found one about 10 inches tall, with a braided white cord. I don't know what they use them for, maybe for ships or something, but it didn't matter. I had found the bell that would announce the end of my treatment and hopefully that of hundreds of other women.

I got the bell and then took it to where you get artwork framed. I chose a beautiful, dark wood for the framing and asked the clerk to please add a small inscription that I found online. The patient would recite the inscription while ringing the bell. When I went to pick it up, the store clerk asked me what it was for, and I explained it to him. He started talking about how his mom had cancer years ago. He seemed pretty moved and gave me a discount for the bell's framing. I guess cancer affects almost everyone, one way or another.

The big day came.

I had finished radiation, and the nurse I had told about the bell asked me to bring it. I was the first to ring it. My husband and my older son came to the improvised ceremony. Because it was the first time somebody had done it in this hospital, the staff didn't know what was going on. One of the nurses held the bell up, and I started ringing it. It rang super, super loud. I was startled. I rang the bell three times and said the inscription words out loud.

Ring this bell three times well, Its toll to clearly say
My treatment's done
This course is run, and I am on my way!

It was so awesome. Everyone started clapping, and we hugged. They also gave me a diploma, which indicated that I had graduated from radiation therapy. Wow! A degree I never expected or wanted to have. But I had done it! I was finished. I hugged the nurses and asked them to please hang the bell so that other patients could ring it, just as I had done.

I left the hospital, almost running from it, not looking back. The whole process had been so intense; I just needed time to process everything that had happened. A couple of months later, I went back to the radiation department for a follow-up appointment. As I came to the door, I wondered about the bell. Had they even hung it on the wall, or had they just thrown it into the maintenance closet? I was greeted excitedly by the nurses. They seemed to remember me clearly. I asked them about the bell.

"Hey!! Did you guys use the bell with other patients?" I asked.

"We sure did!" one of them answered. "Patients have responded very well to it. Two patients have rung it so hard that it fell from the wall twice. We had to reinforce it to the wall to prevent it from falling."

I was elated to hear this. It is so meaningful to have a simple, clear goal in these long, hard weeks when the finish line sometimes seems so distant. I love the idea of ringing bells - the catharsis of so much effort, the sound of other patients ringing them, giving you hope that soon you will be there, hearing the same sound. When you ring the bell, you get closure, you hear the sound of triumph, of a fight well fought, the blessing of being able to do something that maybe others won't be so fortunate in doing. You are one of the lucky ones.

Also, I thought of the staff and doctors working in the hospital. Every time they would hear the bell, they would be reminded that someone else had crossed the finish line. They could hear that their work, sacrifice, and dedication were bearing fruit. I wish I could give a bell to every cancer center that doesn't already have one.

I have so much admiration and respect for all the people who work in the cancer world. It is a tough place to be, but I found angels in my course, and I will be forever grateful. People sometimes refer to cancer patients as warriors. I think that the professionals who dedicate their lives to fighting cancer in whatever modality it may be are also warriors. The doctors, PAs, nurses, and staff who are on the frontline of the war against cancer.

If all the warriors out there are like the ones I have met, I have full confidence that one day they are going to win this terrible and painful war. The patient either survives or does not, but eventually, we all move on. But these warriors stay and fight. They treat another patient, another battle, another win or another loss. It can't be an easy job, yet some of them remain as warm and compassionate as they were on their first day on the job.

I was overwhelmed by the infinite gratitude and love I felt for all the doctors and staff who supported me throughout my journey. They saved and changed my life. I salute their sacrifice, their character, their knowledge, and their service. I will be forever indebted to them. I pray that everyone will be blessed to have the same healthcare and outcome that I did. It is fortunate to feel well cared for during one of the most vulnerable times of your life.

CHAPTER 28

I Made It, Now What?

Life is amazing. And then it's awful.
And then it's amazing again.
And in between the amazing and the awful it's ordinary.
That's just living heartbreaking, soul-healing, amazing,
awful, ordinary life.
And it's breathtakingly beautiful.

—LR Knost

As strange as it sounds, after completing my treatment, being given a clean bill of health, and no longer actively fighting cancer with chemo, radiation, and whatever else doctors threw at me, I felt that a security net was taken away when I stopped. I was terrified that cancer might come back and hit me with a vengeance.

"You need a mammogram and a checkup every six months. If something hurts or you notice something out of the ordinary, call us," Dr. Wang said calmly.

"What, like a headache?" I asked, petrified.

When breast cancer recurs, it can come back to your breast, even with a mastectomy that I hadn't had. It can come back to any part of your body, and typically, when this happens, it is much more serious than the first time around. I was so weak and depleted that my mind couldn't fathom having to go through all of this again. Plus, my type of cancer, which was uncommon and very aggressive, was more likely to recur than other breast cancer types. I had just turned forty, and my life had radically changed.

My mom told me about a story she read in Mexico about a woman who had cancer at forty, just like me. The woman described a type of eagle that, when it reaches forty, retreats to a cave, destroys its own beak, and sheds all its feathers. The eagle stays in the cave until its beak and feathers grow back stronger, so it can survive for another 40 years. I felt exactly like that eagle. My former self had become ashes, and I had to start molding myself from the ashes into someone new. The old version of myself was gone. I had to create and welcome a new version of myself, and I hardly knew who she would be.

My big dreams in fashion weren't important anymore. I was enjoying the ride of Solei; I had been able to get to places that existed only in my wildest dreams. But Sofia was becoming increasingly unpredictable and volatile. Either she was the most gracious and generous partner and friend, or she became enraged by the most inconsequential mistakes of others. On the other hand, when she made a mistake, she would laugh it off and make fun of her missteps.

My priorities had shifted, and what I really wanted was to spend time with my kids, husband, and family. The catwalks, ruffles, ribbons, and everything else could wait. What was most important to me was my health, regaining my strength, and processing what had happened. I continued working as hard as my wounded body permitted me. We were preparing the new collection and making all the deliveries that were ordered at Coterie. Sofia was super stressed with all the new work and responsibility, and she would lose it constantly.

"Why is the hem of this dress sewn like this? It looks like it was made by the town seamstress! Who did this?" she would ask.

The seamstress would try to explain her thinking.

"Well, we don't pay you to think. This is not the way I wanted it," Sofia said. This was the third seamstress who wanted to leave. Sofia didn't know how to sew, which was probably why she found it difficult to communicate what she wanted. I would take over and be the translator between Sofia and the seamstresses. Now she would berate *me* if something was not the way she liked it.

"I need to have more pieces, more options, more dresses, all of this is crap," she would shout in the middle of the atelier. With all the commotion, the seamstresses would not finish on time. I started sewing to help. I sat down at the sewing machine and suddenly felt a hole inside me. I had escaped cancer, and I didn't want to be stressed out to the point of no return, sewing until nine o'clock at night. Tears started flowing down my cheeks. This is why I only wanted 20 percent of the business. I didn't want to kill myself anymore.

Sofia saw me, and I called her discreetly. "What is wrong?" she asked.

"Sorry, Sofia, I know you are stressed out, and it is a lot, but I think I want to scale back. I am exhausted and not feeling well. I wish I could do more," I said while I kept sewing.

"No, Moni, what are you talking about? Remember, we are family. You are just tired. Don't worry. Stop sewing. You can go home now. Tomorrow you will feel better," she said, understandingly.

"I don't want to dump everything on you. I need to regain my strength. I really want Solei to succeed, but my health is first," I explained to her.

"I get it. I promise to keep it together, I am super stressed," she apologized. I knew I couldn't abandon her. She had been so wonderful to me in the most trying time.

I am going to stick by her. Just take it a little bit slower... if she'll let me, I thought.

After Coterie, we received many new orders, but they were mostly just enough to cover our investment. The relationship between Adi and Sofia was suffering. Adi was pressuring Sofia. They had these blowout fights that seemed to me more like a lovers' quarrel than a business disagreement.

"You need to increase the number of orders. I can't produce fifteen dresses of one kind and twenty of another. The minimum is at least 150 pieces per style. If you don't reach the minimum, I'm not going to produce the Coterie orders," Adi threatened.

I didn't know the exact nature of Adi and Sofia's relationship. They loved each other, or they hated each other's guts. I could manage her fine; I would play along. At the end of the day, I couldn't care less if she chose green or blue for the dress. Honestly, I had more important concerns, like my health, and I learned to choose my fights with her. We ended up doing what she wanted, anyway. I thought my role in the business was to support Sofia so that she could take on the world. I was the woman behind the woman, if that even makes sense.

I thought about reaching out to Londres in Mexico on a long shot to help with the minimums.

"Don't worry, Sofia. I'm going to call my contacts in Londres, and with them on board, for sure we are going to hit minimums," I said confidently, putting on the table the biggest department stores in Mexico.

"That would be awesome, Moni. Adi is driving me crazy. We are not going to survive."

I didn't confess to Sofia my misstep with Londres. I had screwed up big time, but I would try anyway. I wrote them explaining that I was part of a new fashion line and attached the line sheet. I made a little prayer and hit send.

Miraculously, a couple of days later, I got a reply. The assistant informed me that her old boss was no longer around and that there was a new director of women's wear—a lucky break. She suggested I email her. The stars aligned.

I emailed the new director, presenting the line and myself. They were very interested and gave us an appointment for two weeks later. I had just finished radiation, but I planned a trip to Mexico to show the collection. If we wanted to continue in business, we had to make this sale.

Additionally, I contacted all my previous fashion contacts with various magazines and shared the story about how I met Sofia and the Chinese aspect of the story. They were very interested and wanted to interview us and conduct photo shoots. One magazine, Elite, was going to photograph me with my wig and all. I wasn't stoked about it, but I took one for the team to create buzz around the brand and sell to Londres.

We arrived in Mexico City and were immediately embraced by my sister and parents. Sofia and I stayed at my parents' house and prepared for our meeting. We arrived at Londres headquarters with two suitcases, just in time for the appointment. The waiting room for suppliers was like an airport waiting room. A lady was working behind a glass, in a large waiting room with all the vendors hoping to make a sale.

Londres is the largest retail chain in Latin America; they had a reputation for squeezing suppliers on price, but were well-organized and paid promptly. If you sold to Londres in Mexico, you had it made. Finally, they called my name: Monica Ocejo from Solei.

We entered a vast space filled with numerous small meeting

rooms. We walked the hallways and settled in a small meeting room with wires on the wall where we hung the clothes. The director of women's apparel and four more ladies came into the room: the buyer squad.

Sofia took the stage, presented herself and said, "We want to give women the opportunity of having excellent quality clothing at affordable prices, and owning a factory in China gives us that advantage. We are strong Latin American women trying to make a mark in the fashion industry, and we would do anything to support Londres to promote the brand."

She was very convincing; she knew her stuff.

The women were pretty impressed. "We want to do a test drive. We have a section where we test brands, and would like to make an order for Mother's Day," the main buyer said. We were absolutely delighted.

"But we want to make some adjustments to the prices. We need fifteen percent off your suggested wholesale," she continued. They had shaved almost all our profit, so we were basically selling them at cost, but we needed volume to satisfy Adi. We came out of our meeting stoked.

"I can't believe we are going to be selling to Londres!"

"Me too, Moni," she answered. "I'll call Adi with the news. We can meet his production requirements, and we can continue with the next collection."

CHAPTER 29

Strong Is the New Pretty

My hair was starting to grow, a new beginning. It was not even half an inch, but when I touched my head, I would feel fuzziness, not cold, bare skin. The new hair that was coming out was mostly greyish. A lot of greys.

My sister Isabel told me, "I think it is time for you to put away your wig. Who cares? Liberate yourself."

I have to admit that hiding under a wig was more comfortable, but she was right. I had to embrace my new reality. I took the wig off. It was very hard for me. I felt like a Christmas present without wrapping or a bow, exposed for everyone to see. But I was alive. *I am not my hair*, I thought. I had survived and gone through a tough process. And I had done it while working and creating a new venture.

I took a selfie with my new look, including the greys, and inscribed a text on the picture.

Strong is the new pretty.

Now I was stronger, wiser. I am not my hair. I am not my looks. I am the spirit and the strength that resides within me. What lives within me is what makes me. Although I looked very different, I still view the world through the same eyes. But now I recognized in other people the pain they were going through, and it made me more compassionate; it helped me grow. I didn't fully understand what compassion meant until this moment.

The first shipment of Solei was delivered, and we had a lot of inventory left. As usual, we needed money, and the expenses were always more than our earnings. I suggested to Sofia that I could do a trunk show at my house and sell all the remnants. I invited everyone I knew. I was part of my community, and many women came. When I opened the door to welcome them, I could see it in their faces—the shock. Their eyes widened slightly when they saw me with barely any hair. The pity was unmistakable.

I sincerely didn't care; I was alive. I moved on and greeted the next guest. That night, I experienced firsthand how one's appearance can change the attitude of some people towards you. You forget whether you have long blond hair or thinning grey stubble; you are the same person inside. Over time, I could feel people avoiding me, even strangers. I began to notice how much kinder people were when I looked healthy, how much more comfortable they were when I had long hair.

Fall came, and I arrived in Mexico City to celebrate with my sister and friends, and Chayanne! I had not seen anyone since my diagnosis; it was a little bit emotional for everyone to see me. We hugged and cried, then headed to the Auditorio Nacional, ready to party.

"Don't you dare arrive late, or I myself am going to kill you," Claudia told me.

"I won't, don't worry," I said.

My sister and I arrived early for the meet-and-greet before the concert. We entered through the back door of the venue, where we met Claudia and were ushered into a small holding room. In front of us were three older women—older than us, anyway. Suddenly, a sliding door opened, and we caught a glimpse of Chayanne. The older women were called in first, and the door slid shut behind them.

"You know who those women ahead of you were?" she asked. "The sister of President Enrique Peña Nieto."

"Figures," we said, rolling our eyes.

Then—just like that—the sliding door opened again.

And there he was. Hunky Chayanne.

Poor Chayanne.

My sister and I squealed and ran toward him like we were sixteen again. We practically tackled him in a hug.

"What's happening? What's going on?" he asked, clearly startled but smiling. I looked at my sister, then at him.

"A few months ago, I had breast cancer," I began. "I missed your last concert because I was in treatment. But now I'm here with my sister and friends."

"That's incredible," he said warmly.

"More than anything," I added, "I just want to thank you. Your music helped carry me through my hardest days. It gave me joy when I needed it most."

He paused and said, "Stories like yours are the reason I keep doing this."

They snapped our picture, and we floated out of that room on Cloud Nine.

Later, the concert began. We met our friends at our seats and danced the night away. We celebrated life. We celebrated Chayanne. And yes—we celebrated with tequila.

Back in Miami, I had a follow-up appointment with Dr. D. My mom came with me. We were patiently waiting, and I was reading a book on my cell phone; I don't even remember what it was about.

"What are you reading?" she asked me. "Something to do with angels?"

"No, why do you say that?" I said.

"Because I thought I read the word angel in there." She responded.

"No, it has nothing to do with angels." I continued reading.

But she kept going, calm, very matter-of-fact. "You do remember we saw your angel, right? That day at the hospital, the day that you felt so bad after chemo." She said.

Instantly, I thought, *OMG, she has gone completely mad*! But at that precise moment, an image flashed into my mind, clear, undeniable. I was lying in the hospital bed, my mom by my side, and behind the bed, a tall, glowing figure stood—a figure made entirely of light. It had a small, almost childlike head, disproportionate to its long body. Its massive wings were folded upward behind its back, arching over and above its head. I can still see that image in my mind today as clearly as if it were a photograph.

My mom then said, "Yes, you were lying in the hospital bed, I was by your side, and the angel was behind the bed. He was very tall and large, and he had a relatively small head. His wings were closed and over his head."

After she stopped talking, I was frozen, speechless, as she continued casually looking at her iPhone. I saw it then. I can still see it now. The strange thing is that I didn't feel or see anything in the hospital. On the contrary, I felt totally alone and abandoned, but I was not. I saw that vivid, uninvited image before she even started talking. If I hadn't seen that image so sharply in my mind, I wouldn't have believed her and would have thought she was crazy.

How unfortunate for me that I had to see to believe.

That night, I told El Mada what had happened. He wisely told me that when people are sick or in extreme distress, they are between worlds. They are more in touch with the spiritual side. They are more open. People in dire circumstances can see or feel things that people in normal circumstances cannot. He had also experienced it firsthand when he was sick. This explanation made sense to me. After that day, my mom and I never discussed it again.

Back to worldly matters, I continued to wonder about Adi and Sofia's relationship. They were very close. It was a hot-blooded relationship. Sofia frequently flew to China. It amazed me how she'd go for weeks and stay with Adi and his wife, Pryanka, in their apartment.

"Moni, it is so tough staying with Adi and Pryanka. They drink so much at night."

"Why don't you go to a hotel?" I said.

"No, Moni, we need to save money, and Adi looks out for me there."

"Sofia, sometimes I think he has a crush on you. He calls and texts you endlessly, saying he needs you and urges you to go to China."

"No, you are crazy. He is family; he is like a brother to me. I was his best woman at his wedding last year, remember? We could not do what we are doing without him, without all the help and resources he is providing to Solei."

"I understand the advantages that Adi gives us. Without him, we couldn't be doing this. But just take care of yourself. It must be so hard being so far away."

"You can't imagine how hard it is, Moni. We are lucky to have Adi, but I miss home, the food, and José," she said.

As we hung up, I realized that my job was to create a support system for Sofia. Even psychologically, with Adi being so volatile, she needed someone to confide in. Sofia couldn't tell José anything because of his strong opinions and harsh judgment. I was also worried about Sofia's cancer. She didn't talk much about it, but, like everything with her, she was very matter-of-fact.

"You know, Moni, I don't understand people who go through cancer and then call themselves survivors. I have never called myself a survivor. Imagine if people who have had polio or a heart attack called themselves survivors. In a way, we are all survivors. Everyone continues their lives, not reliving every day what they went through. For me, it is something that happened, and it's over," she said.

"I haven't thought about it that way, but you're right. Many people go through different things, and they don't call themselves survivors," I said. At this point, I didn't consider myself a cancer survivor. I was still trying to survive the aftermath, but her strength to move forward and face things so coldly amazed me.

If I was asked why I got cancer, I would say it was because of all the stress I was going through at the time. So much stress for such an extended period of time, I think, drained my immune system. Because of this, I promised myself that I would never stress terribly about anything again. Nothing is worth compromising my health, not even worrying about the kids. If I stressed excessively about them, and then I got sick, I wouldn't be helpful to them. So, for the well-being of my family, I had to learn to take things calmly. That wasn't possible for Sofia. She was always very stressed, and she demanded a lot of herself. I worried that all the stress she was carrying would take its toll on her as it did on me.

"Please, Sofia, take it easy. You work so hard, I sometimes worry about how you stress excessively."

"Moni, Solei is my life, my baby. I don't know how not to stress. I want everything to be perfect, and Adi is driving me crazy," she said. "I talked to José, my husband, and he said that you and El Mada need to do more for Solei. What are you doing?"

"Well, Sofia, I am managing the office in Miami, making samples."

"Moni, you need to step it up. We need money. Londres is not going to pay us until we deliver. We need money for the next season of Coterie."

"Don't worry, Sofia. I have some money saved up. I can transfer it to the company as a loan, and when we get paid by customers, Solei can pay me back."

"Thank you, Moni," she said. "That would help a lot."

I was so grateful for how Sofia had stuck with me during my treatment; I couldn't let her down. I had suggested to Sofia that we should start selling our clothes on our website. The fashion industry was changing rapidly, and I thought investing in a webpage where we could sell directly to the customer was a great idea.

"No," Sofia said. "I don't think it is going to work. We can't compete with our own customers, the boutiques that are selling our product," she said.

"But we have some inventory left; it would be so easy to sell," I pressed on.

"No. I love Instagram. We are investing in buying followers. I think it is important to have a lot of followers because if anyone looks us up, it gives a great impression."

She was right. She loved Instagram, and every month, a charge for the Instagram followers she continually bought would appear on the Amex. She had a formula for determining how many likes a post needed to have to make the Instagram page appear legitimate. For likes in each post, she would get them in ways I wasn't even interested in asking. I would see her liking posts, as if she were playing Nintendo, to get likes in return for Solei's posts.

I wasn't on board with buying followers on Instagram, but, as with many things she did, she didn't ask me. When I saw the charges on Amex, I would let it go. Besides, she was right that many people judge you by how many Instagram followers you have, even though they are fake. To me, it was an astonishing fraud.

I was looking at QuickBooks while doing the accounting. As always, we struggled to make payments to Adi or Coterie, continually scrambling for money. Sofia and I were still working without salaries, but I didn't mind. I wanted to make this work. I noticed that Londres had made a mistake and paid us $6,000 twice. I told Sofia about the mistake, and I thought it was best to tell Londres and return the money.

"I don't think so, Moni. We need that money to pay for Coterie. We are struggling for cash," she said.

"I know Sofia, but I don't feel comfortable keeping that money."

"They are a multimillion-dollar company. They are not going to notice."

"That's not the point; the point is that it is not ours," I said.

"Let me think about it. Don't even think about telling anyone in Londres about this in the meantime, ok?" she said seriously.

"I wouldn't do anything we didn't agree on, but giving the money back is the right thing to do," I said and walked away.

The next day, Sofia said, "I thought about the money. I struggled with the decision, so I called my mentor, Jimmy Hannover, the vice president of Bloomingdale's. I told him about the mistake that Londres made. He said that we shouldn't give it back, as giving it back would make the people of Londres suspicious of us. They will think that maybe we asked for it, or wonder why we didn't tell them about it earlier. He said it is best to keep the money and not say a word. When things like this happen in Bloomingdale's sometimes they would cut the account."

"Suspicious how? We are returning the money," I said.

"When was this payment made? Three weeks ago, and you just realized it now?" she insisted.

"Well, yes . . . I was just checking the accounting. " I said sheepishly

"Three weeks is a long time. If you want to give back the money, go ahead. However, if we lose Londres because of this, it will be on you. Londres is the only thing that is keeping us afloat, and it will be your fault if we lose it, so go ahead, tell them if you want to," she said menacingly.

As I left the office, it was clear that Sofia was lying about talking with her ex-boss at Bloomingdale's. There is no way an executive would give that advice; it didn't make any sense. And besides, we were struggling to land big accounts, yet she talked to him about this. Why didn't she send our line sheet to him at Bloomingdale's? I didn't buy her explanation that we weren't ready for Bloomingdale's anymore.

I knew Sofia had lied. I was even suspicious whether Jimmy Hannover existed, or if Sofia had even worked at Bloomingdale's. I went online and searched for Jimmy Hannover at Bloomingdale's, and there he was, just as Sofia had said: Vice President of Operations.

I wasn't sure what to believe anymore.

I wasn't ready to strain my relationship with her for $6,000. If I went against her decision, I didn't know what she would do. I felt intimidated by her; I was afraid of her. I decided, against my better judgment, not to tell Londres about the money. If they had realized their mistake, we would have instantly given it back, but they never did.

Even after landing Londres, Sofia was still under a lot of stress to land more accounts and meet Adi's demands. I thought about Gabriel Rivera Barraza and Tim Valle. I was finally in a position to produce large quantities and face big retailers.

"Sofia, I could reach out to my contacts in New York. I am sure they can help us land big accounts," I suggested.

"That would be awesome, Moni. We need more orders. Adi is driving me crazy," she said.

I called Gabriel, and I told him everything that had happened in the two years since we last talked: about cancer, Sofia, and Solei. As usual, Gabriel was gracious and assured me that he would arrange an appointment with Tim Valle. I sent Gabriel the line sheet, and he later told me that the appointment was settled. We were ready to see Tim Valle and flew to his upscale New York showroom with part of the collection. Gabriel was already there.

"This is Sofia, my partner," I said proudly.

Tim came into the room, Sofia did her pitch, showed the collection, and went into the "we own the China factory" bit. Tim started asking very specific questions, and Sofia became uncomfortable. Tim finally said, "I really like what you are doing. To be honest, this showroom has a higher sales point. We sell to more exclusive boutiques, but the market is going towards this type of fashion."

"We need you to appreciate our work. We are looking for big retailers, not a small boutique. We have a ton of those," Sofia said, bothered.

"I know, Sofia; let me finish," Tim said. "I have contacts with every big retailer, but specifically with Macy's. Our fee is $9,000 and 15% of the sales. These are my terms," Tim said.

"Do you think you can get us an appointment with Macy's?" Sofia said, doubting him.

"Yes, Sofia, I can get you an appointment with everyone in the retail industry," Tim said.

"Thank you, Tim. We will think about it and we will get back to you," Sofia said.

Later, Sofia was doubtful. "I don't trust him, Moni. I don't know what to do," she said.

"Look, Sofia, let's try him for at least one season," I suggested.

"Yes, you're right. Let's see if he can deliver a big retailer, and I can get Adi off my back." We signed with the Tim Valle showroom.

I finally met Adi in person when he arrived in Miami. Adi was fun, made jokes, and was lovable. He was a middle-aged Indian man who looked like a preppy Freddie Mercury. He spoke softly but was very determined and business-oriented. When I met him, I immediately liked him.

"You could be Mexican," I told him.

He laughed and replied, "I love Mexico and Mexican food."

We went to dinner—Sofia, Adi, El Mada, and I. El Mada and Adi hit it off; they liked each other.

"I told you that you were going to love him," Sofia said. Still, she ended the evening with a warning. "He's really nice, but you have to be careful, because his drinking doesn't suit him."

CHAPTER 30

Healing in Lourdes

It was the Summer of 2016, and I felt like I was walking on eggshells, raw, afraid that cancer would strike back. I looked forward to fulfilling my promise to Our Lady of Lourdes in France. We hadn't had a break or vacation since we immigrated to Miami. It would be uplifting to go and give proper thanks for my health. We booked our tickets to Paris and then took a train to Lourdes, France, with the kids and my mom, who tagged along for the ride.

As we were leaving the train station in Paris, I stared out the window. The old historic buildings of Paris flew by, giving way to the countryside exploding with yellow sunflowers, looking and turning for the sun, searching for warmth and survival. I was like those sunflowers desperately seeking light, needing it to continue growing. Letting the sun soak my face and fill my heart.

We arrived in the town of Lourdes, nestled in the middle of the Pyrenees mountains. My kids were excited to be in a foreign country and on a train. I was floored by the beauty of this little town and the majestic mountains covered with noble trees that shaded the landscape like silent guardians.

We soon realized that the whole town exists around the Lourdes Sanctuary. Many pilgrims were seeking healing, and others were helping the sick bathe in the healing waters of Lourdes. I was asked if I wanted to immerse myself in the water of the spring. Volunteers, elegantly dressed like nurses from the First World War, would submerge the sick in the waters of the spring. I was not ready for such a profound experience. I just wanted to give thanks.

We approached the Church, which looked more like a Disney castle with a blue ceiling and multiple vaults. The Cathedral was framed by the mountains and surrounded by the river, a stunning scenery. Pilgrims appeared in the thousands, in whatever way they could, some in wheelchairs and even hospital beds. The volunteers ran around everywhere. We settled in a hotel just a few meters away from the sanctuary. Everything in town is within walking distance, centered in faith. My heart was beating fast. I hadn't seen so many people moved by faith in such a long time. We saw people from all over the world, from Africa, dressed in their local attire, to South America, singing cheerful songs.

We walked, looking for the grotto where the Virgin appeared to little Bernadette. As we approached the cave, I held El Mada's hand super tightly. A statue of the Blessed Mother, engraved on the rock, stands where she appeared. I thought it would be bigger. We stood in line to access the cave, and as we entered, I touched the wet, cold stone and cried.

In the middle of the cave, a small stream of water emerged, sprouting from where there was none. Hope sprouts where sometimes there is none. That is the miracle of the human spirit: to move forward when you have been burned. Light cracks the darkest places. I touched the stone as if I was absorbing miraculous love and healing. As I watched the spring, I thought about the unending blessings and love I had encountered on my journey and left inside the cave a second letter. From the bottom of my soul, I thanked Her.

Multiple boxes full of candles burned, simply as an expression of gratitude. In the boxes that held the candles, the following words were inscribed in different languages: "This light prolongs my prayer." I bought as many candles as I could and lit them for anyone I could think of. Seeing so many lights, so much faith and hope, was uplifting. Sadly, today's world is often steeped in cynicism, pessimism, and materialism; just turning on the news can feel unbearable. A rosary was going to be prayed at night, so they gave us little candles. We would walk, praying, as thousands of people from all over the world, speaking different languages and backgrounds, all joined by faith and hope. I can't describe what an amazing experience it was. We walked, praying, to the highest point of the cathedral, and looked down at the sea of lights below. What a sight.

The office of miracles is located a few meters from the Cathedral. There have been 70 confirmed miracles in Lourdes. Not everyone who goes becomes physically healed, but for me, watching the volunteers helping others, the faith of the very sick, and receiving the healing love of our blessed mother, I felt renewed. I had gone to war, and afterward, I came home to her, and it was a balm of love, hope, and faith. She healed me spiritually. I was broken, and she healed me.

I promise to go back and volunteer to help others throughout my life, I promise.

We went back to Paris to spend a couple of days with the kids and my mom. Unsurprisingly, Sofia was not happy about my trip. "When are you coming back? I am stressing out," she said. "Adi told me that if we didn't get into Macy's, this would be our last collection. He needs more than Londres. Also, did I tell you that to land a better location in Coterie and be a sponsor, I offered to make five thousand promotional bags in China, because Adi told me that he would pay for the bags?" she concluded, almost crying.

"Yes, I remember," I said suspiciously.

"Well, he is not paying for them anymore. If we don't deliver the promotional bags, we are out of Coterie."

"Sofia, just tell your contact in Coterie that we can't afford it," I said, worried over Sofia's overspending. Even El Mada was not helping us anymore because Sofia tended not to abide by anyone's suggestions.

"No, Moni, I can't do that."

"Sofia, at this pace, we are going to be out of business."

"I have a plan, Moni. Your Mom is with you in Paris, right?"

"Yes, she is here with us."

"Tell her that I will give her five percent of my percentage of Solei if she pays for the bags," she suggested. "It is our only option, Moni."

I was taken aback by her proposal. The business had enormous potential. We had landed Londres, different boutiques around the world, and a prestigious showroom in New York. But the relationship between Adi and Sofia worried me. It was unstable. Also, Sofia wasn't receptive to financial advice.

I wasn't sure if I wanted my mom involved in all of this. On the other hand, my mom had always loved fashion. She was very enthusiastic and supportive. We had already delivered to Londres. If we got our things together, we could be huge. I decided to tell my mom about Sofia's offer.

"And what does El Mada think? Does he think it is a good idea?" she asked me in the lobby of the hotel in Paris.

"Well, he says that if we manage it correctly, it could be an excellent business," I said.

"What do you think?" she asked me.

"There is always a risk, Mom. I don't know. A lot of things can go wrong, but I trust Sofia. She will make this happen. She can be difficult, but I have never seen anyone fight for something as fiercely as she does. She is devoted to Solei. I would bet on her every time, but that is a choice you have to make."

"Well, I trust your judgment. If you guys need the money for the bags, I will invest it in you."

"Thank you, Mom. Welcome to the Solei team. I am so happy that you are part of this project." I said.

* * *

Coterie in New York was here. My mom joined us; she was going to experience the magic of the fashion world. Adi was determined to go because he didn't believe Sofia that we were in talks to land Macy's. He thought the last meeting that Sofia had with the Macy's buyers in Tim Valle's showroom was a sham. It seemed so drastic that he didn't believe Sofia about such matter-of-fact things. We rented an Airbnb for the first few days while we set everything up. I told Sofia that I preferred staying at a hotel with my mom, but she pleaded with me not to leave her alone with Adi.

"Ok," I said. "I will stay with you guys for the first days, and then we can move to the hotel with my mom."

"Ok," she said. "I will move to the hotel with you and your mom."

The Tim Valle–Sofia relationship had been very combative from the start. He ultimately got us an appointment with Macy's buyers. The buyers seemed interested and would visit our booth at the show, making a decision afterwards. Sofia was so excited to be a sponsor with the freaking bags; for me, it was an absolute waste. The big opportunity was Macy's visiting the booth. If we didn't land a big account, Adi would not do the production for us. "I lose money even with Londres. I need more quantity," he insisted. Once again, this was make or break.

With my mom on board, with both of us having 25 percent of the brand, I felt more protected.

Sofia, Victoria, and I worked on setting up the booth. I rented a bus and went to Ikea to pick up the furniture for the booth. Just as I arrived, I received a frantic call from Sofia. She and Adi were at Tim Valle's showroom, where our collection was being held. Sofia said that Tim rudely demanded $5,000 if she wanted to stay in his showroom. She vowed never to return. Their relationship imploded, and obviously, we were out of the showroom for good. There was no going back.

Coterie started, and Sofia and Victoria were busy with clients. Adi asked me to help him get drinks for everyone.

"Please come with me for some hot dogs outside Javits Center," Adi said.

"Ok, Adi, just please hurry. I want to go back to the booth," I said.

"Why? Are you afraid of Sofia?" he asked as he smiled.

"I am not afraid of her, but I just don't want to upset her. She is under a lot of pressure." To be honest, I was a bit scared of her.

"I bet she hates that we are having a hot dog together. She can be very possessive," he said.

I laughed. "I am heading back with the water. I don't want to miss Macy's." I ran back to the booth. Their dynamic was so complicated and weird, I didn't want to be involved. I hoped that whatever it was, it wouldn't affect Solei.

Finally, we noticed an entourage of six buyers coming at us. It was the Macy's team. Sofia welcomed the head buyer and showed the collection. It seemed to go well, and then I heard one of them tell the other, "This line is amazing. I think it will do very well."

WILL DO were the keywords. I let everyone on the team in on what I heard. We freaking landed Macy's! Macy made huge orders, and that made Adi very happy. We were working harder than ever, but still broke. Macy's and Londres paid late, and Adi produced large orders without deposits. Fashion finances were brutal.

"Sofia, we need to manage the money better," I said.

"Manage what? We have none," she replied. Clients were paying, but we still saw no profit. I suspected poor money management.

El Mada showed how, with Adi's help, we might break even in three months. Neither Sofia nor I had taken a salary. I kept loaning money to Solei, trusting I'd be repaid. We kept working, but every morning before Sofia came into the office, my stomach would turn into knots. I dreaded what mood she would arrive in, like a child waiting to find out if her alcoholic father would come home drunk, as if the fate of my day depended on her mood.

If I heard her at the door happily greeting us, "Hellooo, Hellooo!!!" I would breathe a sigh of relief. When she came in quietly and slouched, I would walk on eggshells, anticipating who would be the target of her anger. Normally, it would be one of the seamstresses, and I would bend myself backward to calm her down.

We were two years into our partnership, and as Solei was growing, her relationship with Adi was deteriorating fast. She continued to go to China because it was going to get a Starbucks. She would jump on a plane and leave. Sofia called me from China one day, crying.

"Moni, I can't take this anymore. I am going to a hotel. I can't stay with Adi and Pryanka. He drinks so much that his whole personality has changed. We got in a fight about the deliveries. We can't be late now. We have to deliver on time to Macy's; if not, we are toast. He keeps harassing me about every little detail. I am looking at other factories, Moni. We can't just produce with him."

"What are you talking about? He owns thirty-five percent of Solei."

"We never made a contract. Legally, he doesn't own Solei; there is nothing written down between him and me," she said.

"Sofia, but you can't do that, just drop him," I said.

"I am not dropping him. He told me today that he doesn't want to be a part of Solei anymore, that he was going to hang me in a tree upside down naked. I am still shaking."

"What do you mean?" I thought I hadn't heard her well.

"Yes, we had a discussion, it escalated quickly, and he threatened me," Sofia said, crying.

"This is crazy. You need to come back. What if he turns violent?"

"He doesn't know where I am. And Ling, his assistant, who runs the factory, is willing to come to work for us. It turned out for the better."

"So Ling is helping you?" I asked.

"Yes, Moni, he pays her peanuts. I made a plan. He still has to deliver Macy's orders, but we are producing new orders from Macy's with other factories. The real problem is Pryanka, his wife. Since he married her, he has changed. She drinks with him every day. I am worried for his well-being, but I am not going to let his drinking ruin Solei."

I was flabbergasted, but Adi did enjoy drinking. When we met, he had a couple of beers every night, but he seemed a drowsy drunk, not an aggressive one. Nevertheless, I was scared for Sofia.

"Moni, can I ask you a favor?"

"Sure, anything," I said.

"I don't want to deal with Adi anymore. He said he only trusts

El Mada. Do you think he could deal with Adi?"

"Let me see if he would like to help." El Mada reluctantly agreed to act as a broker between them, but wasn't too happy about it.

"Monica, this is getting ugly. Sofia doesn't listen to any advice from anybody. I don't like what I am getting into," he said.

"Please help us. He is abusive to her, and she is alone there. We are figuring out how to manage everything that is happening."

"If you don't get your numbers straight, you are going to drown. Sofia is still using my Amex, and it is now $80,000 in debt. If she doesn't pay, I am going to cut her off."

"Honey, we have hundreds of thousands of dollars in orders. This year, we are looking at $1.5 million in sales. Of course, she is going to pay." I said.

"You have that in sales, but what is your revenue? Companies can have millions in sales but still make no money. I don't understand how Sofia manages everything, and when I suggest anything to her, she gets super defensive."

"Please just send a couple of emails to Adi. Sofia brought me the title to her car and wanted to give me her huge diamond ring to pay off her Amex debt. I made her sign a letter stating that she is personally responsible for the debt. Here is the letter. She won't leave us hanging." I gave him the signed letter stating that Sofia was responsible for any debt.

"Ok, I will help out with Adi, but I only do it for you. I am done with Sofia."

"Thanks," I said. Adi and El Mada exchanged a couple of emails about the remaining order for Macy's. El Mada assured Adi that when we got the order, we would pay the $40,000 the company owed him. We received the order, and by then, Sofia had returned to Miami.

"Now we need to pay Adi," I said.

"Moni, Adi has detained another order at the port, and he won't release the shipment. I am not paying him until he releases it."

By now, El Mada was super tired of all the drama and withdrew from it. Since I had El Mada's iPad, I would communicate with Adi as if I were him, writing back with his email everything Sofia told me.

"You are getting into so much trouble; you are in such a big mess." El Mada said, because he knew I was doing this.

"Don't worry, Sofia has everything under control," I said naively.

At long last, Adi agreed to release the detained order, but first needed to be paid the $40,000.

"Sofia, please make the transfer. When he sees the transfer, he will liberate the merchandise," I said as I was coordinating this incoming disaster. Sofia made a transfer right there in front of me through the bank account. *Thank goodness she paid him*, I thought. *Finally.*

"Adi, please now release the merchandise for Londres," I wrote from El Mada's email. "Sofia has made the transfer."

"Here is the document saying that the merchandise is now in our hands," he wrote back.

"Perfect, Adi, thank you. Here is the document for the transfer of $40,000 for the Macy's order." I pressed the send button with the screenshot of the transfer from the Solei account attached. As soon as Sofia recognized that the merchandise in the port of Hong Kong had been transferred to us, she immediately stopped the transfer for the payment.

"I just stopped the payment. He's not getting the money," Sofia said.

"What are you talking about?!? We have to pay him; that was the deal."

"No, Moni, sorry. He has been abusing us. He is the only one making money from Solei. You and I have not gotten a cent, and he is the only one making money. He has been overcharging for production while he plays golf and drinks. I have talked to other factories, and they will be doing our production. Adi is out of Solei, and we need those forty thousand dollars."

I couldn't believe what I was hearing. I was shocked that she would do such a thing. "Sofia, this is wrong; we need to pay him. El Mada gave Adi his word. He is going to kill me if we don't pay," I pleaded.

"Sorry, Moni, my mind is made up. He never invested in Solei. He was milking us, abusing us. We deserved those $40 000. Good riddance to Adi; we can make it on our own. It is you, me, and your mom. He is not in Solei anymore."

"But Sofia, please, pay him. This is wrong." I pleaded with her.

"You need to choose right now, you either are with him or with me. Think about it carefully."

"Obviously with you, Sofia, but we gave him our word." My head was spinning.

"You should be happy. Solei is you, your mom, and me. But remember, I own seventy-five percent now."

I had been warned. I couldn't do anything for Adi even if I wanted to. I had to think about myself because I had to pay the Amex debt of $80,000. If I didn't play by her rules, it would be the highway like she had done with Adi.

El Mada didn't speak to me for three days when I told him that Sofia had stopped the payment. He wanted to pay or talk to Adi, but I pleaded with him not to.

"You don't understand that the only thing I have in this world is my word, and now my word doesn't mean anything because of you and Sofia," he said, disappointed and mad at me.

"Adi is abusive toward Sofia. He was overcharging us." I made up excuses to try to repair the damage, even though all the blind trust I put in her was already gone.

"I don't want to hear it. I am completely disappointed in you."

This broke my heart. He was right. I let him down.

"I just want Sofia to pay me back. She is going to do the same to us," he said. I knew he was right.

"No, she won't. I promise." As I was saying those words, I knew that they didn't mean anything. My words were not reliable anymore.

Since Adi was no longer part of the company, we had to do the collection ourselves. By then, I had been cut off from Londres and Macy's emails, or any other vendor for that matter. Since we didn't have enough money for a seamstress, I was the one who started making the alterations to the samples she brought from China. It was not what I signed up for.

The management of the funds was what worried me most. I wanted to bring in a professional bookkeeper to properly manage the accounting because a significant amount of money was coming in, but a substantial amount was also going out. We had to manage it correctly.

"What money do you want to manage? There is no money to manage," she said. "I handle the money to pay for the orders; we don't have money."

"Then, how come we don't have money to pay ourselves a salary?" I asked.

"Do you think you work for your twenty percent of Solei?" she asked. "I do everything; you do nothing."

I was fed up with hearing this again. All my money and savings were in Solei, but I wasn't heard and didn't belong. After Adi was out, she felt more powerful. Before, there were three of us, and I had the deciding vote; now, I was a small minority.

"I AM Solei," Sofia announced.

After what happened with Adi, I didn't trust her anymore. I couldn't believe she stopped the $40,000 payment for the Macy's order. And we involved El Mada, who was still furious with me for getting him entangled in this shit show. I was worried about the Amex card, so I brought it up to her carefully.

"Sofia, we need to start paying off the Amex. El Mada is livid, and the expenses are to the roof." I said

"I will pay, I promise. You even have the letter I signed, which states that I am personally responsible for that debt, not Solei. What do you want as a backup? The title of my car? I can give you my engagement ring."

"No, Sofia. You don't need to give me your engagement ring, but $80 000 is too much; we need to pay a chunk of that debt."

Thankfully, after that, Sofia started paying a significant amount of the $80,000.

Solei was still in the office that I owned. It had been two years, and Solei had never paid any rent. El Mada and I agreed it was time to lease the space to someone else, especially since Sofia refused to pay. Fortunately, we were growing rapidly and needed more room to fulfill all the orders. My realtor came through and found us a massive warehouse in the same building. Sofia was thrilled with the deal I made, and with help from Pepe, our handyman, I moved the entire office there.

Coterie was approaching again, but now we couldn't count on Adi anymore, so I was working on the alterations of some of the samples and also received Macy's order. Victoria was spending most of her time in New York with her boyfriend.

One afternoon, I was taking my sons Ignacio and Alex to the orthodontist. Alex dreaded the orthodontist, and I liked taking him myself to prevent a meltdown. As I drove down Coral Way with a lot on my mind from work, I felt guilty for taking time to take the kids to the orthodontist.

"Mom, you work too much. We never see you anymore," Ignacio said.

"What do you mean? I try to be home at five every day. It's only when we have trade shows that I stay until late in the office."

"No, Mom, you are always stressed, and Sofia is always at our house," he said.

Ignacio had been complaining for a while, and he was right. Just then, I received a call from Sofia.

"Where are you?" She sounded mad.

"I am taking the kids to the doctor."

"I am at the office, Monica. I can't believe what I am seeing."
"What's wrong? What happened?" I asked, scared.

"Why did you sew the bow like this? I told you to do it one way; it is not the way that I wanted," she said, pissed.

"I thought that way wouldn't be as bulky."

"But I didn't tell you to do it that way, did I? You keep doing everything wrong, not the way I want it to be done."

"But Sofia, the result is the same."

"But it is not the way I told you to do it. You don't get to decide, I do. If I tell you to do it one way, you do it that way. And why are you taking the kids to the doctor? Don't you have Tita to take them? You need to come back to the office right now," she shouted.

"You know what, Sofia? I don't want to work like this anymore.

I am DONE. Nobody is happy. My kids aren't happy; you are not happy. I am not happy. I am done. I am done, Sofia. I can't do this anymore."

She hung up the phone.

I continued driving to the dentist. Ignacio asked, "Mom, what happened?"

"What happened? I quit!! That's what happened. I can't deal with so much anymore. I feel like everyone's pulling me in every direction. Nobody is happy. I am done." I said.

"No, Mom, please don't quit," Ignacio said.

"Of course, I quit. I am done."

The car was silent. Now that I write this, I feel so bad for my kids and how I reacted. I made so many mistakes at that time in my life. We arrived home, and I knew I had to be careful about how I exited Solei. We still had significant debt on the American Express card, and I didn't want to walk away under strained circumstances.

I texted Sofia: *If you want to talk calmly after you finish at the office, I'll be at home waiting.*

"Ok," she replied. "I'll come to your house to talk."

She showed up late—around 10 p.m. El Mada was already home, but he didn't want to see her.

"Sofia," I began gently, "I think it's time for me to step away from Solei. This isn't working anymore. I can still support you, but from the outside."

"Does El Mada know about this?" she asked sharply.

"Yes, Sofia. He knows."

"He's home, right? Tell him to come down. He needs to hear what you're doing."

"What am I doing, Sofia? I'm sewing and receiving boxes. You could hire anyone to do that."

"You should call El Mada," she repeated.

"You don't want him to come down, trust me. I'll stay until you find someone to replace me."

"But you can't leave. If you do, you lose your twenty percent. You don't deserve it—you haven't earned it. I do everything; you do nothing!" she snapped, then quickly softened. "I'm sorry I shouted. I'm just... overwhelmed. Adi left us hanging. He's an alcoholic. He abused me..."

"Okay, Sofia. It's late. Let's focus on finishing this collection, and we'll figure out the rest after that."

CHAPTER 31

"Congratulations, You Are Cured" A Mastectomy, Please!

Since finishing my treatment, I was due for a mammogram every six months to confirm the cancer hadn't returned. These checkups were torture. I would start having nightmares a few weeks before every checkup. Sometimes I would wake up in the middle of the night shouting, and El Mada had to calm me down.

"AAAAAAAA!" I'd shout.

El Mada would wake up and say, "What's wrong? Are you ok?"
"Yes, sorry. I don't know what happened."

I got the chickenpox when Alex was born. I was so stressed before the mammogram that painful shingles would break out on my legs or arms. Dr. Wang would prescribe something, but they were quite painful. I remember I couldn't even stand a sheet on top of my legs.

It had been two years since I was declared cancer-free, but this checkup felt critical. The type of cancer I had was aggressive and more likely to come back, but if two years passed, I was likely in the clear. I could start considering that, maybe, I was out of the woods. I didn't realize that surviving cancer was almost as difficult as fighting it. When you are fighting it, you have a lot of support and attention, but when you are given a clean bill of health, everybody moves on, as they should. But you, as a survivor, are still dealing with the aftermath, the destruction, depression and anxiety that was left behind.

The checkup was scheduled at the end of the summer. We had experienced an amazing summer so far. My sister came to Miami, and we went to the Bahamas. One of the best vacations I have ever taken. We snorkeled, visited a beach with glorious pigs, and swam with sharks; well, I didn't swim with the sharks, but El Mada and others did. I thank God for these moments: nature, the sea, and feeling alive. Slowly but surely, I was regaining myself. The mammogram was next week, but I was cautiously optimistic about it. I was living again and enjoying the trip, as we talked, laughed, and danced. Life was good.

We returned to Miami, and Cris came with me for the mammogram. I was nervous, back at the place where everything had started - the same robe, the same waiting room, waiting for life-altering news.

"Hi, come in," the nurse said. The same cold machine. . .

She started with my right breast; that was the one where I had cancer. "HOLD your breath, I am going to push, hold, squish, release. Ok,

we are done. Now the other breast," she said.

"I know you are not supposed to tell me anything, but is there anything I should worry about?" I asked.

"No, honey, everything is fine," she said,

"Now the other breast. Hold your breath, hold, hold. Ok, you can get dressed now."

"Is everything ok?" I asked anxiously.

"I can't tell you. I am going to show them to the doctor, and I will come back. Please, take a seat, but don't get dressed."

Crap! Don't panic. Everything is fine, everything is fine, I reassured myself.

"Can I call my friend? She is outside. Can she come in and sit with me?" I asked.

"Sure," she said.

Cris came in, and we started talking mostly about dumb stuff, but I was distracted. The nurse called me again.

"The doctor told me that she needs to take more images." "Why? Did I move?" I asked.

"No, she wants to rule out something in your left breast."

"In my left breast? That is the breast that I didn't have cancer in."

"Yes, we just want to rule anything out," she insisted.

Suddenly, my legs weakened, and I felt lightheaded. I started seeing little black and white spots. I knew what was coming, and I gently started sliding myself to the floor. The nurses started to panic, running around, getting me alcohol. But Cris knew how to handle it and calmed everybody down.

"Don't worry, she is fine," she said. "Sometimes it happens when she freaks out. It is called syncope; just put her legs up."

I slowly came back to my senses so they could take the extra images needed to determine if I had cancer again or not.

"Listen, there are tiny spots in your left breast. Don't jump to conclusions. We are going to send the images to your oncologist. But we think it is best to have a biopsy to rule everything out," the nurse informed me.

Fuck, not again. Same place, different boob, I thought.

We came back home and tried to ignore what had just happened. They were probably being super extra cautious. My cell rang.

"Hi, Monica, this is Dr. Wang." My blood froze when I heard her voice.

"I received your mammogram, and I need you to do a biopsy." I felt sweat rolling down my back. "Listen, it is a small spot, but we have to be careful. Schedule your biopsy as soon as you can."

"Ok, Dr. Wang, I will."

We ended the phone call. Was lightning striking again? Receiving a call from Dr. Wang made everything much more real. I called the center to schedule my biopsy. After what happened with Dr. Shitty, I had been seeing Dr. John, but Dr. John was on vacation. The only one available to do the biopsy was Dr. Shitty.

"Is there anyone else who can do the procedure?" I asked. "Sorry, no, she is the only one available."

"Ok, put me down as soon as possible. I want this to be over."

I was back in the hands of Dr. Shitty. She was doing a guided biopsy with contrast. They injected iodine into my body because the spots were so small, and they needed to see them better. Dr. Shitty introduced her large needle into my boob and then vacuumed.

"I don't think it is anything, but we need to check... I see two more spots near the nipple. Do you want me to take them out now, or do you want to come back another day?"

"What do you mean, come back another day? Take them out, please." *I never want to come back*, I thought.

I got dressed, and the technician told me, "Don't worry too much. It doesn't look like anything."

"Thanks," I said. Somehow, I knew it wasn't serious, but we still had to wait for the official results.

After a couple of days, my poached boob was purple like an eggplant. Then came the call. I was in the clear; it was a whole lot of nothing-burger . . . my boob being the burger, of course.

I was relieved, but decided that I couldn't live like this anymore. Every six months, with a deadline, a question mark: continue as is, or go into survivor mode. I was given the clear every six months, and then gasped for air after being underwater. It wasn't about cancer coming back anymore; it was about deciding how I wanted to live the rest of my life: living in a cycle of fear or getting the root of the problem out?

In Mexico, I lived in fear, and we had gone through so much to come to the US; another kind of fear, but nevertheless, fear. I wasn't going to lock myself away with the fear of the shadow of cancer. I wanted my boobs gone; I wanted a mastectomy. I wanted my life back.

I had been seeing a therapist for a year at that point. She also had cancer in her early forties as a young mom. Now she was in her sixties. She had had a double mastectomy and said it was the best decision she had ever made. She helped me come to the decision of getting a mastectomy. She even showed me her boobs to see how mine would look.

She looked amazing; sign me up if I am going to look like that! I loved her for helping me through it. Talking to someone who has lived the same experience makes all the difference in the world. You speak the same language. I went to Dr. D. to tell him my decision. I didn't consult with anyone; my mind was made up. I was going to have a mastectomy even if I had to drive myself to the hospital. Dr. D. came into the examination room and sat down.

"Hi Monica, first of all, I want to apologize on behalf of the medical community for what happened with your biopsy. You didn't need to go through that. But sometimes, because we want to be extremely careful, we end up hurting the patient."

I love this man. I *really, really* love him.

He got up, grabbed me by the shoulders and looked me straight in the eyes.

"You are cured. After being clear for two years of triple-negative with your history and response to treatment."

"Thank you so much for that. I appreciate it. But I want a mastectomy," I said firmly.

He took a deep breath and walked back, taking a seat. He didn't look ecstatic about my decision, but he understood it.

"Ok, stand up." He then grabbed my fat pouch where my belly button is and said, "You don't have that much fat, but we can work with this. Because you had radiation, we need to take tissue from your tummy and create breasts with the flap. You can't have the normal implant because it may encapsulate."

This was not going to be as easy as I thought. It never is.

"Because the hospital expanded the cancer center, we have recruited talented doctors from all over. We have just hired two amazing young plastic surgeons who have joined our team. Make an appointment with Dr. Medina, and I will do your surgery with him," he said.

"Perfect, so it is settled. I will make an appointment for next week. Thank you, Dr. D., you are the best."

Dr. Medina had been recruited with his team from Harvard, making it one of the most innovative and progressive cancer centers in the country. The new building was amazing, and to my surprise, huge bells were hung all around the new cancer center. I guess the bell thing had taken off.

Dr. Medina entered the room. He was young, calm, and soft-spoken.

"In your case, what we need to do is a mastectomy with flaps from your tummy. That means we take fat from your tummy, and we turn it into implants and make new breasts with them. We make a large incision in your pelvic area, and then we..." He continued talking, but I didn't hear any more. I disconnected.

It would have been better if I had brought someone with me to the appointment to ask questions later. There was so much information, but I was on a mission, so I hadn't told anyone about the appointment.

"Ok," I said to Dr. Medina, stunned by how big the surgery was.

"For this surgery, I need the help of my partner, Dr. Salinas. We worked in Boston together. He is going to work on one side of the flap while I work on the other side. At the same time, Dr. D. will be doing the mastectomies. Once Dr. D. is done, Dr. Salinas and I will reattach the flaps to the breast. It's a lengthy surgery, lasting around seven to eight hours, but the result is quite good. A couple of months after the first surgery, we will need to do a revision surgery to clean everything up."

Crap. Two surgeries. The first one is the Godzilla of surgeries; it sounds terrifying. I am not even going to ask about the second one. I need to get through the first one.

"Do you have any questions?" he asked.

"Can I die?" I asked him, dead seriously.

"Do you suffer from some type of blood clotting?"

"No," I replied.

"One risk of a major surgery are clots in the lung, but we are cautious, and we will monitor you very closely, so no, you are not going to die," he answered.

"Does it hurt a lot?" I asked.

"We do a technique where we numb the nerves of your tummy, so, no, normally it doesn't hurt. It is like having a tummy tuck."

"Can I keep my nipples?" I asked.

"Yes, we can keep them," he said.

"Ok, I want to go through with it."

Then he took out his phone and showed a before-and-after picture of a woman. In her first picture, the woman had a mastectomy without reconstruction and was completely flat. They had taken everything from her chest, leaving instead two big horizontal scars. The after picture was the torso of two perfectly rounded breasts. You could never imagine it was the same woman. I noticed she was standing tall, more confidently, proud in the second picture.

"You changed the life of this woman," I said, stunned. He smiled.

"Well, you need to meet my partner, Dr. Salinas. I will coordinate with Dr. D. so we can schedule your surgery, and you need to have all these exams done."

"Ok, sounds good. Thank you, Dr. Medina."

I liked Dr. Medina. He seemed serious and responsible, but at the same time, he was kind. I needed to get El Mada on board with this surgery. He agreed that having a mastectomy was a good idea because of all the fears we had in the past, but this was another story. Three surgeons were going to be working on me at the same time, and it was going to be a very long surgery.

On the bright side, I was going to have a complete mommy makeover. I was going to have a tummy tuck and a boob job at the same time. That made me kind of happy. Dr. Medina told me I was not going to die, so we were golden. I couldn't wait to have my boobs removed. I wanted to get it over with and never think about getting a stinking mammogram again.

I guess for me, the pain and trauma of the decision to get a mastectomy had been processed for two years. I kept waiting for those destructive, petulant cancer cells to come back to my breasts. The first time you hear the word mastectomy directed at yourself, as in, "You might need a mastectomy," the word sounds menacing, an amputation of your womanhood, of your sexuality.

How am I going to look? How am I going to feel about myself when I look in the mirror? How will my husband take it?

It is terrifying. A part of me that symbolizes womanhood, motherhood, even my sex appeal, will be taken away. These thoughts crossed my mind. But I was over them. The fear of those cancer cells coming back would entirely shut up those thoughts in my head. Nothing was more important than regaining my peace and security.

I am not my boobs, I thought.

So, while getting a mastectomy is such a hard and painful decision for any woman to make, I can assure you that for me, it was the key to freedom, my only option. Knowing that I was going to do absolutely everything in my power to strip away anything that may compromise my physical well-being, as well as my mental health, would set me free. I deserved to be healthy and happy. My husband and kids needed me healthy and happy; nothing would stand in my way. And besides, I was going to keep my nipples, which was super important for me. I was going to be no different than any other woman with a boob job.

CHAPTER 32

Hurricane Irma: The Perfect Storm

A monster hurricane was roaring and churning in the Atlantic, one of the biggest and deadliest in decades. I was skeptical at first; the media tends to overhype hurricanes hitting Miami. We would stock up on essentials, sometimes evacuate, and eventually, the hurricane would dissipate or veer off course. This one was different. It was the size of Florida and had left a path of death and destruction through the Caribbean. Now the beast was looking at us, a direct hit like a raging bull running towards us, plowing with all its strength.

It was a chaotic scene: women in supermarkets fighting for water bottles, gas stations had run out of gas, and the police were handing out sandbags to avoid flooding. We lived in a particularly vulnerable area prone to flooding, so we were on the lookout for mandatory evacuation orders. Two years prior, we had been evacuated due to another menacing hurricane. After hours and hours of traffic and driving, we sheltered in a motel near Naples, Florida. The hurricane diverted, and we went back home blissfully, less than 24 hours later.

We weighed our options. If we drove away, it could hit us anywhere from Naples to Orlando to Tampa. We needed to get out of Florida altogether. El Mada booked tickets for his parents—who were visiting—and the kids, as well as me, through Fort Lauderdale to Mexico City.

"You are taking my parents and the kids to Mexico City tomorrow. This thing is getting worse by the second. If we don't leave soon, they are going to close the airports," he said.

"Ok, but I have to secure everything in the office. Sofia is vacationing in Spain, and I have to receive merchandise from China and send some pending orders," I said.

"I get it, but you also have to prepare the house for the storm," he wisely advised.

"I can't do everything if I am leaving tomorrow. I am sending Tita for the sandbags and to move the furniture and electronics to higher ground, but you need to help me before you leave."

"Ok, I will take care of it before I leave for Mexico."

"What if they close the airport before you leave? You don't have a plan B."

"I must stay and help the sales department set up an office in Santo Domingo. I can't leave sooner. I will make it to the plane, don't worry, Flaquita," he assured me.

When a Category 5 hurricane hits, water and electricity can be out for weeks. This storm had the capacity to blow roofs off houses, and experts predicted a 10-foot storm surge. Meanwhile, Sofia was blissfully vacationing in Spain. Even though things weren't going well anymore, I was worried about her coming back to this pandemonium.

"Sofia, this thing is going to be outrageous. Don't come back to Miami; try to fly somewhere else safe. They are evacuating half of the city." I warned her through text.

"Is it that serious? What about the orders we have pending?" she asked.

"I've sent the boutique orders, but the Macy's order is going to be delayed because they are closing airports. I think we need to ask

Macy's for an extension due to natural disasters. Watch the news. It's all over CNN. I'm not kidding."

"What about all the alterations for the new collection? We have to show the new collection to the buyers in two weeks in New York."

"I've done all the alterations that you wanted, but since you told me not to touch the other pieces, I am waiting for you to come back so we can finish them," I said.

"Yes, I need to be there to see that everything is done perfectly, how I like it. I will figure out where to fly. Take care, Moni."

"Take care, Sofia, and let me know where you end up. We are going to Mexico City and staying with my parents."

I hustled and finished all Solei's errands. Everything in my office was secure, but when I went back home to pack, I had a feeling of dread. I was so busy securing Solei that I left my house totally unprepared for the hurricane. I hoped El Mada could get everything prepared and ready for the storm. As I drove to Fort Lauderdale with the kids and my *suegros*, I prayed for everyone and everything that I was leaving behind in Miami. I hoped that all those horrible predictions that the media were making would not come to pass. This was now my home, my happy place. "Please let everybody be ok," I implored.

El Mada took the last flight that left Miami for Mexico City. He saw friends left behind because their flight had already been canceled. We spent our days in Mexico glued to the phone, following Irma's destructive path. At the last minute, it diverted and hit the Florida Keys and Naples with all its force. We were so sad to see the images of towns destroyed and flooded. The ocean woke up and devoured them.

Even though Miami was spared a direct hit, the hurricane's outskirts caused vital damage. Electricity was out, and trees, roofs, and construction cranes were ripped apart like paper. The sea decided to make an entrance, and Brickell became unrecognizable. Instead of a modern avenue, it was now a river; it was mind-blowing.

The day after the hurricane, Giuliano, Cris's husband, who was holed up in Miami, called us. "Hey guys, I can drive by your home to see if it is still standing," he said.

"That would be awesome, thank you," we accepted.

He phoned back later. "The house is still standing. A tree fell on the rooftop. There is some damage outside the house. I looked through the window, and as far as I could see, it looked like there was no flooding."

"What a relief, we still have a place to live," I said to El Mada. "I want to go back as soon as possible. Sofia needs me to finish the collection because she and Victoria are leaving for New York next week. There is so much to do."

"Monica, are you crazy? The roads are closed; there is no electricity in the house."

"I don't care, I can sleep in your parents' apartment. That building has a generator," I said. "The office is on safe ground; I have access to it."

"Everyone is staying out of Miami, and the schools have been canceled. I am so tired of you being so committed to Solei, and Sofia treats you like shit."

"I know, but you don't get it. If I don't return, there's no way we'll be able to complete the collection. After this season, I will talk to her calmly. I want to do this right and leave Solei on good terms. I don't want to poke the bear. You know what she is capable of. If I don't go, things will get worse."

"Ok, I will get you the ticket. Stay at my parents' apartment, and please be careful."

As soon as I could, I left Mexico City. When I arrived in Miami, I was shocked to see the damage that Irma had caused. Boats were thrown into the middle of the street as if they were toys. Centennial trees became rubble. Electrical lines were torn like chopsticks. The taxi dodged wreckage on the road like a video game. I wondered about my house. It was late, and I went directly to my suegros' apartment.

Early in the morning, I called Pepe, my loyal handyman. He was as reliable as a faithful husband. Pepe was waiting for me in his car parked outside my desecrated home. The tall tree that framed the house had fallen onto the roof, but luckily, it had damaged only a small part of the structure. Trees, debris, damage everywhere, a war zone.

I opened the door of my house, and immediately, a stench of humidity hit me. Everything was soaking wet; the house was completely flooded. Dirty water had seeped in and stained everything inside the house, reaching a minimum height of twelve inches. Furniture, walls, rugs, everything soaked, rammed, and lost.

"I am sorry, señorita," Pepe said as he grabbed the soaked rugs and placed them outside.

What had happened? How did so much water come in? Why did Giuliano tell us that everything was fine?

I started cleaning and mopping up all the muddy water, as if I were trying to erase what had happened. I called Tita, who had stayed safely in her sister's house, and asked her if she could help us clean up. Although I should have been freaked out about how all our stuff was destroyed, all I could think about was that I wanted to go to the office and finish the collection.

Sofia was on her way back, and I knew how she overreacted. As soon as Tita arrived, I left her with Pepe, cleaning, but it was clear that we couldn't move back in. We were going to have to stay somewhere else until we could rebuild our home.

I arrived at the office and started working on the unfinished pieces. I also called Rafaela, the seamstress, to help with the sewing. Sofia hadn't arrived, but there was still a lot of work to be done. I felt a pit in my stomach, worried about her reaction. When she arrived, she hardly greeted us, rapidly went to the rack where the collection was hanging, and started staring attentively at the pieces. I hadn't seen her since she went to Spain. She turned to me and said:

"So, can you explain to me what you have been doing all this time?" she said with her hands at her waist in a power position.

"I did the work we agreed on when you left for Spain. This rack is finished, and this rack I haven't touched, because you told me not to touch it, that you wanted to be here for the alterations," I said, while she became more enraged by the second.

"So, are you telling me that all of this rack needs to be finished by tomorrow when I leave for New York?" she asked.

"Yes, I think that between Rafaela and me, we can finish it," I said calmly.

"You are kidding me, right? I can't believe you; this is all your fault!" she barked.

"What are you talking about? Do you think this is my fault? You told me not to touch that rack because you don't trust me, and now we are behind. I could have finished it, but you didn't let me," I said, exasperated.

"Yes, it is your fault, because you can't do anything as I tell you."

She took a breath as she tried to calm down, figuring out that if I left, she would be in big trouble because she didn't know how to sew a button.

"Ok, let's forget about it and continue working. We need to finish," she said, as she went to the computer to see the pictures of the collection.

Rafaela and I sewed without pause all through the day, while Sofia approved our work. She started packing everything needed for Coterie in New York.

It was seven in the evening when Rafaela said she couldn't work anymore, that she was leaving.

"Please, Rafaela, don't leave me. We still have a lot of work to do," Sofia begged Rafaela to stay extra hours.

"Sorry, Sofia, my back is killing me, and we have been working non-stop. I have to go home," Rafaela replied.

"I will pay you extra. How much do you want?" Sofia asked.

"Nothing, Sofia. I am exhausted, my eyes are tired, my legs are tired," Rafaela said, as she stood up and left. Sofia was sitting in front of me, staring as I hand-sewed a top.

Although Irma had come and gone, I felt another storm brewing.

"I am serious; this is all your fault," she whispered in rage.

"Sofia, how is this my fault? Irma set us back a week, and you were in Spain on vacation for two weeks. I was here working, remember?" I said.

"Working? You did nothing! Show me what you did? And everything you do is wrong!" she replied.

"Oh my God, Sofia, I have been killing myself for Solei. I came back from Mexico and left my house destroyed. You still find a way to make me feel like shit. You can't even see it! I am taking all the unfinished pieces home and will work on them all night. I will leave you the luggage with the concierge of the office, so you can pick up the things before you leave for the airport tomorrow," I said, exhausted, packing everything up. I couldn't be around her anymore.

"My plane leaves at 1:00 p.m., so be sure the suitcase is there at 11:00 am with the concierge. If you don't finish, we don't have a collection. It will be all on you," she said.

"Everything will be here," I said.

I went home to my suegros', had dinner, turned on the TV for company, and started working. I stayed up all night sewing skirts, tops, and pants. I finished the details by hand and, finally, sewed the labels. I sewed the night away, and around 7:00 a.m., I finished and went to sleep. I set my alarm for 10:00 am. I woke up, and thankfully, Tita had arrived.

"Tita, please take this suitcase to the office and leave it with the concierge. It has to be there exactly at eleven am. I can't drive. I think I am going to be sick," I said.

Tita left with the off-the-cuff collection, and I went to the bathroom to throw up.

How did I get here? I have no idea. I have asked this question many times, as if I have not made the decisions I made through my free will. As if life has thrown me into different circumstances and moments that I had no control over, and I am watching incredulously as the consequences of my decisions unfold. But this time, I couldn't fool myself. In this situation, I was a willing participant and an active and silent accomplice. I was living my dream of owning a fashion line that would sell worldwide, with two major department stores, Macy's and Londres, in Mexico.

But now I know dreams have a very hefty price to pay. And by God, I had paid the price, but it seemed I was still in debt. Getting here had taken so much money, effort, and hard work that now that I had achieved it, it felt painfully different from how I thought it would feel.

It was early Saturday morning, and Sofia and Victoria would

arrive at any moment. They were back from New York. We hadn't communicated much, just exchanged cold texts. She had informed me that we had received large orders from our biggest clients. Good news, I guess. *How is it that with million-dollar sales, we still couldn't afford to earn salaries, Sofia and I?* I was still working for free. She had control of everything: finances, clients, factories in China, and undoubtedly, she also had control of me.

While they were in New York, I stayed in Miami and received the largest Macy's order yet: 101 boxes. I had counted the boxes six times by then, totaling 101 boxes. I was nervously rearranging the rows and rows of huge boxes with different models by style, size, and color. How come this dream had come true, yet felt so awful, so distant? I had given up so much and worked so hard to make it come true, and now I just wanted to be anywhere else but here.

After breast cancer, my self-esteem suffered, and Sofia took advantage of it. I was faking happiness to ensure a peaceful exit. I knew that she was capable of anything; I had already witnessed how she screwed Adi out of $40,000 and how she appropriated his shares of the company. I just wanted to leave in peace and for her to pay the $30,000 that Solei still owed my husband on the credit card.

Sofia suddenly came in looking rather serious. "Good morning," she said crisply.

"Good morning," I replied. The environment became icy. "How are you?" she asked.

"Good, working," I replied as I kept arranging boxes, feeling a drop of sweat plunge down my back.

I heard her scuff as she said, "You, working?" She laughed. I ignored it. "Did you arrange the boxes as I told you?"

"Yes, there are a hundred and one boxes, and I have divided them by styles." As we agreed. She walked around the huge room and noticed that I had opened some boxes.

"Why are those boxes open?" she asked me.

"Which boxes?"

"Those over there." She pointed.

"Oh, those boxes are not for Macy's. I opened them to start building the orders for the other boutiques."

"Didn't I tell you to wait for me before you open anything? Why did you open those boxes?"

My heart was beating really fast, and my head was boiling.

"I thought I would start preparing those orders so I would advance the work we have," I said patiently.

"Work? Really? You are the only one here who doesn't work. What did you do while we were in New York, selling the collection?"

"What do you mean? I received and carried up a hundred and one boxes. And then I organized and arranged them. That is why I stayed and didn't go to New York, remember?" I was exasperated.

"You don't deserve your twenty percent of Solei. You don't work

for it."

"I am sick of you telling me that! I don't need to work for my twenty

percent of Solei. I paid for it, I own it. I have been working without a salary for two years, putting in all my money and family resources. I absolutely deserve the twenty percent of Solei," I said, exploding.

"Well, at this point, you have no idea what orders we have pending or anything that is going on in the company!"

I started to walk toward her, furious, "You did this! You sidelined me from all the accounts and suppliers. You have relegated me completely to sewing labels!"

"I kill myself for this company. I don't have a life outside Solei; this is my life. And your life is not Solei. You have a family, friends, and other priorities."

"I never told you Solei was going to be my life. I have worked very hard to make this brand successful."

"No, you haven't. You do nothing."

"You want to see what it is to do nothing?" I asked her as I started walking toward the door. I snatched my bag from the desk. "Now, watch me do nothing."

As I was walking to the door, I heard her say, "It was my birthday when I was in New York, and you forgot to call me." It dawned on me that all of this particular drama is because I forgot her birthday. I turned around and said to her.

"Well, happy birthday!" And I walked out the door, realizing that another hurricane was about to hit us with all its force. After I walked out that Saturday morning, things with Sofia escalated pretty quickly.

My house had been totally damaged by Hurricane Irma, and so was my self-worth. Irma came with its deadly winds, all its anger and forceful energy, and bent sturdy, chunky trees like twigs; I felt like those fallen trees. Sofia's words decimated me. The reality was that I was afraid of her, that I partly believed her damning words about me not being good enough, not really being a fashion designer. I had to stand up to her, but I didn't want to go back. I didn't want to talk to her. She would twist everything and make me feel like shit, always. She preferred the version of me: sick, vulnerable, dependent, and weak. As soon as I regained my strength, she was threatened with the healthy version of me and all that that entails. She pushed me out. I was of no service anymore.

El Mada said not to worry, that he would talk to her so that she would make the Amex payments, and that I should concentrate on getting better emotionally, rebuilding the house with the insurance money, and my upcoming mastectomy. We would figure everything else out later.

"I emailed Sofia for the first payment of the Amex, and she paid three thousand of the thirty thousand dollars left. I am going to try to get the rest of that amount as soon as possible," El Mada said.

The payment for the 101 boxes for Macy's had probably come through by now, and because we had access to the Solei account, we saw that there was more than enough money for her to pay us. We also discovered that she finally obtained a business credit card and was making payments of up to $20,000 in a single payment.

El Mada emailed Sofia asking if she would please pay the $30,000 debt in six payments. Meaning in six months, it would be done. Sofia answered that she would only pay $1,000 a month. She added that since Solei's official papers stated that I was still vice president, and El Mada as treasurer, she was going to hold a board meeting, and things were going to change. She expected us to attend.

"OMG! Board meeting? Who does she think she is? Warren Buffett? She is crazy!" El Mada erupted. "We need to send her our resignation letters as soon as possible. We need to separate immediately from Solei."

Then he responded to Sofia, telling her that if she didn't pay at least $3,000 this month, he would involve a lawyer. El Mada was beside himself. He felt so frustrated, angry, and disrespected. One thousand dollars didn't even cover the interest! I was also beside myself, furious. El Mada, who had helped us so much, didn't deserve this, so I emailed Sofia.

"You need to pay the debt. If you don't pay what you owe, this is going to escalate." I wrote.

"Don't threaten me. I won't pay what you want," she answered. The deadline for payment arrived, and she hadn't paid anything, not even the $1,000 she had offered.

Wow, that escalated fast. We needed a lawyer.

As we discussed options with a lawyer recommended by our neighbor, he told us, "Sometimes it is best to lose the money. Fights can be very

costly, but this is a piece of cake because we have proof and a paper that she signed that she was responsible for the debt," he said.

"No worries, easy peasy."

I had been completely ousted from Solei at that point. I didn't know anything that was going on; she wouldn't even let me see any paperwork. I decided to hire a lawyer to determine where all the money was going. I knew there was at least $1 million in sales. Where was all the money?

"Solei is still broke," she argued.

El Mada sent her an email again, insisting she pay at least $3,000.

Nothing worked; she ignored everything. We were iced out.

Lime Icebox Cake (Carlota de Limón)

For when you are put in the freezer and need something sweet.

Ingredients:

- 2 cups sweetened condensed milk (about 620 grams)
- 240 grams (8 oz) cream cheese, at room temperature
- Juice of 5 limes (strained)
- 2 packages of María cookies (about 400 grams)
- 1 stick of butter (about 90 grams)

Instructions

1. In a blender, combine the cream cheese, sweetened condensed milk, and the juice of the 5 limes you squeezed. Blend until smooth. Set aside.
2. Take one of the packages of María cookies and crush it into powder using the blender or food processor. Add the melted butter and mix until it has a crumb-like texture.
3. In a mold or dish for assembling the Carlota, start with a layer of the crushed cookies as the base. Then pour a layer of the lime cream mixture on top. Add a layer of whole María cookies on top of the cream.
4. Continue layering: one layer of cream, one layer of cookies, repeating until you use all the mixture or fill the mold.
5. Place the dessert in the freezer for a couple of hours to set.

Optional: Decorate with lime slices and crushed María cookies before serving.

CHAPTER 33

Dear God, I Am Pissed. . .

For a star to be born,
there is one thing that must happen:
a gaseous nebula must collapse.
So collapse. Crumble.
This is not your destruction.
This is your birth.

—Zoe Skylar

Sometimes life places people disguised as coincidences, so you can't miss them, you can't avoid them. That's how I met Sarah. She lived two blocks from us, and I met her when we bought our house. She was married to the son of the previous owners. Ignacio, my son, slept in the bedroom where Carlos, Sarah's husband, grew up. When pregnant with her first child, Sarah was diagnosed with breast cancer. She got treated and went into remission, but months later, the cancer came back. When I got sick, El Mada's cousin told me about her high school friend Sarah, who had cancer, so that she could share her experience, and gave me Sarah's cell phone number. I realized it was the same Sarah when I called her. She held out her hand to me when I needed it. I once called her in tears, asking her how to handle the fear of cancer coming back. She dropped what she was doing and walked to my house with her dog Candela.

"I have debilitating anxiety, even though the doctors tell me I am fine. I don't believe them. There is a threatening, gray cloud hanging over me," I told her.

"Oh, look! Candela recognizes the garden from when my in-laws lived here," she answered. "About the fear of it coming back, the only thing to do is to wait and see."

"But I've been told by the doctors that it's unlikely it's coming back."

"Well, I was told the same thing, and it came back," she said.

Perfect; just what I wanted to hear, I thought.

But she was right, you never know.

When you get breast cancer, you connect with women who have been through the same. It is tough to understand if you haven't gone through it. It's like when you're having a baby for the first time: other moms tell you about the overwhelming love at first sight of your baby, the sleepless nights, the struggles with breastfeeding, changing diapers, and the life-altering event of becoming a mom. With any life-altering event, you can imagine what it's like, but you haven't experienced it. With cancer, the same thing happens. Until you experience it for yourself, you can't understand the depth of it. You're a member of a club that no one wants to join, part of the "it sucks" group.

But since becoming a member, I have come to experience that when two souls meet and recognize their deep pain and suffering, they instantly embrace and console each other. They connect in a way I haven't felt before. I learned that compassion involves understanding and connecting with someone else's pain, as you have experienced your own. The more time passes by, the prouder I am of belonging to this club.

Sarah's cancer came back with a vengeance.

"Cancer has metastasized to my liver, and I am going to have chemo. I loved how you handled your hair loss with your wig. Can you take me to Gilberto so he can do mine?" Sarah asked.

"Of course," I said. "I will take you so he can work his magic as he did on me."

When Sarah told me about her cancer coming back, all of my worst fears became her reality. I was still fragile emotionally and wasn't in the best position to help her out. Sarah was a young mother of two children under five, a tragedy. I decided to accompany her on her journey, just as she had accompanied me. Even though it would pain me to see her slip away, I decided to take her hand and accompany her, and give her love and affection in the last weeks of her life. I witnessed how she fought for her life and her children. As cancer was ravaging her body, it didn't defeat her spirit. She kept fighting and living with that smile, that beautiful smile that defined her.

To say I was in the dumps was an understatement. Hurricane Irma had flooded my house; I was out of Solei, and Sarah was shutting down right before my eyes. Even the book I was already writing, originally intended to be a light read, was now a fucking tragedy. It was supposed to be a moving comedy, not a freaking drama. The only thing I looked forward to was the mastectomy. It gave me comfort. I was finally getting rid of my boobs that had served me well, but had reached their expiration date. How can I be in such a dump that I am so excited about getting a double mastectomy?

"WHAT THE FUCK???" I shouted in my car, reaching my breaking

point. I don't remember where I was driving. I parked the car on the roadside and started crying, bawling, tears coming from the deepest, darkest part of my soul. I didn't want to go there, but I finally arrived.

I turned to God, pissed, and asked him.

"What more do you want from me? I don't understand what more you want? Really? Is this your plan? I've been a good person. I've offered you everything I've ever done. I thought you had a plan for me; is this your plan? Okay, I don't have cancer, thank you, I appreciate it. But I feel I've lost so much, I feel so lost, so little, I don't know who I am. I thought you had my back. I am pissed," I cried.

And at that moment, crying, I finally hit rock bottom, full of despair.

After a while, I heard the ding of a text on my cell phone. Wiping my tears, I grabbed the cell phone and saw the text from my friend Bertis, who had recently arrived in Miami with her family. I knew her from back in Mexico because she attended the same Catholic school I did, and just like me, she was expelled. When she was in sixth grade, she discovered a glow-in-the-dark condom in her parents' dresser. She decided to explore her discovery further with her classmates in the school bathroom. The teacher caught them red-handed, or, better yet, glow-in-the-dark-handed, and poor Bertis was expelled at the tender age of 11 years old. Her mom was so mad that the UROs didn't appreciate Bertis's natural curiosity that she also took Bertis's two sisters out of the school.

We would laugh, comparing stories, bad-mouthing the UROs. Bertis is cutely short and has big, bright blue eyes and brown hair. She has a very sweet, pretty face, but is extremely funny and has a foul mouth. When I am with her, my swearing instantly increases by 200 percent. Mexican swear words exist in a universe of their own, and it's so much fun to relish them. Bertis and I had become very close.

"Hey, Byatch!!! Send everyone to hell, and let's do the tortilla business! Ándale, my husband Rodrigo told me that he would help us set up the business. He is excited about the idea."

I read the text, and although I could have attributed the timing to an answer from above, I decided that I would never again make decisions by throwing the ball to God. I had done that with Solei, and look where it got me. But I couldn't completely ignore the obvious timing.

"OK, Bertis. I am having the mastectomy in a few weeks and will be out for a while, but if you still want to do this, let's do it," I wrote.

"Yeiii!" she wrote with cornets and a dancing flamenco girl emoji. "Don't worry. Let's bring the tortilla machine from Mexico, starting slow, nothing big."

I can't believe I'm out of one and already into another. That's how Tortilla Bros. was born.

CHAPTER 34

On a Sunday Morning

I learned Sarah died on Sunday morning. I cried so much that at one point, my youngest son, Juan, entered the bedroom to ask me. "Why are you crying so much? Are you ok?"

"A friend of mine died. I am sad, but I'm ok," I told him.

I gave myself Sunday to cry all day. On Monday, I stopped myself from crying anymore. I was having my mastectomy on Wednesday. It was going to be a huge surgery, and I had to take care of myself. I have heard so many times that when you are stressed, your immune system suffers. I learned to remain calm and ground myself to go into surgery as strong as I could. Being a witness to Sarah's death motivated me even more to have a mastectomy. I told Carlos, Sarah's husband, that I wouldn't be able to attend her funeral. I would be in the hospital.

We were able to move back into our house just in time for the surgery. We had been living in a borrowed apartment for a few weeks until all the water damage from Hurricane Irma was repaired. I was happy to move back home and recover there. My mom and my sister Isabel came from Mexico for the surgery. I don't remember much about those days. I was once again in survival mode.

We arrived at the hospital, and Dr. D. came in to say hello. "How are you today? Are you ready?" his smiling face asked me.

"Yes, Dr. D., I am ready when you are," I replied.

In one of my pre-op appointments, he discussed with me the

option of taking my nipples out completely, and he had printed thirty pages to make his case.

"Dr. Medina talked to you about the possibility of keeping your nipples with the surgery. I thought about it, and the best option for you is to take your nipples out," Dr. D. said.

I took a big breath. His suggestion was unexpected. I was excited about keeping my nipples, and now he was suggesting that the best option was removing them.

"I printed all this literature for you about the subject." He handed me a pack of printed paper with medical studies. "My reasoning is that you are doing this mastectomy as a precaution, because you need to feel safer. Although it would be extremely rare, we leave some breast tissue under the nipple, so it would be wise to take out the nipple for your total peace of mind. Read the literature. You can think about it and later let me know what you decide."

"But if you take the nipples out, how are my breasts going to look?" I asked.

"Well, Dr. Medina, in a later surgery, will reconstruct your nipples, and afterward, you will get a tattoo. The work that some tattoo artists do is surprisingly realistic," he said.

I took the literature home, and I threw it in the trash. I hated the fact that I had to give up my nipples. I never read the lit Dr. D. gave me so kindly. I didn't need to read it. I knew I would do what he suggested. I never thought I would have to discuss my nipples with so many people. It was weird and it sucked.

I had to remind myself of how fortunate I was to have this surgery with these wonderful doctors. At heart, I am still a Mexican girl who marvels at American technology and advances in medicine. So even if I was going to lose my nipples, I was still thankful to be able to have the surgery. I am not sure if this type of surgery is even available in Mexico.

So once again, in my typical manner, I closed my eyes and offered up my nipples to God. I chuckle about how that sounds. I have been offering everything that I have been losing to Him, with the hope that He knows better than I. If I offer the pain of losing something dear and close to me, maybe the pain will become less and will make more sense in the future. Perhaps I can find some purpose in the pain. I had been losing so many things that by now it wasn't even funny anymore; I could write a book called *The Art of Losing*. But still, I continued to offer it up. *I am not my body,* I thought. I imagined my two nipples with little angel wings flying away to heaven. Fly high, little nipples, you have served me well.

The day of the surgery was here. I was hooked to various medical devices that made beeps.

"So, you decided to take out your nipples, right?" Dr. D. asked, reaffirming what I had informed him earlier.

"Yes, Dr. D., I trust you. Do whatever you need to do."

"Ok, so we are ready. I will do the mastectomies, and then I will inform your family. Dr. Medina and Dr. Salinas will start the reconstruction as soon as I finish. Don't worry, you are in very good hands."

"Thank you, Dr. D. I know." It has been such a gift to have him by my side on this journey. He gave me security, comfort, and guidance, making me feel that everything was going to be fine. I will never, ever be able to repay him for the magnificent care he gave me. I love Dr. D. I will always be grateful to him, and I am not the only one.

They took me to the operating room, and they worked on me for most of the day. I don't remember much. I remember waking up in intensive care with my mom and El Mada.

Dr. Medina entered the room. "How do you feel?" he asked.

"Good, considering. What am I doing in intensive care? Why am I here?" I asked him, freaked out.

"You are doing fine. You are here so we can keep a closer eye on you. You have two new implants, think of it like an organ transplant, and we are monitoring the pulse of the implants. A nurse will come in every hour to check that blood flows to the implants. Hopefully, they will hold. If not, you would be in a standard room," he said.

His explanation made sense. I was not in intensive care because I was gravely ill, just to monitor me meticulously. I relaxed a little bit. El Mada and my mom said their goodbyes. They wanted to go home, rest, and tell my kids that everything went well. It had been a brutal day since dawn in the hospital.

That night in intensive care, I didn't have pain, but I had horrible nightmares. I dreamt that Sofia was chasing me, harassing me. I felt as little as she always made me feel. I didn't want to think about her anymore; it hurt so much. She was haunting me.

I opened my eyes. I was alone in the room. A nurse came in with a little pen to check if the implants were still alive. She would search for the pulsating vein with a pen-like instrument, making sure the implants were still in place.

"Perfect, I hear it, it sounds like they are still there. Now to the other side." She measured the other breast. "I hear it." *Tuck, tuck, tuck.* "They sound great, that is good news." She left the room.

I closed my eyes, tried to sleep, again with Sofia stalking me. Please go away... please leave me alone.

While in intensive care, they covered me with a blanket that would inflate and deflate. At home, my dog Mini was always by my side or at my feet at the end of my bed. That night, while Sofia was chasing me around and the nurses kept checking on me, I imagined that the inflatable blanket was Mini, my dog. She was at the foot of the bed, keeping me company.

I stayed at the hospital for five days. During my stay, I was happily pumping morphine until the machine decided it was enough for the moment. Dr. Medina was right; I was never in pain. Dr. D. drove in from the Keys on Sunday to sign me out.

"Wow," he said. "You look remarkably well."

"Thanks, Dr. D.," I said, smiling. "I feel good. You know I love you, right? Do you realize how special you are? You have been such a blessing to me," I said, wondering if he understood the difference an extraordinary doctor makes in a patient's life.

"Please, Monica, don't say that. Thank you for letting me treat you. My dad always told me that we were the lucky ones, that patients let us help them and treat them."

"Well, I disagree with your dad. The lucky ones are your patients. There are not many doctors like you." Then I turned to El Mada. "Can you please take a picture of me and Dr. D?"

He took my phone and took a picture of both of us, sitting in the hospital bed, hugging and smiling.

That morning, every patient wanted to check out as fast as possible to get home. The hospital didn't have enough wheelchairs, and we were waiting for a long time because they needed to wheel me out.

"But I feel fine. I could walk out," I told the nurse.

"Are you sure?"

"Yes, I am sure. I want to leave and see my children, please," I pleaded desperately. She finally agreed.

On a Sunday morning, with the help of El Mada by my side, I walked out of the hospital to a new beginning, after having a literally life-changing surgery.

CHAPTER 35

Tortilla Bros.

Since we arrived in Miami, I had stopped eating quesadillas or anything that involved tortillas. The only ones we could find were in the supermarkets and had nothing to do with the original. Because the Mexican population in Florida is scarce, we didn't have authentic Mexican food like in California, Texas, or Chicago with so many Mexican *changarros*. As a business opportunity, it was an interesting thought, and I also enjoyed sharing part of our culture with everyone here in Miami.

My friend and I decided to bring an industrial machine from Mexico. When I contacted the salesperson of an industrial tortilla machine, they informed me that they had sent tortilla machines to Africa, China, Europe, and Australia. Funny enough, they had sent industrial tortilla machines to every corner of the world.

The industrial machine was on its way, so we started looking for places near La Calle Ocho. However, after inquiring about construction permits and local adaptations, the investment amount skyrocketed. Nevertheless, I called the real estate agent who rented me the space we were using for Solei. Maybe she could help find a space for the tortillas.

"Hi, Monica, nice to hear from you. How are you doing?"

"Great, Angela. I was looking for a small place around La Calle Eight."

"I think I can help you. How are things with Solei?"

"I am taking a break from it right now," I answered.

"I don't want to intrude, but I've known you for a long time, and I thought of calling you after Sofia called me. She said that you are no longer part of Solei. She needed the locks changed in the office. I asked her why, and she said things have been missing, that someone is stealing dresses. I told her that was impossible. We have cameras, a concierge, and those offices are completely isolated. She said that she was being robbed and that she needed the locks changed. That if not, she would be leaving. I didn't want any trouble, so I changed the locks," she said.

My heart sank. When I left, I didn't even take my computer. I just left. All the office things that I had brought from Mexico, my sewing machines, computers, everything in that office, I had bought. And now I was locked out of it. I felt a thousand daggers stabbing me inside.

"Thank you for telling me, and be careful. She might stop paying rent," I said.

"Yeah, I think so too. I want her out, as quickly as possible."

While I was dealing with my post-mastectomy care, my new partner, Bertis, and her husband, Rodrigo, found an industrial kitchen that would rent us space where we could set up the machine and charge us an affordable rent. The great advantage was that we could get started right away, and the owners of the industrial kitchen would facilitate the permits. The disadvantage was that we only had three hours a day, starting at 8:00 a.m., and we had to leave by 11:00 a.m. at the latest. Another team of "cooks" would take over our station and make Argentinian empanadas.

I wanted to get back into the saddle of entrepreneurship, but I was still in the aftershock of the Solei situation and wasn't sure if I was ready to invest in something again. I was hurt. I had trusted

Sofia, but she had walked all over me and left me for dead. I was pushed out of something that I helped create. I understood now how Steve Jobs felt when he was kicked out of Apple. Could the tortillas be my Pixar? I really hoped so.

I talked to Bertis about my insecurities. "I don't know if I am ready to put myself through a business again. I feel super weak and freaked out. It's like I just went through a massive breakup, and I'm throwing myself into a new relationship again. Maybe I am skipping the healing process," I said.

"Look, Moni, I understand, but please don't compare me with that witch. I want to think you know me better than that. It is not such a big investment, and we will start small and try to grow organically from there."

"Bertis, you are nothing like her, but I feel so powerless. I doubt myself constantly. How could I not see what she was doing? I thought I was an amazing judge of character, but now I feel stupid and fooled."

"Everyone can be fooled. You have to let that go. She fooled a lot of people, not just you. I promise we will have a fun time making tortillas, you'll see."

So, as I usually do, I threw myself back into the ring. We signed the lease for the communal kitchen and brought the machine from Mexico, as we began researching how to make tortillas. It can't be that difficult, right? It is just corn and water.

Wrong.

It turns out tortillas have science and technique to them, so we dove into it.

The science behind it is that, for some reason, when lime is added to corn and boiling water, an alchemy process called nixtamalization occurs, a complex term even for native Spanish speakers. It took me a couple of weeks to remember to say it correctly. When you see how the corn changes when the lime is added to the boiling water, I can't describe it, but it's short of magical. How did the Mayans come up with this? The color and texture of the corn instantly change, making it perfect for smashing to make the tortillas' masa. I have summarized the process here in a very simple way that I am sure would cause tortilla specialists in Mexico to cringe. There is so much tradition and history in the tortilla that I was completely unaware of. It takes hours and hours of work to get the masa right, and I summarized it in a short paragraph.

When we set up the tortilla machine in the industrial kitchen, all the other cooks were very intrigued by the machine and what we were going to do with it. I suspected that they thought we didn't have a clue, and they were right.

I usually went to work wearing cute little outfits, such as mini dresses or shorts. I was in fashion and lived in Miami. I first appeared in the industrial kitchen with a short-printed dress and, of course, heels. Bertis saw me come in, and she thought nothing of it. She had on a pair of jeans and a white t-shirt, but as I walked by all of the kitchen stations, I felt how the cooks gawked at me, up and down. What is wrong with these people? Why are they staring at me? I left my purse at the steel table.

"¿ *Qué onda*, Bertis? What's up?"

"The owner of the kitchen just came in and told me we had to wear gloves to handle the masa, and we have to wear nets on our hair, so we don't contaminate the masa with any of our falling hair. . ."

"You're kidding me, right? Those nets are awful. It's like we're serving meals in prison."

"I know, and honestly, I think you have to change your working outfits. You look like Elle Woods in *Legally Blonde*. You work in a kitchen now, so I think jeans and a t-shirt would be more appropriate. Our buddies in the next stations, over there, think you look kinda ridiculous."

I laughed. "Yeah, I got the vibe when I walked in that I was a little out of place. I will definitely bring jeans tomorrow. But I refuse to use the net, maybe a baseball cap?"

We started experimenting with our own recipe, and once we had it down, we did a tortilla tasting with a couple of our Mexican friends. We made different types of tortillas and assigned them a number. The participants were asked to identify which tortillas had the best texture, taste, and aroma. We also judged color and flexibility. We all agreed on a winner. Incredible how a good tortilla could bring us all back home.

Now we had to figure out how to work the machine to make industrial quantities of tortillas. We made 50 pounds of masa, and we started feeding it into the head of the machine. Tortillas started coming out like crazy, spitting them everywhere. They would fall folded into a comal, that is, a huge griddle. Because they came out folded, they were of no use. It was like that episode of *I Love Lucy* where she and Ethel were going crazy trying to catch all the food that the machine was throwing out at them. We couldn't keep up. After making 50 pounds of masa, we took home only three decent pounds of tortillas. The rest went to the garbage: burnt, folded, some too thick, too thin, or broken. We ended the day with masa all over our clothes, sweaty and exhausted. We sat on the floor next to the machine, between exhaustion and laughter.

Bertis told me, "How funny to see you with your hairnet, gloves, and making tortillas. From fashion designer to tortillera."

"I know, right?" I replied. "I don't know whether to laugh or to cry." And we both started laughing.

To be super honest, I hadn't been this happy and liberated for a while. I was again productive and creative. And I didn't have the pressure of Sofia consuming me. I was free again.

It took some time to learn how to make the perfect tortilla. We told our Mexican friends and neighbors about our new venture. We offered subscriptions online, and with Tita's help in the kitchen, we were going to deliver fresh tortillas, salsas, guacamole, and our famous taquitos to homes every week.

We got various clients and subscriptions from the Mexican crowd, but it was not enough to do business. I was part of a neighborhood chat that had a waiting list to join. The chat was comprised of Miami natives, not Hispanic immigrants, who were mostly my acquaintances, so this was a new market. In this chat, they would ask about everything from plumbers to hurricanes, accidents in town, or any important event in the community, such as a kitten in a tree, or how to solve the problem of an iguana eating the flowers in your garden. I posted about my new business and thought nothing more about it.

Soon, the chat lit up with questions about fresh tortillas. Salsas? Where? Who? What!! Delicious!!! Other friends in the chat started complimenting the tortillas, and Amelita, my good friend, even posted a taco on her Instagram. Suddenly, we had a flood of orders from people from all over the world. I loved that a woman from the UK wanted to make tortillas to accompany fresh fish tacos with fish her husband had just caught. A person of Hindu descent purchased a weekly subscription for salsas and tortillas. I was elated to share part of our Mexican heritage with people from all around the world and experience how they enjoyed it. We soon got into some Mexican restaurants and convenience stores.

We made tortillas in the morning, and afterward, we would

deliver them. We captured the interest of a chain of Mexican restaurants, and I obtained the contact information of a small chain of supermarkets. But the way we set up the business in the industrial kitchen was not going to be enough; we needed to expand if we wanted to grow.

I had my second surgery with Dr. Medina. I wasn't thrilled to go under the knife again, but my tummy incision got infected. Dr. Medina grafted fat from other parts of my body and injected it into my breasts to perfect them. When I told my friends that they would take fat from my waist and thighs to inject it into my boobs, they all made the same joke.

"If you need extra fat, I can donate mine to you," they said.

"No thanks, I have enough fat of my own. But if I need more, I'll keep you in mind," I joked back.

Dr. Medina created a new nipple. He pinched some skin, and voilà, he made my boobs and tummy better than ever. He cleaned the tummy incision and made the scar smaller. After a couple of months, I went and had my tattoo done. A lady added pink color to recreate my nipples in 3D. Later, I went to my ob-gyn for a checkup, and because my boobs looked so natural, he actually forgot I had the mastectomy.

"Hey, remember I had a mastectomy," I said to him.

"Oh, that's right. If you hadn't told me, I would have forgotten. It is one of the best mastectomies I have seen."

I smile now proudly at my boobs. It was a long and difficult process that I blocked out when I was sans nipples. I thought that how my body looked at that moment was temporary; I didn't focus too much on the process, I waited for the result. I trusted my doctor. For the months between surgeries, before the final result, I tried to power through it. Mind over matter. The best part of all is I don't have to have those sucky mammograms anymore, and that fact alone was life-changing. After all was done, with my new boobs, I started to feel good again. My body was no longer a weapon. El Mada, amazed, would say, "Dr. Medina is an artist, a genius."

In one of the post-ups with Dr. Medina, I was waiting for my car in the valet area. The bell celebration that I started in the hospital has become so successful that they now have massive bells throughout the new cancer center. My heart was full every time I passed by and witnessed somebody ringing the new massive bell in the new facility. Now, the patient would invite family members and their nurses to their ceremonies. It had become a big deal.

While I was waiting for my car, I sat near a lady who seemed tired and in treatment. I struck up a conversation with her.

"Hot day, huh?" I said

"Yes, and humid also," she replied. We started talking, and she told me she had throat cancer, was having radiation, and was exhausted.

"Look at my neck, do you see it? It's all burnt," she said sadly.

"Yes, I see it. You need to keep going. I know how tough it can be." I said.

"Three more days and it is over. Three more days and I am done with radiation."

"That's amazing! When I was doing radiation, my sister told me about a bell and...."

She interrupted me, super excited. "I know!! The bell, right? I'm looking forward to it. I have been waiting for so long to ring it, three more days...," she said hopefully. I was stunned she was so excited.

"You know, I was the one who donated the first bell to the hospital. Not the big one, but the first one in the old building," I said to her.

Her eyes started to tear up. "You're kidding me, right? You got the bell?"

"Yes, I got the bell!" I told her excitedly. Tears started to flow down her face. By now, I was almost crying, but I held back my tears.

"Thank you so much for your words," she said.

My car had arrived, and the valet guy was waiting for me. I hugged her and said, "Remember, three more days. You made it, you got this."

I got into my car and drove away, crying. I didn't think that the bell could mean so much to people going through cancer. I then called many Miami hospitals asking if they needed a bell. Most of them had one or weren't interested. Later, I helped a Brazilian friend take a bell to Brazil, and we donated them in Mexico, too. I hope that many people ring the bell full of health, love, and pride in their amazing feat.

CHAPTER 36

The Devil Wears Zara1

Sofia was blocking us hard with the subpoenas of El Mada's case for the payment of the $30,000; she was running and hiding like a pro. It seemed she had been through this before. We didn't know what to do next. It was scary. I hadn't realized how little I knew of Sofia. I thought I really knew her; heck, I sometimes knew what she was thinking or what she was going to say next, but I didn't know where she lived. She never once invited me to her house. She said they were renting because they had just sold their fabulous house in Coconut Grove. But the reality is that we didn't have an address for where she lived.

We didn't know who she was.

Michael, the lawyer, recommended conducting an investigation to find out more about who we were dealing with. The results came in, and I was floored, flabbergasted. I couldn't believe it. Sofia, on any governmental record, had never worked at Bloomingdale's; she had worked at a pizzeria in Hialeah. She had never worked at any of the places she claimed to have worked.

She did own that apartment in Coconut Grove, but she and her husband had stopped making mortgage payments on it. The bank fought them for two years to reclaim the apartment, but they kept blocking the letters and bills they sent. After two years, they finally sold the apartment and paid the bank. That is exactly when I met her. They now lived in a rental apartment in a not-so-good part of town.

Who was this woman? How could she lie so naturally?

In hindsight, now, I see everything clearly. How she was always short on cash, the way she charged Starbucks and every meal to Amex. She always seemed so eager to demonstrate that she had money. Deep-seated insecurities, raw ambition, and an amoral hunger have no boundaries and become dangerous.

It was never about money for me, never. I couldn't care less where she lived or her bank account. It was about trust. Everything that came out of her mouth was a lie, a complete fabrication.

Who did I have sit at the table to eat with my kids? Who did I take to my parents' house in Mexico City and let sleep in the same house as all of us? Who is this woman without any limits or constraints?

I welcomed her into our lives, into our house, into our finances. How could I have been so gullible? So blatantly stupid? I wanted everything she said to be true. I ignored the signs because it suited me. I had even sometimes followed the lead in her lies. But all the stories she told me about working at Bloomingdale's, her work experience, everything was a lie. She was lying, and I was lying when I convinced myself that I believed her lies. Lies are toxic and destroy what they touch.

We were dealing with a professional con artist.

CHAPTER 37

Keeping the Faith

I know that the God that I worship is able to deliver me, but if not, I am going on anyhow, I am going to stand up for it anyway.

—Martin Luther King, Jr.

From all the fallout of Sofia, I experienced so much loss. I lost my work family, my friends, because I considered Sofia and Victoria as friends. I lost my business, my identity as a designer, my job, my money, my furniture, and my ego.

I am not my job, I tried to convince myself. There was so much loss, but everything paled in comparison to the fact that I had lost my faith.

During my cancer journey, I had prayed so much, and I felt so close to God. I had clung to the spiritual, the signs, and hoped that the universe would make everything better, but now I realized that I was wrong. Not everyone has their happy ending, and not everything happens for a reason.

That was what hurt the most. I felt as if Sofia even took that away from me. I felt like a victim—how could I have been so stupid to believe everything she said? I gave her all my savings. I even got my mom involved, and Sofia took her money. I left my husband with thousands of dollars in debt on the American Express card.

I always prided myself on having a strong sense of knowing people's intentions. I was so off with her; I wanted to believe her, as it was convenient for me to do so. I conceded to her all responsibility, and when something didn't sound right, I chose to believe her rather than trust my own intuition. She had fooled me, every one of us. I felt so much pain, pain and loss that was now my close companion from my cancer journey.

In a time of constant loss, I felt how pain hit me all at once, consuming me, squeezing me, and surrounding me with darkness. There was no hope, no way out. It hurt to blink, it hurt to think, in these moments of deep pain and despair.

I felt like a tsunami came unexpectedly and rolled me over, and the floor under my feet shattered. This unbearable pain didn't let me move; I was paralyzed, couldn't move forward, couldn't move backwards, and the only way out was to breathe.

I kept breathing, one breath at a time, all I had to do, concentrate on breathing, keep breathing in, keep breathing out. Keep breathing, until finally one day I didn't feel so much pain. Keep breathing, so a time came when it didn't hurt so much to move. Keep breathing, so after many days of darkness, I found a spark of light that, with time, grew bigger and bigger. Holding on to the light, holding on to what gives me joy. After a while, one day I woke up and realized that I no longer had so much trouble breathing. Then, I knew that I had survived.

For now, I would only continue to breathe, taking one breath at a time, and giving myself space and time to heal my wounds. I would never again extend to God the responsibility of my decisions. Because of how I met Sofia, I thought I had to stay in Solei and went against my own wishes. That's where I was wrong. They were all my decisions, I made every one of them, and I had to take responsibility.

And it hurt.

CHAPTER 38

Rising from the Ashes

*My mission in life is not merely to survive, but to thrive;
and to do so with some passion, some compassion, some
humor and some style.*

—Maya Angelou

The new tortilla business was flourishing. We got the hang of the machine, and we were rapidly growing by selling tortillas. It's funny how life works, how many times you have to reinvent yourself. In Mexico, women grow up in small towns around the country, hoping that their futures amount to something more than making and selling tortillas. Being a *"tortillera"* in Mexico is viewed as humble and low on the social scale. After many ups and downs and twists and turns, I finally found peace in making tortillas. The smell reminded me of home; the flavor gave my family and friends a gift that we had lost when we immigrated to Miami - the warm feeling of home. It gave me comfort to create something so common in our Mexican lives, and I loved sharing that part of our culture with non-Mexicans.

One day, El Mada said to me, "Please, whatever you do, don't stop making tortillas. You have changed my life in Miami. You improved my quality of life with tortillas."

Over the last few years, Mexico and Mexican immigrants have been pounded in the US ethos. I was proud to remind and introduce people to a part of our culture that they liked. I was thrilled when we discovered that many of our most loyal customers were not Mexican. We also started delivering to a fancy hotel that featured a Mexican restaurant and an upscale market, promising freshly made tortillas.

I had told Bertis from the beginning that my idea was to have a free-standing *tortillería* in Miami. It would actually be the first one. But Bertis wasn't ready to make such a huge commitment. Her husband was dreaming of going back to Mexico, and she was dreading the idea. Like me, she was happier here in the States, where, although we worked much harder, it was a much simpler life.

I can say, "Hi, it's me, Monica, the tortilla lady," and I didn't feel judged.

Imagine in Mexico: "Hi, I'm Monica, the *tortillera*." They would have a field day after being a fashion designer. But, I can say I am happier making tortillas than I was making dresses in the conditions that I worked under Sofia. It was simpler work, and everybody was happy with their tortillas. Perhaps it was also the circumstances in which I was thrown, building a fashion business from scratch without a clue about what I was doing. I was burned out with fashion and the whole Sofia thing, so I hung up my stilettos and short skirts for a while. Now, I was more at ease in skinny jeans and tennis shoes, happily selling tortillas.

I had also continued writing my book; it was almost complete. *I am not a writer; who is going to care about my story? All this work, and it is never going to get published,* were constant thoughts in my head, which I sometimes ignored and sometimes believed. But in the end, the idea that my story might help someone out there would bring me back to the computer.

One day, Bertis invited me for a cup of coffee. I saw her almost every day, so that she would ask for a scheduled time to talk kind of worried me.

"So, as you know, Rodrigo has made up his mind, and he wants us to go back to Mexico," she said.

Crap! I thought. The situation in Mexico had been deteriorating since we left. Sadly, President Enrique Peña Nieto and his cabinet had brought the level of corruption to a new high and emptied the country, stealing whatever they could over the last couple of years. It was just appalling. Mexico was now outraged with the president and his wife, a former telenovela actress, who had allegedly spent Mexican taxes on high fashion and fancy houses. She never bothered to help Mexican women or children.

It was an election year, and by the looks of it, a new president was coming: Andrés Manuel López Obrador. It was the third time he had run for president, but because of the mess Peña had made, he now had a chance. People were sick and tired and wanted a drastic change. That is exactly what Obrador promised: a transformation and an end to corruption. It was a platform that Mexico needed, but sadly, we knew Obrador would never make true his promises. On the contrary, the country would go backwards, because of his populist views, people warned that "Lopez Obrador was going to make Mexico the next Venezuela." We had been hearing this threat for years. The prospect of going back to Mexico now didn't seem great.

"Rodrigo has his business there. We need to go back to Mexico. I would love to stay, but he needs to attend to his business. I was the one who thought that maybe we could have stayed longer," she said.

My heart sank, but I had kind of known this was coming.

"I'm sorry, Bertis. I just hate the idea of you leaving. I am going to miss you so much," I said.

When you don't have family in the US, your friends become your family, and as had happened with Sofia, I had become close with Bertis. You see each other every day. Bertis and I were friends before partners, and we always will stay that way. She had been more than a friend to me; she helped me heal a lot of the pain I felt from Solei's falling. It was funny how Bertis helped me get back on my feet. She helped me heal in a way that nobody else could at this point. She was the yin to my yang.

"But I wanted to talk to you about the business. I discussed it with Rodrigo, and the most important thing for us is our friendship. We have grown significantly and established a solid base of clients, but we are essentially breaking even. We agreed that the best for all of us is that, if you want, you can

keep the business. If you don't want to carry on, then I think we should close it."

I didn't expect this. I was blown away by her generosity in leaving me the business, but on the other hand, I didn't know if I wanted to take it on alone. We were breaking even, but I thought we had tapped into a market segment that was previously non-existent in Miami. I was again torn with the decision. Doing it alone and investing a significant amount of money to establish a freestanding tortillería or close the business altogether.

"Oh, Bertis, I hate all of the options. Doing it alone or closing it. Let me think about it and talk about it with El Mada. I have no idea what to do," I said.

Again, I was faced with a big decision: go big or go home. We had recently received some money from a real estate investment that had gone our way, but I still wasn't feeling like myself. All the blows I had received to my self-esteem, the loss of my business, the voice of Sofia in the back of my head: "You are not good enough." I was still rebuilding my sense of security with my health and my appearance, as if I was reborn again after cancer, and I had to rebuild myself piece by piece, brick by brick.

"I am confused about what I want to do," I told El Mada. "I mean, I see economic potential in the tortilla business. I think we could make money, and right now, what I want is to recover all of the savings I lost in Solei."

"I also see the tortillas making money. The thing is, do you like making tortillas?"

"I mean, it was never my dream, making tortillas, but I kinda enjoy it. I can be creative with the recipes, and I love bringing Mexican culture to Miami. What I want is to have a healthy business."

"It is your decision; we have the money from the sale of the property. I believe you can do it."

"I don't want to lose any more money. I'm not sure if I believe in myself. The real question is, do you prefer the amount of money we would have to invest for a stand-up restaurant in the bank or invest it in the tortillería?" I asked.

"I would invest it in you," he answered.

I don't think I deserve this man, I thought.

So now, I would have no partners at all, just me and, of course, El Mada. I was terrified of taking the leap again, and creating a budget was going to be a significant investment, but I did my numbers. If I could sell what the tortilla machine produced, we would have a more than profitable business.

I looked around the famous Calle Ocho, where Cuban history is embedded in every corner. I liked that street, a far cry from the snobbish Brickell office I once shared with Sofia. Many Central Americans were living in that zone who also ate tortillas, and it was a convenient spot to reach Brickell, Coral Way, Coral Gables, and Key Biscayne. I felt happy and comfortable there. I decided to stay.

CHAPTER 39

Thrown into the Flow

Although the tortilla business was going well, I still felt that something was missing, and I wasn't reaching my full potential. After a cancer diagnosis, the trajectory of your life changes, and I found myself with a strong urge to help fellow breast cancer patients. I felt a deep compassion and a strong desire to help other women who were going through what I had gone through. I wanted to help, but I didn't know how. I was already writing my book, but sometimes I thought I was writing it for my own healing and doubted whether it would even get published, let alone help someone else.

One day, Amelita, my gorgeous Argentinian friend, sent me a video through WhatsApp. This video blew my mind and rocked my world.

It was an Argentine news clip about a woman named Paula, who had long blonde hair and deep blue eyes. She spoke energetically to the camera, smiling and telling her story.

"I was diagnosed with breast cancer, and like many women, I immediately thought, what is to become of my hair? I determined that cancer was not going to take my hair," she said as she grabbed her long, silky hair. "So, I made a cold cap with gel packs to wear during chemo. The theory behind it is that the cold transferred through a cold cap to the scalp constricts the blood vessels, which reduces the amount of chemo that reaches the hair follicles. This reduces the effects of chemo on the hair follicle, and as a result, prevents or reduces hair loss."

My mind was blown. After she wore the cold caps during her chemo, Paula didn't lose her hair. The camera then showed how Paula, along with fellow cancer survivors, would make a "cap" out of cold gel packs that can be found in pharmacies. A woman would be sitting down, and Paula would wrap her head with tape and the gel packs. They would have to wear at least six caps to keep their scalp cold during chemotherapy.

Another woman came on camera and said that she had also kept her hair using this method, which Paula had coached her on during her chemotherapy. The woman then asked Paula how she could repay her after keeping her hair, and Paula responded, "You can repay me by helping other women keep their hair." This selfless act created a chain of women helping other women.

The video floored me on so many levels. First, how creative, gritty, and courageous of them to make these caps. It didn't look easy to make them. I remember the night before my chemo, I was scared shitless. I would not be in the mood for making six cold caps.

Suddenly, as I watched the video for the thirtieth time of one woman wrapping another woman's head with tape like a UPS package, I got an idea. I saw the pattern in my head of the cold cap, just as I had seen the pattern of the dresses I made before. I decided to make gel caps, so these women wouldn't have to struggle as much on the eve of their chemotherapy. It was as if a bolt of lightning had struck my head. I drew it down and showed it to El Mada.

"Look what I drew. It could be made so easily. Imagine how much it could help women in Latin America if I designed an affordable cold cap to preserve the patient's hair during chemo," I said, excited.

"Wow, that is a great idea. That would be amazing. But have you researched to determine if it really works?" he asked doubtfully.

"Yes! I have been doing a lot of research on the subject. In the last couple of years, cold caps have been growing in popularity in the USA. In Canada and Europe, they have been using them for many years now. They are now even offering it in the hospital where I was treated, but the total cost, on average, is $2,500. Although insurance covers it, what about the women who don't have insurance? Or the women in Mexico or Argentina? These machines are only available in high-end hospitals. There are no alternatives except for rental cold caps, but they are still very expensive. Would you have worn it when you were sick?"

"Yes, I would have," he said.

His answer surprised me. I thought men's hair wasn't so important to them.

For me, without a doubt, it was one of the hardest things to overcome. Hair loss during chemo affects your self-esteem, confidence, and emotional state. It is a traumatic experience for the patient and family. It also prevents the patient from fighting the disease in a private manner. Everyone notices that you are going through something, and you see in the mirror how serious the disease is and what it is doing to your body. Then, your short hair coming back is a reminder of what you went through weeks, months, and even years after. In a way, I began to regain myself when my hair grew back.

My head was going 120 miles an hour. I couldn't stop thinking about the idea and how it made perfect sense for me to do something like this. How could I ignore this idea that could potentially help women on a massive scale? I was in the flow for a week, as if I was high on cocaine and couldn't stop. I had a name, logo, and business plan in a flash.

A couple of weeks passed, and I continued researching the cold cap project. I also continued with the tortillería project. I found a perfect spot on La Calle Ocho and began planning, obtaining all the necessary permits for a tortillería bakery. Although it seemed I was taking on a lot of projects, the City of Miami took so much time reviewing the plans that I had time to spare. I continued working on the cold caps while waiting and managing the new locale. I stopped making tortillas altogether and let my customers know that I was in the process of constructing a new kitchen, and I would return soon.

"Aren't you getting yourself into too many things?" El Mada asked. "You have the tortillería going on, and you are writing the book, and now this?"

"I know, I think I am kind of crazy for doing this, but I can't just put off this idea. It is too important. Having gone through it, if I could help women keep their hair in such a difficult time, I would be utterly and absolutely happy."

"Ok, just please don't go overboard. We are investing in the tortillería. I think you should wait; we don't have money for this."

"I won't use any of our money. I will get the money somewhere else. I have already filed for a US patent on my design and found a company in Indianapolis that specializes in plastic welding. I called and made an appointment. I need someone to do the actual prototype," I told El Mada, excited.

I bought a round-trip airline ticket to Indianapolis on the same day, and off I went. I rented a car and entered the address into the car's GPS. I drove through the middle of fields of corn, in the middle of nowhere. I started to chuckle; am I crazy? What am I doing here? But what was driving me was the force of all those women, their determination to keep their hair. I thought about them receiving their diagnosis, and the fear and anguish they would feel for themselves, for their spouse, for their children. If they could learn that one big burden of this whole experience was going to be lifted, that they would not lose their hair, now there was an option. That was what was driving me to Indiana, the women I hoped to help.

When I got to the factory, I was impressed. It was a beautiful factory. Some of the medical devices I used in my surgeries were manufactured there. WOW! I used that inflatable sheet when I was in the ICU for my mastectomy, cool! They said they would be able to develop the cool cap and were excited about the project.

"How much is it going to cost me for you to develop the prototype?"

"It is two development stages, but around thirty thousand dollars."

Crap! I don't have that kind of money. I will have to get it from somewhere, I thought.

CHAPTER 40

American Express on Trial

A couple of months passed, and it became clear that everything that pertained to lawsuits takes ages and is a little nightmare, plus Sofia didn't make it easier with her Houdini tactics. On the positive side, the less I heard from Sofia, the better. Between the tortilla business and the cold caps, I had my hands full. I was focusing on getting back on my feet and reinventing myself. To find some sense in all the chaos.

I received a call from Michael, my lawyer.

"Hi, Monica, listen up. I found out something that might change the game. Did you know Adi is suing, in federal court, Sofia and Solei?"

"No, I had no idea." I got panicky. "Is he suing us also?"

"No, just Sofia," he said. *Thank God*, I thought. I couldn't manage to fight Adi in court as well. I wouldn't have blamed him if he sued us; as far as he knew, we were in on it with Sofia.

"So that means they haven't made up, right?" I asked.

"It looks like it. I mean, being sued in federal court is a whole different ball game."

Their relationship was so mysterious to me that I never thought about contacting Adi. I thought they probably had made up by now.

"Do you want me to contact his lawyers? This can be big for us. We can join forces against Sofia; you can testify on Adi's behalf. He can claim his percentage of Solei, and then we could destitute her, and you could take over Solei," Michael said.

"Let me think about it, and I will get back to you." I talked it over with El Mada and decided to contact Adi directly.

Aside from Sofia, I felt I needed to apologize for what had happened. I had no clue how he would react, but I wanted to give it a shot, so I sent him a WhatsApp.

M: Hi, Adi. How are you?

K: Good. Hope you are well too.

M: Thanks, I've gone through a really rough time over the last couple of months.

K: Sorry to hear that.

M: I heard from my lawyer that you are also suing Solei and Sofia. K: Let the lawyers deal with that. Please.

M: Ok, I just wanted to say sorry. K: I have no issues with you.

M: We have no issues with you. We also got played. She also owes us money.

K: Well, good luck with that. Sofia called me and told me that she has in-house lawyers who will make a blood bath out of this, and I just said, "Bring it."

At that moment, I got a call from him.

"You are also suing!? I can't believe it! I knew she was going to stick it to me, but I can't believe she betrayed you."

"Well, believe it. She is crazy," I said. "And Victoria?" Adi asked.

"She is still with her."

"Shit, does she have in-house lawyers?" Adi asked

"She doesn't have crap, Adi. She's running out of money, mismanaging everything. She has a ton of legal fees to pay; she doesn't have an accountant. Everything is a lie. All that shows about her and José having all this money is a lie. We had her investigated. She never worked in Bloomingdale's."

"I knew it! She said that you were dumb and lazy. She told me to lie about how much the collections were so she could ask you for more money." Adi said.

"Yes, she told me you were a drunk and that you were closing your factory," I said.

"You knew that we had an intimate relationship, right?"

CRAP! I thought.

"Well, I kind of suspected it, but I asked her about it a couple of times, and she always denied it. She said that you were like a brother to her, and another time, she said that you were gay," I explained.

"Well, we had a relationship for a long time, and that is how she got away with so much. When I told her that she needed to pay the $40,000 that Solei owed me, and the $20,000 that I had lent her personally, she said she wasn't going to pay me. I told her I would sue her, and she threatened to tell my wife of the affair and show her some pictures. For a while, I didn't do anything, but afterward, I told my wife what had happened and sued Sophia."

"And did your wife forgive you?" I asked.

"Yes, she forgave me. And I sued Sophia's ass," he said.

"Well, I am glad she forgave you. Now we have to pick up the pieces."

"I know, but I kind of understand she did what she did to me. I was

playing with fire, but you? You were only nice to her."

"Well, that's what I got for trusting her," I said.

After we reconnected with Adi, I felt much better. After my conversation with him, everything made sense. Of course, they were having an affair all this time. That is why she needed to fly back to

China so often to keep tabs, why their relationship was so passionate. El Mada called Adi and apologized for how we enabled Sofia to screw him. He graciously understood.

"We were all fooled," he said.

We discussed how we could band together to take control of Solei, but we were now years into litigation, incurring lawyers' fees. Honestly, I wasn't even interested in managing Solei anymore. We just wanted to get paid.

Sofia had reluctantly delivered the documents of Solei that we had asked for, but the information was incomplete, false, and useless for finding any kind of investor.

"What do you want to do?" Michael, my lawyer, asked. "I can complain to the judge and pursue this year's information, because she just sent us last year's. Now we have to ask her for this year."

"Michael, I don't want to keep doing this. I am wasting my time and money. I have come to terms with the fact that I lost Solei and all the money I loaned the company," I said, "Please, let me think about what I want moving forward."

I realized that I had lost Solei and everything that it entailed. It had been such a deep, devastating, painful blow. I didn't want to keep fighting and being involved with such a toxic creature as Sofia. I didn't want anything to do with her. But I couldn't walk away empty-handed. I thought about all the extra inventory she always ordered to reach minimums. When I left, the office was full of extra inventory, so I might be able to sell it. I called Michael and made my last attempt at getting something back.

"Michael, I know what I want to do. Tell Sofia that I will leave her alone and never ask for papers again if she buys my and my mom's part of the company with all the inventory that she has in the office."

"Are you sure?"

"Yes, I want her out of my life. I don't want to spend money on legal fees. I can sell the clothes, donate them, or give them to the nurses at the cancer center. I don't want to waste my life chasing her."

"I will reach out to her lawyer and ask her if she agrees."

Surprisingly, Sofia agreed to my proposition. She didn't have enough inventory to cover my mom's and my Solei investments, so we agreed on having two different deliveries. One right away and the other delivered the year after, but I agreed. I just wanted to rescue whatever I could and leave. Sofia and Victoria prepared a document that listed all the inventory and its associated costs. The clothes weren't worth what they claimed, but it was approximately 300 pieces of clothing for the first delivery, not bad at all. Solei had moved from where we had the office before, and I didn't know where the new office was or if there still was one.

We set up the delivery time, and I expressly asked for Sofia not to be there. I asked Amelita, my friend, to help me pick up all the merchandise. It was going to be a lot of work.

At the last possible minute, almost half an hour before the delivery time, we still hadn't been given the address of the place where we were going to pick up the clothes. I dreaded going into the huge, new, shiny office of Solei with its many young interns. What lies about me would she have told everyone?

"Michael, I need the address; hasn't her lawyer given it to you?" I asked.

"No, Monica. You know how everything is with Sofia. We will be lucky if she doesn't cancel."

"UGGGH! Ok, let me know if you hear anything."

Eventually, Michael texted me an address very close to Brickell and our old office. I summoned the courage, and with Amelita in tow, we drove to the address. What would be a surprise is that the address was a warehouse building. We parked and, at a distance, saw Sofia's Mercedes-Benz with Sofia inside. She stared at me and quickly drove away.

We went to the third floor. Michael and a lady representing Sofia were already there.

She opened the warehouse—and to my heartbreak, all the furniture, racks, mannequins, cutting table and everything that I had brought from Mexico was inside that abandoned warehouse like garbage. I turned to Sofia's representative.

"All of this stuff is mine. I bought them from Mexico," I said angrily. "I have no clue. I am here just to give you the inventory," she said.

"Well, just so you know, you are working for a thief. She stole all of this from me!" I was beside myself.

"Monica, calm down. As I told you, we could put a motion for theft, but today we can't take any of this stuff. It is legally Solei's," Michael said.

"I understand, Michael, but she just dumped it here like garbage. I have asked her for my things, and she is not even using them."

"If you want all of this back, we can fight for it later." "No," I said. "Let's just take the clothes and go."

We loaded the car with twenty boxes of clothes, some of which were samples, and 100 dresses of the same style. I didn't care; it was a victory. I didn't leave empty-handed.

I told Amelita to take as many clothes as she wanted. That night, Amelita went to her house with a full-blown new closet.

El Mada was determined to recover the Amex money. He had been paying off the Solei debt for two years. After Sofia fought tooth and nail—like a wounded animal—we finally secured a trial date with the judge, who would determine what she owed. By that point, El Mada had already spent a significant amount on legal fees, but the silver lining was that if Sofia lost, she'd be responsible for covering those costs as well.

Michael asked me if I wanted to be a witness for the case, and I happily agreed. He prepared me, and there were a couple of charges on the Amex that we didn't recognize. Most of them were minor charges, but one stood out. It was $9,000. It said "family clothing in New York." We looked everywhere, and nothing. El Mada, as brilliant as he is, found where the money was spent, and we were going to use it in court.

The day of the trial arrived. I waited outside the courtroom on a wooden bench. I couldn't hear what was being discussed in the courtroom. Then, finally, I was called in. I walked to the stand, swore to tell the truth, and took a seat. My lawyer asked me some questions. I answered as he instructed me—short, concise, and don't give extra information.

Then it came to Sofia's lawyer's turn to grill me.

"Ms. Ocejo, here we have a charge of $3000 for furniture. Sofia doesn't recognize that charge. Do you recognize it?" she asked.

"That charge was made to buy the Londres furniture for display."

"Sofia says that it is furniture for your house."

"She is lying," I said, looking at Sofia right in the eyes. She couldn't hold my stare.

"You say she is lying. How can you prove it?" she asked.

"I have in my phone the WhatsApp message of Sofia approving that charge on the date the charge was made."

"You are telling me if I ask you for your phone, you can show me the texts?"

"Yes, I have them here. Do you want to see them?"

"Yes, please," the lawyer said incredulously. It seems that she had her lawyer fooled as well.

I gave my cellphone to Sofia's lawyer. She looked at it and handed the phone back to me.

"Thank you. I want to continue," she said. "Is it true that you have three children?"

"Yes, I do," I said.

"Does Sofia have any children?" "Not that I know of."

"Do you recognize this charge of $9000?" she asked. "Yes, I do," I answered, looking at Sofia with a smile on my face.

"Did you make that charge?"

"Yes, I did."

"So you admit you spent $9000 on clothes for your children in a store in New York."

"No, of course not!"

"Then what is that charge for?"

I looked at Sofia straight in the eyes and said, "I made that payment to the Tim Valle Showroom that represented us in New York. That is the name that appears as the holding of the company for his showroom," I said triumphantly, stripping Sofia and all her lies. "And for the record, I would never spend $9000 on my children's clothing."

Her jaw dropped, and I felt like jumping, dancing, giving the judge a hug, and moonwalking in the courtroom. Sofia's lawyer approached Sofia nervously, as she was probably feeding her more lies.

"Thank you, Ms. Ocejo. You can step down," the lawyer said.

The judge ordered Sofia to pay El Mada the whole $30,000 plus the $20,000 he spent on lawyer fees in the couple of years that she fought like a madwoman and drowned us in a sea of anxiety and betrayal. The judge gave El Mada a default payment. If Sofia didn't pay, he would be able to freeze Solei and Sofia's bank accounts. Sofia, through her lawyer, kept trying to negotiate with El Mada.

"You have the power, Sofia never complies when you are nice to her, she only understands with concrete consequences, freeze her bank accounts, so let's see if she doesn't start paying," I said to him.

"You are right. I am telling Michael to freeze her bank accounts," he said.

I like to imagine the moment Sofia tried to withdraw money from the ATM or pay for her Starbucks and found out her bank account was frozen.

I imagine her shouting, "NOOOOO!!!" staring blankly into the air with her closed fists. I rejoice in that image.

A couple of hours after freezing her accounts, Sofia's lawyer proposed a payment plan. She asked if she could pay $4,500 a month for a year. She argued that she didn't have the money available. El Mada agreed.

"You are too nice," I said to him. "I would have made her pay at least a twenty-thousand-dollar down payment. She dragged us through hell for two years," I said to him.

"I agree, I just want her out of our lives. I want to get paid and forget about her," he said.

Thankfully, it was over. Sofia paid El Mada religiously every last cent.

After everything we had gone through together, Adi and I remained friends. We would laugh, imagining Sofia's reaction to knowing we reconnected. He invited El Mada and me to visit Hong Kong. We kept in touch, and one day he asked me, "Do you think I should continue going after her?" Adi's lawyers were in New York, and even though I had given them her address, they couldn't serve her with papers.

"Listen, Adi, I think you will waste a lot of money and effort in suing her, and in the end, I don't think she even has the money she owes you. If I were you, I would drop the suit and cut my losses. We got her, but it took a long time and a lot of effort. I don't think it is worth it for you, being in Hong Kong."

"You are right. Here in China, she has left many people in debt. They are going to catch her eventually, and it's not going to be pretty," he predicted

Some time passed, and we joined Adi and his entire family in Orlando. They wanted to visit Disney World. We got to know Pryanka, Adi's wife, as well as his sister and nephews. It closed a circle for me, at least in the wake of Sofia's path of destruction. We had gained friends from a family that lives on the other side of the world.

Tortilla Soup for the Soul

Ingredients:

- 2 tablespoons vegetable oil
- 3 ripe tomatoes, chopped
- ½ an onion chopped
- 2 cloves of garlic
- 1 pasilla chili (seeded and chopped)
- 3 cups chicken broth
- 2 epazote leaves
- Salt and pepper to taste
- 3 corn tortillas (preferably day-old), torn into pieces
- 3 tortillas cut into thin strips fried (for garnish)
- Panela cheese, cut into cubes
- Mexican crema (or sour cream), to taste
- 1 avocado, diced
- Strips of Chile guajillo for garnish

Instructions:

1. In a pot, heat the oil. Add the chopped tomatoes, onion, garlic and pasilla chili. Sauté for a few minutes until the flavors come together.
2. Pour in the chicken broth and bring to a simmer over medium heat. Add the epazote leaves, salt, and pepper to taste.
3. Cook for 5–10 minutes. Transfer everything to a blender, add the torn tortilla pieces, and blend until smooth for a thicker texture.
4. Return the mixture to the pot and reheat until it comes to a gentle boil.
5. Serve hot and garnish with crispy tortilla strips, cubes of panela cheese, a drizzle of crema, and fresh avocado.

CHAPTER 41

Welcome to My Tortilla House

As the courthouse drama with Sofia unraveled, I continued to reinvent myself and work on my two new projects: the tortillería and the cold caps.

I continued to develop the cold caps to help women preserve their hair during chemotherapy. I sold a lot of the inventory I received from Solei, and with that money, I paid for a good part of the prototypes. However, they were expensive, and I was frustrated. After a few failed prototypes, I was on the right track, but I needed more money. My son Ignacio helped me fundraise so that we could continue with the project.

I kept on doing research and talked to different women who had done the cold capping during chemo. Some were happy they had done it; others complained about the process or the caps being very cold. I was sometimes deterred from the project because I tried to use them, and it was very, very difficult for me. It pained me to put women through more distress during chemo. But I knew the results would outweigh the uncomfortable coldness.

I followed the Instagram community of women in Argentina doing this amazing work. Different groups of women in different cities in Argentina would help women use cold caps. This group of women would lend the caps, help them learn how to use them, and support them during their process. I saw the pictures of these courageous women on Facebook and Instagram. Some of them saved their hair, some lost it, and some didn't want to continue with the cold caps, but they all supported each other. I contacted one of the women who was in charge of a group in the small city of Tucuman, located in northern Argentina. Her name is Gaby, and I told her about what I was doing. She helped me with all my questions.

"Gaby," I told her, "when the caps are done, I would love to donate some of them to you guys in Argentina. You have been the architect and inspiration for this project."

"Thank you, Monica. We have grown so much all over; we don't have enough cold caps for all the women who want to do this."

The tortillería, after dealing with the horrendous bureaucracy of the city of Miami's building department, was finally slowly taking shape. I was excited and decorated the tortilla place really cute. I had never dealt with the permits required for food management or building a small restaurant that involves grease traps, different sinks for various purposes, and large industrial kitchen hoods.

I had already had two meltdowns in the City of Miami due to frustration over the permits. My wicked luck was that the whole building department had changed its system, and it took ages for them to issue the permits. Finally, after the building and permits were done, I painted "Make tacos, not war" in pink and white on the wall,

I waited for Bertis to visit Miami to do a small "inauguration." I couldn't do it without her. Before everyone arrived, Bertis gave me a charm necklace in the shape of a mini corn; God knows where she got it. Only Bertis could be so thoughtful and funny at the same time. I cherish my friendship with her. My close friends came to celebrate: Cris, Amelita, Ana, Ariadna, Ana Cristina, and Gaby surrounded me with love and laughter. I don't think my life could be the same without my friends. They are and always will be an endless source of happiness, joy and support.

CHAPTER 42

Your Dreams Are Not Always Your Purpose

I always thought that part of my purpose was to be a fashion designer. I loved the creativity, the process, and making women feel beautiful. I had worked so hard towards that dream that when I accomplished it, and life unraveled, I discovered that my purpose was so much bigger than that dream. After assessing the damages, I discovered a newfound purpose that made me so much more whole. Even though I went through dark times, doubted myself, and distrusted the journey, I can say I am stronger, more like myself than I have ever been.

El Mada and I applied to be American Citizens. I am proud to be part of this wonderful country, which has welcomed us and now calls us home. Mexico is the family I was born into. It runs through my veins. Everywhere I go, I carry it with me; it's who I am, profoundly proud to be born there. The United States is the family we have chosen to be a part of. We have sacrificed, worked hard, and followed every step to be part of this family that welcomes people from every corner of the world, seeking a safer and better future for their children. I am eternally grateful to the United States, a place where you can be whatever your heart calls you to be. It has given me, my husband, and my children opportunities that we wouldn't be able to find anywhere else in the world.

I try not to look back, and I am not interested in the fate of Sofia and Solei. If I were to look into her Instagram, I know it is all lies. It's the lies Sofia wants to put out in the world of Solei and her. My entire relationship with her was based on fabrications, and as time passed by, things clicked in my brain, and now I have twenty-twenty vision.

Sofia told me she had cancer in the spleen, that the tumor was probably there when she was a child and grew through the years. Yet, she never had chemo or lost her hair. I started doubting everything she ever told me, but could she have also lied about having cancer? I did my research, and it seems that cancer in the spleen is very rare because the spleen is an organ that purifies blood. It is most probable that if you had cancer in the spleen, you would also have cancer in the blood; it is called leukemia. You need chemo for leukemia, so if this were true, everything she told me about her cancer and how she was treated was also a lie. Maybe that is why she didn't like to be called a survivor, because she never was a cancer survivor.

I have no idea why Sofia is the way she is, and I never will. But I have let go and found peace with what happened. I forgive her even though she probably isn't sorry. I can't carry so much contempt for her. It harms me, not her. It is like a snake bite; you carry the poison in your body. I want that poison out. She has to live with herself; that is punishment enough. I have moved on to another life and have let go. Sometimes to win, we must lose and rebuild over that loss. I have left an old version of myself to welcome and celebrate a new one.

After all, I have realized it doesn't matter if I make dresses, tortillas, write, or do nothing at all. It doesn't matter if my ventures succeed or not.

What I have come to realize is that what truly matters is that *I am still here*, watching my children grow, surrounded by people who love me and whom I love in return, and finding purpose in daily life.

What defines me is what lives within me, whether I choose love over hate, whether I choose hope over despair, whether I choose to stand up again or stay on the ground, whether I choose to forgive and let go, or whether I choose to be thankful or complain. We all have a light engraved within, but it depends on us, through our actions and love, to grow that light into a beam of light, or we can choose to let that light die. I have chosen to grow my light. At the end of the day, what lives and grows within us all is what defines us and what really matters.

Surviving:
Cancer as a Teacher

Cancer is the toughest, most grueling, demanding and destructive teacher I have ever had in my life. I remember, back in school, I'd ask my friends about the teacher who taught each class. Depending on the teacher's reputation, I would carefully select each course. Without shame, I would aim for the easiest, most comfortable courses.

The thing is, with cancer, I had no choice. I didn't choose to take this "course." I don't think anybody does. Cancer sucks, and nobody wants to be in this daunting classroom with this horrific teacher. If given a choice, I would have preferred to live in blissful ignorance. I would have opted to stay as I was and not evolve into what cancer might make of me. The only choices I had left were how I was going to behave in this classroom and what I was willing to learn. The lessons are incomprehensible, the pain almost unbearable. But maybe if I stay still, if I pay attention and observe, I might learn something from this mess. I might even find meaning in the whole experience.

So, what is the legacy of cancer? Is it pain, loss? Devastation, destruction, sorrow, misery, grief? Yes, all of the above, but after the aftermath recedes, and you can breathe again, the legacy of a tragedy or hardships is what we make of it.

Pain can be the seed that motivates us to take action to help others. So many good things that have changed the world have been born out of loss and pain. Almost every charity, association, and foundation has been the direct result of somebody's misfortune.

Anyone can transform their pain into enlightenment, even if it's just by being more compassionate and grateful every day. It takes a lot of time and effort first to process, then to heal, but eventually it will happen.

People who were with me in the cancer classroom in general are doing great, but some have relapsed, and some have not made it. Women with breast cancer who may have had a better prognosis than I have died since. For these reasons, I have learned a valuable lesson: nobody is safe, not even I. But nobody is safe, even if you haven't had cancer. No one has tomorrow guaranteed. You don't need to be in the classroom to learn the lesson.

Failures can become successes, and successes can become failures. Money comes and goes. Live as fully and as truthfully as you can. Do good. Have a grateful heart. Life is just a second to be enjoyed, for yourself and your loved ones. I particularly feel that I have been given extra time. I need to make the most of that time, however long it lasts, whether it's one day or 50 more years. Surround yourself with people who make you feel good, who love you. Run away from negative energy.

So, when people say that everything happens for a reason, it is not up to God, the Universe, or life to reveal that reason to us, although sometimes they will. It is up to us to find out or even create a reason and meaning for our loss and pain, making it valuable. It is up to us to find out the meaning and purpose in our lives. I do believe God will be with us, supporting and accompanying us in our journey. But this is our path to travel, our journey to complete, not

His. Try to make sense of the unthinkable, seek meaning in the incomprehensible, and find peace within yourself.

I have found that the richness of experiences is what makes life worth living. To experience deep love, deep compassion, joy, and overcome pain, and reach goals that give life meaning. You might have heard that some cancer or near-death-experience survivors say, "You learn to appreciate the moment more, not sweat the small things."

It is true. If you choose to, you live more freely, enjoy more, and worry less. So, whatever you are going through, just breathe, sit still, and try to be open to whatever you are about to receive. Endure the horrible lesson, and I promise you that you will be stronger, tougher, and more resilient by the time the course has ended.

Cancer is limited
It cannot cripple love
It cannot shatter hope
It cannot corrode faith
It cannot destroy confidence
It cannot kill friendship
It cannot erase memories
It cannot silence courage
It cannot eat away peace
It cannot invade the soul
It cannot reduce eternal life
It cannot lessen the power of resurrection

—Dr. Robert L. Lynn

CHOOSING
A LANE

THE SEED
OF FEAR

STEPPINNG ON
CRAP CAN LEAD
YOU TO LOVE

MIAMI
FASHION
WEEK

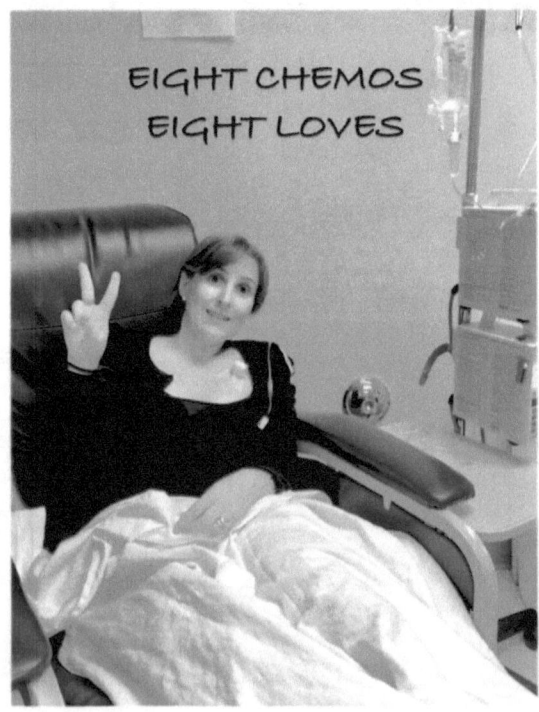

EIGHT CHEMOS
EIGHT LOVES

FOCUS ON CHAYANNE

two months before chemo

two months into chemo

last chemo

FREE AS MY HAIR

two months after chemo

three years after chemo

today

HEALING IN LOURDES

WELCOME TO MY
TORTILLA HOUSE

YOU'RE
NOT
ALONE

How You Can Flourish as an Online
Learner with Faith and Success Strategies

Dr. Remilyn Mueller

Published by hope*books
2217 Matthews Township Pkwy
Suite D302
Matthews, NC 28105
www.hopebooks.com

hope*books is a division of hope*media

Printed in the United States of America

First paperback edition.
Paperback ISBN: 979-8-89185-255-6
Hardcover ISBN: 979-8-89185-256-3
Ebook ISBN: 979-8-89185-257-0
Library of Congress Number: 2025942718

hope*books